New Playwriting Strategies

"The exercises Paul Castagno provides are eminently usable. They're direct, clear, and I'm gonna steal them for any playwriting classroom I'm in front of in the future. They can be the ax Kafka talked about to break the frozen sea within us, let the writing loose, and demand that he or she let the mind hit the page in some new and yet somehow familiar ways."

Len Jenkin, *Professor of Dramatic Writing, Tisch School of the Arts at NYU*

New Playwriting Strategies has become a canonical text in the study and teaching of playwriting, offering a fresh and dynamic insight into the subject. This thoroughly revised and expanded second edition explores and highlights the spectrum of new techniques that inform contemporary theater writing, as well as their influence on other dramatic forms.

Paul Castagno builds on the innovative plays of Len Jenkin, Mac Wellman, and the theories of Mikhail Bakhtin to investigate the groundbreaking approaches taken by a broad range of modern dramatists, including Sarah Ruhl, Suzan-Lori Parks, and Young Jean Lee. New features in this edition include in-depth studies of the adaptation of classical texts by contemporary playwrights, and of the utilizing of new technologies, such as YouTube, Wikipedia, and blogs, to create alternative theatrical shapes.

The author's step-by-step approach offers the reader innovative models for:

- narrative
- dialogue
- character
- monologue
- hybrid plays.

This is a working text for playwrights, presenting a range of illuminating new exercises suitable for everyone from the workshop student to the established writer. *New Playwriting Strategies* is an essential resource for anyone studying and writing drama today.

Paul C. Castagno is Professor of Theater at UNC-Wilmington, where he served as founding chair of the Department of Theater. He formerly served as Director and Head of MA Programs at the School of Theater at Ohio University, and headed the MFA Playwriting/Dramaturgy programs at the University of Alabama. He teaches playwriting and dramatic literature, directs, and has published books and articles on playwriting and *commedia dell'arte*.

New Playwriting Strategies

Second Edition

Language and Media in the 21st Century

Paul C. Castagno

Routledge
Taylor & Francis Group

LONDON AND NEW YORK

Second edition published 2012
by Routledge
2 Park Square, Milton Park, Abingdon, Oxon OX14 4RN

Simultaneously published in the USA and Canada
by Routledge
711 Third Avenue, New York, NY 10017

Routledge is an imprint of the Taylor & Francis Group, an informa business

First edition published by Routledge 2001

British Library Cataloguing in Publication Data
A catalogue record for this book is available from the British Library

Library of Congress Cataloging in Publication Data
Castagno, Paul C., 1950–
    New playwriting strategies : language and media in the 21st century / Paul C.
Castagno. — 2nd ed.
        p. cm.
    Includes bibliographical references and index.
    1. Playwriting. I. Title.
    PN1661.C364 2011
808.2—dc22
2011013344

ISBN: 978-0-415-49147-1 (hbk)
ISBN: 978-0-415-49148-8 (pbk)
ISBN: 978-0-203-80301-1 (ebk)

Typeset in 9.5/13 New Baskerville
by Saxon Graphics Ltd, Derby, DE21 4SZ
Printed and bound by Edwards Brothers, Lillington, N.C.

To my three sons who inspired me during the writing of this book:

Andrew, for the joy and talent in which he pursues his dreams

Peter, for his unflappable courage, strength and will in his battle with cancer

Chris, for his youthful wisdom and fun-filled, loving companionship

Contents

Tables

Preface

I met Paul Castagno briefly at the New Directions in Theater conference in Key West, Florida in early January of 1990, and he invited me to Tuscaloosa, Alabama at that time, when he was teaching in the theater department. He wanted me to do a workshop with his students, and he had some money for it, and expenses. For a New York City boy, this was an invitation to visit America I couldn't refuse.

It was surprising to me that a theater professor in Alabama was inviting me to teach his students. I had a thickheaded, pretentious preconception that the students at the University of Alabama would make no connection to me and my particular way into theater. I wasn't famous, though my work had gotten around some, and I was a bit worried it was going to be "Who the hell is this guy? Lets get drunk at the sorority cotillion and throw up on the statue of Bear Bryant. Roll Tide!"

I was wrong about the students, and the professor was Paul Castagno, the author of this book. The extent to which he knew and understood my work was a flattering shock to me. And he was a terrific guy to be around—knowledgeable, smart, and a generous host.

His students were extraordinary in their way, deeply southern, but from all kinds of backgrounds, ready for anything I threw at them. I loved Tuscaloosa—the dead downtown, the terrific ribs at John Bishop's Dreamland Café—and especially the brilliant local artists who lived nearby. Paul came along with me to visit Benjamin Franklin Perkins, a wonderful artist and a true gentleman. Talk about theater. Brother Ben had painted his entire house red, white and blue, plus a garage full of blunt, heartfelt , religious pictures on canvas. I bought as many as I could afford. We also visited Robert Cargo, a retired French professor who had an amazing folk art gallery in Tuscaloosa's downtown. The place was dead quiet, and full of unbelievably intense southern folk art—devils and angels painted and carved by people to whom they were something more than interesting symbols. The devil is still out there in the woods in Alabama, and no doubt your neighborhood as well....

My relationship with Paul Castagno continued over the years, and he was kind enough to ask me to write the forward to this second edition of his *New Playwriting Strategies.*

To give high praise to a work like this one is a pleasure. It deserves it. Paul Castagno has written a book that is the most thorough work I've seen on new American playwrights, what they're up to, and how they approach making plays. He's aware of everyone (much more so than this writer) writing for the stage, even brilliant people like Madelyn Kent who have only written two or three very challenging works. His analysis of more established writers like Suzan Lori-Parks and Mac Wellman gets to the heart of their process, reveals their tricks, and treats them with the academic rigor they deserve.

The book is authoritative, and up to date. It is also multi-purpose.

Paul Castagno gives us new definitions that break down playwriting techniques that are usually intuitive (at least for this playwright) and often based in free-floating responses to what is already on the page, or in the plan, or on the stage (if actors are involved early on)—and enables anyone to see these techniques as a usable and learnable approach to making things out of words. I say techniques for lack of a better word—what I mean is methods to increase an awareness of the infinite possibilities in a theatrical moment, the multiple worlds present inside and outside everyone, and the myriad forms of what we call story. This is invaluable, not only for the playwright, but for anyone working in any form of writing or any art form for that matter.

The book is intended for fellow academics, fellow theater practitioners of all kinds, and for students. The exercises Paul Castagno provides are eminently usable. They're direct, clear, and I'm gonna steal them for any playwriting classroom I'm at the front of in the future. They can be the ax Kafka talked about to break the frozen sea within us, let the writer loose, and demand that he or she let the mind hit the page in some new and yet somehow familiar ways. *New Playwriting Strategies* also has the potential to break the frozen sea within critics, within students of contemporary theater, and within that theater's audience.

This book will give anyone who reads it new insight into contemporary theatrical practice in America, and sympathy and affection for its practitioners, who labor in a business (as does the author of *New Playwriting Strategies*) for the love of it, and the joy and hard work of it, and for that moment when the lights come up onstage.

Len Jenkin
New York City, July 2011

Acknowledgments

I would like to thank the playwrights in this book, many of whom I worked with at the University of Alabama, and several of whom I met with during their residencies to Ohio University, including Caridad Svich and Carson Kreitzer, whose works are discussed herein. It now seems a career-long venture extending over 21 years, beginning with the contentious *New Directions in Theatre* conference held in Key West, Florida in January 1990, when even the new millennium seemed a long way off. I discussed that conference in the last edition, and a number of the language playwrights who participated then are still actively creative in the field. When I was director of the New Playwrights Program, I invited many of these writers for residencies: Len Jenkin, Mac Wellman, Eric Overmyer, Jeffrey Jones, Ruth E. Margraff, Nena Beeber, Heather McCutcheon, Peggy Shaw, Matthew Maguire, and many others. I also want to thank my good friends and play-writing colleagues Doug Grissom and Kent Brown for their many years of support and good will in advocating the best in playwriting.

I would like to thank my beloved sons, Andrew, Peter, and Chris, for pro-viding the greatest gift a father can have. Also, deep appreciation to members of my family, particularly my brothers Tony, Richard, and Joe for their ongoing support during the past several years as this project was being completed. At UNC Wilmington my appreciation goes to professors Tom Schmid, Nelson Reid, and Johnson Akinleye for their good will and sincere friendship. My appreciation goes out to UNC-Wilmington where I served as founding chair of the Theater Department and had the opportunity to oversee the building of two beautiful theaters and adjacent facilities in a US$34 million structure.

On a musical note, I extend appreciation to songwriter/performer Brad Heller, who enlisted me to play bass for his terrific rock band The Fustics. Playing bass was the perfect complement to the solitary hours spent on this edition, and helped me through a stressful period when my son Peter was diagnosed with cancer. I extend my thanks to Chris Jones, longtime friend and theater critic extraordinaire, for an inspiring weekend in New York experiencing and discussing American theater. I thank Jerry Rojo, my first mentor, who encouraged me to become a theater artist. My appreciation to

ACKNOWLEDGMENTS

those playwrights who have publicly acknowledged on blogs and list-servs the usefulness of the first edition in improving their playwriting. I want to thank the playwriting instructors who adopted the first edition for their classes, and ask that if you are an instructor of playwriting, I hope you will consider adopting this new edition for your workshop or seminar. I was pleased to see the book's usefulness and adoption in related areas of creative writing, English, script analysis, dramatic literature and dramaturgy. Further, thanks to my playwriting students in theater and creative writing departments who have worked through all the exercises in this book, and surprise me with their "takes" on the material. If you need to spruce up your workshop with some dynamic new excercises you need look no further. While *New Playwriting Strategies* provides the theoretical foundation of my pedagogy, the workshops emphasize constant writing, and the exercises in this edition have all been tested in the workshop setting. To this end, my thanks to *Scripped.com*, which greatly facilitates the teaching and reading of new plays in the workshop setting.

Finally, I acknowledge the great art that is theater, and playwriting that is at its core. Now more than ever, we need the theater to make the visceral connections in the face of a technological age obsessed with electronic communication. Theater compels us to be present at the experience, to revel in what is human and shared. Particularly for the younger generation who grew up on texting and twittering, the theater may become the last refuge for a sustained live aesthetic experience. Perhaps this explains the surge in playwriting programs and new work over the past ten years, as new generations find deeper meaning in the incredible experience of creating and producing live, high-quality theater.

Paul C. Castagno

Introduction

BEYOND THE TIPPING POINT

Over the last decade many of the tenets of new playwriting have been main-streamed into the broader landscape that defines dramatic writing. The effects have been far-reaching, as paragons of new playwriting, most notably Eric Overmyer, have successfully introduced language playwriting techniques to the small screen. As executive producer of the successful HBO series *The Wire*, Overmyer constructed a landscape of street language and juxtaposed narratives into an intertwined political-cultural matrix—revolutionizing the traditional good guy/bad guy, cops versus criminals' format. In the same spirit, another HBO series, Steven Milch's *Deadwood*, reworked the film western genre into a sea of heightened, colorful, and profane language that liberated the genre and its characters from erstwhile cliché stereotypes. This trend continues with AMC's *Mad Men*'s recasting 1950s lingo and swagger; transforming an "old-fashioned cocktail" with its *bons mots* and speech acts. In these three critically acclaimed shows, a specific world of language emerged that defined both characters and themes, the distillation of which was an 'attitude' of urgency and presence that was palpable and forceful. The attitudes of these shows became synonymous with their "ensemble" identities, eclipsing the featured star approach of network television. If attitude marked the style, it was always the language that defined it. In effect, language became the arbiter of character and the *mise-en-scène*.

In the downtown New York theater scene, maturing playwriting collectives such as Clubbed Thumb (who self-consciously promote 'edgy' new work) and 13P have not only survived into adolescence but also thrived, filling a void in the production of new, experimental work. The visibility and success gleaned from these productions is evident in the number of winners or finalists of major playwriting awards among their members, and can be attributed to a broadening in critical reception that was unforeseeable when the first edition of *New Playwriting Strategies (NPS): A Language Based Approach to Playwriting* was published over ten years ago. Several of the most interesting playwrights in these workshops, Young Jean Lee and Alice Tuan for example, have formed their own spin-off production companies. Lee has been featured in several *New York Times* features, demonstrating that critics are taking a longer-range view of her work. Sarah Ruhl, from 13P, has been finalist for two Pulitzer Prizes in Drama (2005, 2010). The goal of these collectives and individuals is to produce challenging work directly, without the rigmarole of endless staged readings as the play is "developed to death."

In overturning the so-called hegemony of the male playwright, the collectives consist of mostly women playwrights, many of them women of color. In the main, their plays are language-based and experimental, working cleverly through theatrical constructs to present racial or cultural themes. For example, Young Jean Lee's *The Shipment,* which opened at the Kitchen in New York City a few days after President Obama's inauguration, used song and dance, minstrelsy, stand-up comedy in the style of Richard Pryor, and cartoon-like caricatures to probe "the blister of race relations" (Ramchandani, June 5, 2009). Her playful and irreverent handling of Asian characters (she is Korean-American) in *Songs of the Dragon Flying to Heaven* (Lee 2009) emphatically suggests, and refreshingly so, that we are in a post politically correct, post-multicultural age.

While the first edition focused on the mostly male progenitors of language playwriting, this edition of *NPS* expands the contributions to new playwriting by a host of woman playwrights who have emerged over the last decade. In addition to the above, works by Sheila Callaghan, Naomi Iizuka, Lyn Nottage, Anne Marie Healey, Lisa D'Amour, Barbara Cassidy, Madelyn Kent, Carson Kreitzer, Rinne Grof, Anne Washburn, and Erin Courtney are considered. This increase in the impact of women on playwriting is noteworthy, and promises to expand as a majority of women playwrights now matriculate into the profession.

The availability of the above work in print is augmented by the huge impact of You Tube over recent years. Some experimental work, such as Suzan-Lori Parks's *365 Days/365 Plays* (2006), has enjoyed widespread dissemination as acting groups in site-specific locations videotape the work and upload across You Tube and Facebook sites. *365 Days/365 Plays,* which represents Parks's novel achievement of writing a short play every day for an entire year, may be the perfect paradigm for a restless age that prefers its entertainment in snippets, via Twitter or the ubiquitous text messaging. Indeed, one may 'tweet' any number of downtown theaters to stay abreast of current developments, read and access scripts, and engage dialogue with theater practitioners either directly or through blogs. Encouraging flexibility in how this work is produced, Parks and other authors, such as the primary figure in the contemporary adaptations of classical plays, Charles Mee, consider the outcome with collaborators as the ultimate reward. (Mee posts his plays on his website with no restriction on usage or copyright.) No longer limited to the downtown loft theaters with 50–60 patrons, You Tube disseminates challenging work like *365 Days/365 Plays* to thousands of viewers, vastly increasing the scale of impact for this experimental project.

As new playwriting techniques and principles saturate the structures of contemporary theater and media, they are becoming more entrenched. The longevity of this phenomenon is secured by the pedagogical shifts over the past ten years. Advances in the pedagogy of playwriting have rendered strictly Aristotelian approaches obsolete; small wonder, when faculty in the most competitive programs are themselves first-generation language playwrights. Mac Wellman, the maven of language playwriting, heads the graduate playwriting program at Brooklyn College and is largely responsible for organizing the anthology *New Downtown Now: An Anthology of New Theater from Downtown New York* (Wellman and Lee 2006), which features many of his former students. Paula Vogel moved from Brown University, where she replaced Wellman, to take over the playwriting program at Yale University. Sarah Ruhl, who is discussed at length in this edition, studied at both Brown and Yale under the mentorship of these innovators. Erik Ehn, whose Saint Plays collection was a breakthrough in new playwriting (and is discussed herein), left his position as dean of theater at California Institute of the Arts (where Suzan-Lori Parks recently was a faculty member) to helm the Brown playwriting program. Alice Tuan who studied with Mac Wellman, is now head of playwriting at California Institute of the Arts. Len Jenkin at Tisch School of Dramatic Writing at NYU is now joined by Rinne Grof who studied with Wellman at Brooklyn College, and is a member of Clubbed Thumb. Erin Courtney, a member at Clubbed Thumb and 13P, also studied with the peripatetic Wellman, and has now joined the faculty at Brooklyn College. Matthew Maguire moved from head of playwriting to chair the Fordham theater department. What seems a game of departmental musical chairs points to a network of connectors and charismatic individuals who have become leaders in the academic field of playwriting. These graduate programs attract smart, ambitious students, in a field that often mandates a slow learning curve where patience and resolve are critical ingredients. In providing a link upon graduation, an early progenitor of new playwriting, Jeffrey Jones, has become a major promoter of the downtown New York theater scene, by helping graduates from these programs in their efforts to get produced in New York.

This "tipping point" in the pedagogy of playwriting translates into new generations of playwrights from highly competitive programs inculcated with recent advances in dramaturgy. The change is not so much ideological as it is ineluctable. As the best new playwrights matriculate through the so-called "elite" programs, they build upon the innovations and pedagogy of their mentors. This has created a sea change in how learning takes place in playwriting. The adoption of the first edition of *NPS* into many playwriting programs provides testimony that teaching values and objectives have drastically changed. Moreover, as blogging surged in the past decade, *NPS* was cited in a number of different contexts as a vital and innovative way to approach and think about playwriting. The evidence is clear that language playwriting and playwrights now represent the dominant pedagogy in training playwrights. In defining the tipping point in physical science terms, a new equilibrium state has been established that is qualitatively dissimilar from old school, Aristotelian orthodoxy.

For Matthew Gladwell, author of *The Tipping Point* (2000), the tipping point is contingent upon several factors: among them the "Law of the Few," "Stickiness Factor," and "Word of Mouth." As the new poetics was given voice in the classroom and workshop, it became the accepted norm for student playwrights over the last ten years. A few key programs and teachers over the last fifteen to twenty years fomented an evolutionary shift in playwriting. As new generations follow the path of their mentors the stickiness factor takes hold. The best students want the most innovative instruction, the most challenging curriculum. With the proliferation of playwriting blogs and online formats, such as Scripped.com, new techniques and ideas are shared and become common practice. National conferences, such as ATHE, LMDA, and TCG, provide opportunities for broader dissemination within academe and the profession. Connectors, like Jeffrey M. Jones at the Little Theater at Tonic in New York, hold monthly features of experimental work that bring together writers and artistic directors. This "word of mouth" spreads what's innovative in small but efficient packages, compounding its impact over time. The outcome then is that new playwriting is no longer the "other" on some outer orbit; but rather, the center core exerting gravitational pull that has altered the shape of the mainstream.

Concomitantly, the tradition of American actor training, for years ensconced in internalized "method," Stella Adler, Uta Hagen, or Meisner traditions; now finds counter approaches vying for primacy. Placing concentrated emphasis on the corporeal actor, these range from Anne Bogart's viewpoints to Suzuki training to holistic approaches that coordinate the voice and body, such as the Fitzmaurice method. These latter approaches mandate that the psychological element of character emerge from releasing tensions in the body and voice, so the approach becomes more psychophysical than internalized. Suzuki training for example places heavy emphasis on the physicality of the voice and musculature of vocal articulators—the perfect instrument for language playwriting. Acting instructors, anxious to receive "certifications" that will enhance their marketability or tenure track, enroll in master class workshops, absorbing and then passing along these methods that have become de rigueur with students. The newer acting training methods have met the demand of new playwriting with its emphasis on theatrically based versus psychologically based characterization. This has opened up writing for the stage, since actors can now seamlessly move across orthodox training boundaries, subverting established pretexts, such as a Meisner actor, a method actor, an external actor.

Recent plays by Suzan-Lori Parks (*Topdog/Underdog*), Naomi Iizuka (*36 Views*), Len Jenkin (*Margo Veil*), Martin McDonagh (*A Behanding in Spokane*), Sarah Ruhl (*The Clean House, In the Next Room, or the Vibrator Play*), and Carson Kreitzer (*Freakshow*), to name just few examples, incorporate erstwhile theatrical traditions that require an externalized or physical basis for the actor. Throwbacks include the use of the *tableau vivant* (Robinson 2009, 33), minstrelsy, *Grand Guignol*, carny typification, *film noir*, and in Iizuka's case, Kabuki theater. The evolution in acting pedagogy can now satisfy the physical orientation required to effect the performative character. These practices are discussed in detail in this edition.

Does achieving the tipping point mean that orthodoxy has been toppled, or that older methods are invalid? If so, what are the implications for the future? This edition attempts to take a forward-looking view with some striking observations. One factor seems clear. The recent generation of emerging playwrights are staking out their own turf from a variety of perspectives. Formal experimentation continues with the rebottling of antique theatrical practices and traditions in the creation of the text. Playwrights are building texts more collectively than in the past. As stated, Young Jean Lee collaborated with an ensemble of black actors in creating *The Shipment*. Madelyn Kent works with Japanese wives learning a second language to develop new work, extracting language that is distilled and syntactically arresting. Her plays *Sachiko* and *Enoshima Island* are explored later in this edition (Wellman and Lee, 2006).

One significant trend is the blending of a new playwriting sensibility with traditional narrative and character development. More playwrights are producing plays that merge traditional and new poetics, the dramatic with the theatrical. A meta-theatrical verve is loosening traditional dramaturgy from its moorings: in a sense, weaning mainstream audiences away from orthodoxy yet still providing them with a lifeline. The most prevalent format for plays nowadays is the hybrid, marking contemporary playwrights' unease with traditional narrative through a conflation of dramaturgies and source materials. Playwrights are exploring the indigenous ways in which theater can communicate theatricality. If the first edition of *NPS* marked a renaissance in how plays are written, this edition acknowledges that this aesthetic has its corollary in the contemporary culture. There is an emphasis on creating unique theatrical worlds, on surprising or shocking audiences, lifting from a variety of sources (Wikipedia, blogs, transcriptions and so on) or working collectively and in collaborations—as befits the mission of companies like Clubbed Thumb, 13P, and Flea Theater. More playwrights are creating through collaborations with actors, or encouraging collaborators to adapt aspects of their work to suit a particular production. The rigid paradigm of the playwright as sole creative source has become less the mantra, particularly with women playwrights like Young Jean Lee and Suzan-Lori Parks. Thus, old school unity has become restive, perhaps passé, as multiple voices and sources shape the playmaking.

The critical success of the rock musical, *Bloody, Bloody Andrew Jackson* (opened on Broadway in 2010) exemplifies how all of the above can be bundled into what has long been considered the most mainstream of formats, the musical. Jackson is no grey-wigged statesman from the history books but a rock-and-roll American idol. *Chicago Tribune* critic Chris Jones described it as "the consummate musical for the Wikipedia age" (October 13, 2010). Rather than reflect history, or simulate the period, the production takes an irreverent anachronistic view that conflates present and past, with no grace given to political correctness or sensitive depictions of Native Americans (the entire cast is white—in itself, enforcing the play's arrogance). *Bloody, Bloody Andrew Jackson* relies upon a performative, urgent, theatrical style to meet the demands of a shifting dramaturgy that juxtaposes a variety of aesthetic styles and approaches.

This crossover poetics bundles disparate theatrical aesthetics into novel formations. In writing *Topdog/Underdog*. Parks reached her largest and most diverse audience as the play sold out houses on Broadway, culminating in her winning the Pulitzer Prize in 2002. *Topdog/Underdog* combines a trackable narrative and thematic with a number of new playwriting techniques; from the speech genre—here, marked by the rhythmic cadence of the three-card Monte game—to hybridization, minstrel conventions, and the use of signature "ticket names" for the characters Lincoln and Booth. Sarah Ruhl, who combines a grounding in new playwriting with the comfortable dramaturgy of mainstream regional theater fare, has enjoyed huge success over the past decade; most recently she was a finalist for the Pulitzer Prize (2010) for her controversial play, *In the Next Room, or the Vibrator Play* (She was also a finalist in 2005 for *The Clean House.*) The crossover trend is pervasive. Naomi Iizuka's *36 Views* sets a traditional narrative in an art gallery, than bombards it with ancient iconographical gesturing and Kabuki interludes. Martin McDonagh's *A Behanding in Spokane* (2010) takes us to the edge of the *Grand Guignol* grotesque, while trapped in the familiar moorings of a seedy hotel room. Because this bundling of dramaturgies has become so prevalent and successful, I have devoted a new chapter to it, entitled "Crossover poetics." This chapter explores the breakthrough plays of Sarah Ruhl and Susan-Lori Parks, work that has now reached a much larger and commercial audience.

I believe it is important for the emerging playwright, or the playwright beginning a career, to maintain an openness to advances in dramaturgy, while not getting too hung up on labels, schools, or "camps." Let the content guide you to the play's optimum form, rather than lock in to a particular approach. If your background or training is traditionally based, you should find this chapter an excellent point of entry into weaving new playwriting techniques into your current work. This book provides a map to discovery and invention, and, an invitation to openness.

Updates in this edition now include language-based playwrights and plays that have emerged over the past ten years, and are readily accessible in print to readers. Significantly, Clubbed Thumb, 13P, and the various anthologies representative of new work are populated by a decisive majority of women playwrights. Many of these plays feature heightened language and characters, with an eroticism that had been hitherto underexplored in new playwriting. This edition looks at how these writers are introducing transgressive subject matter into new writing. It is my hope that this edition avails readers and producers of the many fine, innovative female playwrights that are pioneering a new landscape of opportunity for women playwrights.

As Mark Bly, the highly esteemed dramaturg and former chair of playwriting at Yale School of Drama, noted on the cover of the first edition (2001) that *NPS* "chronicles the seismic shift in playwriting over the past two decades," this volume demonstrates that the "aftershocks" of the last ten years have promulgated a gender shift in the prevailing hegemony.

All the chapters have been updated, although the core from the first edition has been maintained. With the widespread prevalence of hybrid formats in contemporary theater, Chapter 3 has been expanded to include a section on adaptation of classical texts. Significantly, many of the playwrights discussed in the volume have published dramaturgically inspired versions of the classics. Along the way, I have added a number of new exercises that have been successfully tested in the playwriting workshop. Other exercises and examples have been revised or updated. The most recent work of playwrights Len Jenkin and Mac Wellman has been included, as these playwrights are active and still widely influential both as practitioners and pedagogues. I have reduced Eric Overmyer's presence in this volume, as he now works almost exclusively in television. However, his seminal work in language playwriting is significant and paradigmatic; its language basis provides a benchmark for much new work. As such, I have redacted the former Chapter 6 into a new Chapter 5, which is titled "Transformation of character." This segues from the previous chapter, "Theatricality of character," and highlights the two most important features of creating character in new playwriting.

Monologue has become the dramaturgical *topoi* of choice in many recent plays, and understanding its multiple functions is essential for the *au courant* playwright. This edition explores the matter in depth over the last two chapters. I have introduced some variant monologic formats, including the pivot monologue, *skaz, the tour de force* monologue, and the performative monologue. These will provide the playwright with a number of new strategies for not only constructing monologue, but also integrating it as a key structural device. Part II explores the dramaturgy of new playwriting in detail in a system that is both teachable and applicable, securing the foundation of craft that is the *sine qua non* of all good playwriting.

Finally, if the first edition addressed the need for "a new poetics," as David Rush suggested, the second edition acknowledges that this is well underway and entrenched. As such, I don't want to grate on the reader by tearing down an orthodoxy that has been largely displaced. In fact, the chapter "Crossover poetics" is a gesture to the traditionally based playwright in how to incorporate new forms or transform old ones, without requiring an overhaul of your technique. Nor do I suggest that new playwriting's impact on the mainstream has in any way diminished its experimental vigor and urgency. For example, language playwright Mac Wellman continues to find alternatives to traditional narrative structures, while offering uniquely exciting and engaging theater. The range of subject matter for new playwrights is increasingly daring and vitalizing as new generations of playwrights stake out higher ground. In sum, *NPS 2: Language and Media in the 21st Century* celebrates the penetration of language playwriting into the culture; inclusive of the pedagogy, classroom, workshop, downtown theaters, women's collectives, regional theaters, Broadway, contemporary media and internet, cable television, and so on. It is a phenomenon that has increased exponentially in impact over the past ten years. It is inculcated into the best playwriting today.

1
New Playwriting Strategies:
Overview and terms

This second edition of *New Playwriting Strategies (NPS)* continues the exploration of playwriting from an innovative, forward-looking perspective. It presents a fundamentally different theoretical and practical approach to character, language, and dramatic form. The book challenges the underlying premises and assumptions that determine what constitutes a play. But the real goal is to provide you with the confidence and tools to challenge your status quo as a playwright, so that you can write plays with an expanding range of new strategies and techniques.

Until recently, orthodoxy ruled in the teaching and development of plays and playwrights. Many playwriting texts, including those written within the past ten years, rehash the core tenets of Aristotle's *Poetics* (ca. 325 BC) with long-standing "common-sense" dictums like conflict, the central protagonist, and character-specific dialogue. While the teaching of playwriting has advanced significantly over the past ten years, most playwriting texts remain resistant to change and innovation. The positive reception of the first edition, and its course adoption in many top programs, has helped to change this paradigm.

In the face of "common-sense" traditional approaches to playwriting, we find increasing experimentation in the writing of plays not just at the margins, but in the mainstream. The Pulitzer Prize-winning plays of the 1990s, including Margaret Edson's *Wit*, Paula Vogel's *How I Learned to Drive*, Edward Albee's *Three Tall Women*, and Craig Lucas's *Prelude to a Kiss*, used innovative forms and techniques to tell their stories. This trend continued into the 2000s, with Suzan-Lori Parks's *Topdog/Underdog* (2002) and Lynn Nottage's *Ruined* (2009) winning the Pulitzer Prize, while other notably innovative plays, such as Sarah Ruhl's *The Clean House* (2005) and *In the Next Room, or the Vibrator Play* (2010), Will Eno's *Thom Paine* (2005), and Rinde Eckert's *Orpheus X* (2007) became finalists. Clearly, there is a widening gulf between the writing of contemporary plays and what has been prescribed as correct playwriting. Certainly, the best playwriting students want to learn and incorporate the latest, most challenging techniques. Concomitantly, the more seasoned collaborators involved with new play development, including producers, directors, literary managers, dramaturgs, and actors desire a point of entry into the new playwriting—where the language of orthodoxy does not apply. Now more than ever, as plays are made and shaped in different ways, it has become increasingly important to describe this phenomena with a pragmatic perspective toward how things work.

NPS established the basic premise that playwriting is language based. As such, language prevails as the dominant force in the shaping of characters, action, and theme. The playwright orchestrates the voices in the text, entering into a kind of dialogue with characters and language. The playwright is open to language in its widest sense, whether coded in a specific genre, found in another text, historically based, or produced by the linguistic impulses that unleash slang, unusual syntax, foreignisms, discourses, and so on. While "writing through" the other (often multiple) voices, the playwright remains the creative or orchestrating force behind the text. The term *dialogism* describes how the interactive relation between voices in the playtext shapes the play as an act of discovery. Dialogism, in its various manifestations, is the fundamental principle at work in new playwriting.

A new approach to playwriting requires a distinctive set of terms and working tools, most of which are defined in this chapter. The chapters that follow establish a theoretical foundation derived from select plays. We will explore together a new way of thinking about playwriting. Comparative charts demonstrate basic distinctions from traditional or orthodox approaches. Along the way, I provide numerous practical examples and exercises for the playwright. These exercises have been tested over years of workshops and classes. The point of view is from the perspective of the playwright—to establish what useful strategy or technique can be gleaned from a given play. Therefore, the book does not probe thematic questions or underlying ideologies of the plays or playwrights. The result is a pragmatic study of new playwriting that challenges you to expand your imagination and technique.

FROM THEORY TO PRACTICE

While playwrights generally shy away from theory, it is necessary in this case to establish some fundamental principles about the new playwriting. In *Literary Theory: A Very Short Introduction,* Jonathan Culler describes theory as a "critique of common sense, of concepts taken as natural" (1997, 15). *NPS2* questions many assumptions or "givens" about playwriting while offering alternative premises. Further, Culler states that theory is analytical and speculative. This book analyzes a number of plays by various playwrights, demonstrating how these works can spark the playwright's imagination and sense of invention. Herein we speculate on what a play might or can be. Finally, Culler tells us, theory is drawn from other disciplines, where removed from its original context it offers special insights and applications. Along these lines, I utilize the concept of dialogism as the inspiration and organizing principle for this book.

The Russian literary critic Mikhail Bakhtin first coined the term dialogism. He used it as a means to reevaluate certain nineteenth-century

Russian novels that could not be categorized into traditional genres. These hybrid novels juxtaposed sophisticated literary techniques with storytelling elements drawn from folk culture, while other texts featured an array of linguistic styles, dialects, neologisms, and slang. Bakhtin used the term *polyvocal* to describe the divergent source materials that made up the text. (The term *multivocality* is used when multiple speech styles are bulked within a single character.)

Bakhtin assessed that the polyvocal text was an interactive system in which each element was in dialogue or dialogized with the other elements within the novel. Each part reacted with or against other parts in the text to create a dynamic sense of meaning and interest, which could not be distilled into a simple statement or unified arc. Plural, often contradictory, voices gave the dialogic text freer reign than traditional monologic formats. Rather than one narrator or point of view, multiple narrators vied with each other to tell the story. While the hybrid text resisted capture and classification, dialogism had offered a means of describing its inner workings and mechanisms.

DEFINING THE DIALOGIC PLAY

By appropriating a definition of the dialogic novel, and substituting the word *play* for novel, we can establish a working definition of the dialogic play. The dialogic play is "fundamentally polyvocal (multi-voiced) or dialogic rather than monologic (single-voiced). The essence of the [play] is its staging of different voices or discourses and, thus, of the clash of social perspectives and points of view" (Culler, 1997, 89; bracketed text added). Formally, dialogism represents the play's capacity to interact within itself, as if the various components were in dialogue with each other. As we will see in this edition, many of the dialogic principles that defined new playwriting ten years ago, can now be applied to the broader mainstream. Part of this may be due to the fact that dialogism anticipated the globalization of discourse and communication that defines our new millennium to date. Thus, the move to the dialogic play has been a natural extension of factors that have deeply influenced our evolving culture.

LANGUAGE PLAYWRITING

To be credible, a new theory and method need models that "work," or help to demonstrate certain points. The models used in the book largely derive from the plays of writers known as the "language playwrights" or "new playwrights." The language playwrights emerged over the past twenty to thirty years to stake out a significant territory in American theater. Since the 1970s they have been produced (and published) in and out of New York, and have been a major influence on the practice and pedagogy of playwriting. The latter is important because their persistent mentorship has greatly influenced new generations of playwrights. In this edition, we explore noteworthy second and third-generation new playwrights as well the ongoing work of their progenitors. While their influence has been extraordinary within the field, they have been largely ignored for production in the commercial theater, and until the first edition of *NPS* was published had generally escaped further critical inquiry.

Some of the award-winning leading figures from this first generation are Mac Wellman, Len Jenkin, Constance Congdon, Eric Overmyer, Erik Ehn, Suzan-Lori Parks, Jeffrey Jones, Paula Vogel, and Matthew Maguire. Their workshops, classrooms, and influences have been felt by an entire generation of playwrights, many of whom will be considered going forward. As earlier stated, a number of these playwrights head (or teach in) top programs in playwriting at the university level. Wellman and Jones have aggressively championed the works of their students or mentees in the downtown New York theater scene. The newer generations of playwrights are aggressively pursuing production goals. Young Jean Lee, for example, has her own production company established to produce her newest works. This double-edged sword of teaching young writers and producing creative playwriting is already impacting future generations of playwrights.

THE DIALOGIC CLASH

While these playwrights of interest each have a distinctive style, their methods of writing plays are fundamentally dialogic. Two seminal examples of the dialogic approach demonstrate how this process works. Len Jenkin's *Kitty Hawk* represented a breakthrough in terms of defining what constitutes a play, and opened the door for a surge in new playwriting, while Eric Overmyer's *On the Verge* was the most widely produced of the playwright's works, and catapulted him into his successful television career.

OBIE Award-winning playwright Len Jenkin first gained notice from the late Joseph Papp (of New York's Public Theater) and others through plays that were uniquely dialogic in approach. There really is nothing in the Off-Broadway historical avant-garde to compare it to. *Kitty Hawk* began simply by introducing the Wright brothers, inventors of the first airplane. As Jenkin proceeded to work on the play, he decided as an experiment to add various brother acts throughout American history, including such notables as the Smith brothers (cough drops) and James brothers (outlaws). The resultant play was unique in its formulation: dialogic in the juxtaposition and interaction between brother acts, each engaging different historical periods and levels of discourse in American culture.

Jenkin's doctoral background in comparative literature, in particular his interest in Russian nineteenth-century literature, may explain his ease in handling multiple narrators and storytellers within the play. Jenkin's creative process is intuitive; he dialogizes the script by asking, What if this other brother act enters? What interactive dynamic can be energized? The relativity and number of acts is discovered in the making of the script; plot occurs as a kind of frisson or friction between character groups. There was no book that guided him to make plays this way; by ignoring the language of normative "how to" playwrights, Jenkin developed his uniquely dialogic playwriting style. When I interviewed Jenkin during a residency, he stated that in revising his plays he still works dialogically: moving segments or blocks of text, attempting to discover an arrangement that works best for the play.

The most widely produced work of this early group of playwrights was Eric Overmyer's *On the Verge: The Geography of Learning*. Across America, university and regional theaters produced this breakthrough hit in the late 1980s and early 1990s. The play's complex vision was disguised by accessible, attractive features: three major roles for women, and a strong sense of language and period. The acting and design style required of the three women "trekkers" suggested the Victorian romantic adventure genre. Easily identified, this genre provided familiar moorings to a contemporary audience witnessing a revival in nineteenth-century subject matter, particularly in the film industry (for example, films based on the Brontë novels). Even conservative audience members felt comfortable with the independence of these late-nineteenth-century women explorers, their quaint feminism, and the play's literary challenges and references. Overmyer, presumably, was repackaging an old form popular at the turn of the century the time of expansionism and colonialism, when daring independent women smoked cigarettes and struck out on their own. Mainstream directors wanting to try something new flocked to the play since its stylistic appeal blurred the boundaries between the avant-garde and realism, and classicism versus method approaches to acting. *On the Verge*, more than any of Overmyer's other plays, was accessible across the board.

The first act progresses conventionally when suddenly, the characters are thrown into a kind of time warp. Overmyer had subverted the familiar context, and with it the audience's comfort zone. By intermission, the expectations of the audience are totally dismantled. Overmyer's *terra incognita* undermined expectations, breaking the conventions established at the beginning of the play. Overmyer had reinvented the "rules of the game," as this play was no longer about familiar genres. Audiences participated in the characters' journey or were frustrated by the move. Some spectators felt misled, even violated, by the shifting expectations.

Overmyer's play established a model of the *dialogic clash*, which pitted its characters' historically based Victorian phraseology against a rapidly changing, twentieth-century landscape, thus causing it to lose coherence as the characters were hurled forward through a rapidly changing, twentieth-century culture. This shift created a continuing *recontexting* of language through which new objects and experiences were mediated. A simple eggbeater, for example, became imbued with talismanic powers. This clash became the stuff of the play, superseding character development or traditional conflict. Content was factored on a moment-to-moment basis, as language and meaning altered continually through the shifting historical context. By the play's end, the audience had experienced a new form that privileged the journey of language as much as, or more so than, the voyage of the characters.

As playwrights, we can glean something more profound: the play itself is a system of language. Traditionally, the playwright strives for coherence at all costs. Coherence is the by-product of recognizable conventions deriving from rules that set up probabilities and expectations. In *On the Verge*, Overmyer establishes coherence, and then bursts the bubble. Dialogue does more than bring the characters into interaction; it becomes the free radical that "osmoses the future." Characters blurt newly discovered utterances, surprising themselves and the audience with each new value and meaning. It is "through language" (*dia* meaning "through," *logos* meaning "language"), that we experience Overmyer's play.

VIRTUOSITY AND THE NEW PLAYWRITING

A distinction can be made between the new playwriting and more traditional methods: the striving for virtuosity and stunning effects versus the notion of the script as a vehicle for actors and production. Realism favors the more or less unseen hand of the artist/playwright since the goal is to simulate or represent reality. Unfettered by these concerns, the new playwright is able to create an anti-world of their own, and thus allotted considerably more flexibility. Theater seems to be witnessing a renewal of the virtuosic today through increased attention to the uniquely theatrical. The language playwrights are exploring the power of stage language, reigniting the appeal of virtuosic writing for the theater. While virtuosic effects may provide the signature of the new playwright, the truly realized master will combine this with a solid understanding of form and the underpinnings of narrative.

WHY FOCUS ON NEW PLAYWRITING?

Because new playwriting celebrates the playwright as a virtuoso of language, it represents the optimum model for a playwriting study. Moreover, new playwriting techniques offer theatrical solutions to creating *mise-en-scène* or for overcoming aggravating transition problems such as frequent blackouts and ponderous scene shifts. New playwriting promotes the aesthetic nature of play construction over political or thematic content. While a thematic agenda may be embedded in a given play, new writing is devoid of political bias or a particular cause. While many of the plays are thematically rich, they speak "on their own terms," rarely serving as mouthpieces for the political views of the playwrights. As a playwright you can gain specific insights into your craft without feeling cornered into an ideological camp. It is up to you to supply the particular content and thematic focus. It is about the exploration of writing strategies and formal devices, so there is a great deal to study and learn.

Unlike some other contemporary theatrical forms, new playwriting has not totally abandoned narrative. Many of these plays maintain story lines or plots, albeit in nontraditional formulations. To this extent, the plays and methods are more accessible than abstract, suggesting to the playwright new tools and methods of storytelling. As the so-called mainstream theater becomes infected by these advances in dramaturgy, it becomes incumbent on the developing playwright to acquire more innovative approaches to narrative and structure.

LANGUAGE AS STRUCTURE

New playwrights do not attempt to mirror or represent the visible world; rather, they create a theatrical world parallel to it, a world with its own ontology and conventions. This inimitable world enters into a dialogic relation with the "real" world. New playwriting, as does dialogism, "exploits the nature of language as a modeling system for the nature of existence" (Holquist 1990, 33). In this sense, language not only serves to shape the play's universe and fabricate character, but also provides the primary building blocks of the play itself. In the polyvocal play, structure is a product of the relational pattern between building blocks while style is determined by the nature of sequence and transition. The process of determining the best pattern is a major component of revision. Meanwhile, without the need to "mirror" reality, new playwrights are freed to pursue the theatricality of the play, a component that realism tends to downplay.

WIDER APPLICATIONS

Many of the terms that follow can be applied to a variety of theatrical phenomena beyond language playwriting. Performance art is often based on a system of juxtaposition and layering of polyvocal elements. The increasing trend toward "hybrid" performances suggests many instances of dialogic formulation. For example, Cirque du Soleil juxtaposes a variety of cultural and theatrical forms to redefine our notion of what a circus can be. In the 1940s and 1950s the playwright Bertolt Brecht experimented with hybrid forms in a manner that was essentially dialogic. *The Caucasian Chalk Circle*'s narrative is largely drawn from an Asian fable. The synergy of conflict in Lynn Nottage's *Ruined* (2009) derived from a combination of historical accounts and horrific personal narratives. The applications of dialogism are wider than the niche "new playwriting" would suggest. The recent transfer of *Bloody, Bloody Andrew Jackson* (2010) from the Public Theater to Broadway demonstrates that the clash of visual styles, language genres, and theatrical conventions has established the dominance of the hybrid within the new mainstream.

The reception by audiences of the hybrid should come as no surprise; consider that the phenomenon of Facebook, for example, allows individuals to construct a kind of multivocal assemblage of their life, drawing from a variety of sources and backgrounds, some real, some fantasy. Wikipedia is another example of a hybrid, constructed with multiple voices and sources, a true example of the polyvocal text—ever in a state of dialogic flux with its environment of readers and contributors. The hybrid is defining the current culture.

Familiarize yourself now with the terms that are used throughout this book. To progress more quickly, you will benefit by setting aside several afternoons or evenings to acquaint yourself with the plays referred to in each chapter. You are more apt to "get the feel of it" once you have established a frame of reference. The selected plays are published and readily accessible through any university library, or may be purchased through the publishers, at the Drama Book Shop in New York, or downloaded over the internet to your computer or Kindle. When possible, I have referred to a single play in various contexts, so as to facilitate your familiarity with certain techniques, while consolidating your reading time. A number of the newer entries are included in anthologies for your ease of access. For young playwrights, I urge you to reserve judgments like "I don't like this play," because a judgmental attitude will block you from engaging with key techniques. Keep an open mind. It is equally important to not get thrown off track because a given play challenges your comfort zone. This, after all, is the point. A final word on the plays: read with the eyes of a craftsperson. Give a close reading! Pay particular attention to the use of language, how sequences and transitions are made, theatrical devices, and the "raw materials" or sources used by the playwright. A focus on character and device functions will provide insight into the dramaturgy.

If you like, you can proceed directly to the appropriate section in the book for a more detailed explanation and for examples and exercises. Cross-references to other terms in this list are indicated by SMALL CAPITALS.

Absent "other." An offstage character addressed in monologue through indication, symbol, or by substitution. See Chapter 11.

Anchor character. The main character or protagonist in the broadest sense.

Back channels. In the TURNS-oriented approach, back channel refers to a section of dialogue that is recapitulated later in a sequence, after it has been dropped as a topic in the dialogue. The successful use of back channels allows the playwright to thread a narrative while maintaining a TURNS approach.

Beat. The smallest identifiable unit of action, language, or thought that the playwright works with. Can be isolated from other units and is the building block of the script. See Chapter 9.

Beat rollover. The process whereby the actor plays through intermediate beats to create some particular effect or moment.

Beat segment. Multiple beats are grouped together around a given action or topic. A beat segment can vary in length from several beats to a dozen or more. A significant structural component in the development and, later, revision of the playscript. See Chapter 9.

Captioning. A narrative or rhetorical device in which a speaker announces a shift in scene or locale, or provides brief commentary to a stage event. Captioning is a variation of FRAMING. See Chapter 12.

Carnivalesque has to do with strange combinations, the overturning of expected norms, and the grotesque. Usually featured are abrupt shifts from high to low diction, whether slang, specific speech regionalisms, colloquialisms or profanities. Carnivalesque characters conflate bestial and human traits or exhibit other oddities:

1. Santouche in Mac Wellman's *Harm's Way* alternates elevated language with vulgar speech and profanity. Speech is carnivalesque rather than character specific. It masks and unmasks, is impulsive and full of surprises.

2. Characters in Anne Washburn's *Apparition* move between a faux Latin and American English, often to create articulatory effects, or commentary. Foreignisms take on a poeticizing aspect that features the phonic over semantic.

3. The carnivalesque character Human Salamander in Carson Kreitzer's *Freakshow* is part amphibian, part human, indicating a conflation between human and bestial realms.

For more on the carnivalesque see Chapter 2.

Character clash. The juxtaposition of characters from opposing historical eras, genres, or languages to create polyvocality and difference in the play. See Chapter 3. An early example is Adrienne Kennedy's *The Owl Answers*, which juxtaposes characters from various historical eras; another is Young Jean Lee's *The Appeal*, which clashes the Romantic poets Byron, Coleridge, and Wordsworth with a contemporized Dorothy, and shifting levels of speech and profanity.

Character-specific. In traditional play development, character-specific refers to the principle that each character should speak a consistent way or within a certain range, dependent on education, cultural background, occupation, and the like. See Chapter 2.

Chops. The confidence and facility of technique. The playwright's "sound." On a level of force and confidence beyond what is being said, chops give stamina to the play. See Chapter 9.

Commedia dell'arte. A late Renaissance theatrical form that emerged in Italy and was based on specific, predetermined character types denoted by costume, mask, movement patterns, dialects, and behaviors. The harlequin, for example, always wore a patchwork or diamond-shaped costume and a black mask, and was governed by opposite behavioral traits: cunning/stupid; lazy/agile and quick; thief/confidant. See Chapter 4.

Contexting defines how a term or word can shift meaning in a play's text depending on its function in a specific context. In DIALOGISM, a word is never isolated nor a meaning fixed; instead, words are "in dialogue" with other words in constantly changing circumstances. Contexting is derived from Bakhtin's technical term *heteroglossia.* See Chapter 3. As examples:

1. Wellman's Girl Hun in *Whirligig* establishes new meanings for 1960s lingo by conflating it with 1980s vernacular.

2. The alien characters in Constance Congdon's *Tales of the Lost Formicans* are plummeted into a world in which the relation between word and function provides the basis for the humor. The audience delights in the imaginative means given to everyday objects, now imbued with talismanic powers.

3. In Ruhl's I*n the Next Room, or the Vibrator Play,* the nineteenth-century characters have no context for the invention of the vibrator. Mrs. Givings refers to it as a "farm tool."

Contour. Each BEAT SEGMENT suggests a certain definable shape, or contour: jagged, sinuous, flat, rounded, straight-ahead, angular, S-shaped, or elliptical, for example. A stylistic consideration, since it provides the "signature" of the playwright. See Chapter 9.

Crossover poetics. The integration or interpolation of new playwriting techniques within conventional or mainstream formats: *Topdog/Underdog* and *The Clean House* are among those discussed herein. Typical of the style of Sarah Ruhl, Naomi Iizuka, and prevalent in playwrights' collectives such as Clubbed Thumb and 13P.

Deictic language is language that provides orientation: adverbs such as here, there, and now indicate immediate spatial or temporal conditions; pronouns, particularly second person (you, yours, etc.), create presence "in the moment." Deictic language connects characters to each other or to a given environment.

Dematrixing. The device of breaking or fracturing the mold of a specific character through a variety of means. Often, the results will FOREGROUND the actor over the character. See Chapter 12.

Development. The various and intermediary phases of a play's growth, from concept, research, and initial drafts to workshops, rehearsals, staged readings, previews, and ultimately finished production.

Device. Utilizing a physical object or prop toward a dramaturgical end. For example, the cellphone and vibrator, respectively, in Ruhl's *Dead Man's Cell Phone* and *In the Next Room, or the Vibrator Play.*

Dialogism. The play is "fundamentally polyphonic or dialogic rather than monologic (single voiced). The essence of the play is its staging of different voices or discourses and, thus, of the clash of social perspectives and points of view" (Culler 1997, 89). Internal dialogism refers to the play's capacity to interact within itself, as if the various components were in dialogue with each other.

Dialogic clash occurs when language levels, speech genres, or discourses collide in the play's script. See Chapter 3.

Difference. Opposed to unity, difference seeks to establish arbitrary or intentional breaks in convention or expectation, utilizing techniques of juxtaposition or conflation. For example, an eighteenth-century figure enters into a play set in the present. Another current practice is to set an apparent period for a play, then violate it with present day references or commentary. See Chapters 3 and 4.

Disponibilité. A concept term coined by the French surrealists that suggests an openness or spontaneity in the act of creation.

The dominant. A literary device that provides the structural underpinning of the play. See Chapter 12.

Dramaturgy. The construction and articulation of the play and its characters.

Equivocal character. The capacity to switch or transform from one character into another and back again facilitated through some trigger device. See Chapter 5.

Façade. Type of performative approach to character in which an identity is concocted or manufactured to attain a certain goal or information.

Euclidean character. Wellman's derogatory term describes the traditional approach to characterization, whereby every "character trait must reveal an inner truth about the character, and each trait must be perfectly consonant with every other trait." See Chapter 4.

Foregrounding. Giving special emphasis to make a word, device, or character stand out from surrounding factors or circumstances. Foregrounding is achieved through interruption, repetition, intonation, or reversal of expectation.

Formalism. The study of language and language devices as primarily aesthetic concerns. Language is considered as it functions autonomously from meaning or content. The Russian formalists, who emerged in the early part of the twentieth century, influenced developments in futurism and semiotics.

Found texts. Existing works that can be used or appropriated as source materials for new works. See Chapter 3.

Framing. A metadramatic technique utilized to change a spatial or temporal setting. In practice, framing is related to a narrator who "sets the stage" for a theatrical or dramatic event: Shifts levels of "reality" in a play and draws attention to the structure. Other elements such as sound, setting, or lighting can serve as frames.

Free radical. In a TURNS-ORIENTED approach, the free play of words or phrases affects rapid shifts in dialogue and monologue. When language is the free radical the play "becomes a discovery" as Overmyer posits. The free radical SPINS a line of dialogue or monologue in a different or divergent direction. See Chapter 9.

French scene. A structural unit defined by a character's entrance or exit. See Chapter 10.

Grafting. Recycling FOUND TEXTS into new Work. Lifting "strips of dialogue" from their original sources and utilizing these strips as character dialogue. See Chapter 3.

Groove. Unlocking the essential rhythms and pace of the play through close attention to the integration of language with spacer beats, such as pauses, rests, and silences. Most notable in Suzan-Lori Parks's recent work, especially, *The Red Letter Plays, Topdog/Underdog* and *365 Days/365 Plays*.

Hybridization is the mixing or clashing of different genres, cultural or historical period styles, and techniques. For example, the farcical mixes with the serious, the high-toned with the vulgar, the sophisticated literary with traditional folk tales; Eastern performance traditions exist side by side with Western approaches.

1. Iizuka's *36 Views* juxtaposes East Asian iconography and Kabuki characterization within the realistic depiction of a high end Western art gallery.

2. Jenkin's *Poor Folk's Pleasure*: in this ensemble play a mélange of characters performs various roles. The play mixes futurist performance, children's songs, a game show, carnival sideshow, and scripted and scenarioed sketches with a linguistic range from gibberish to Finnish.

3. In *Topdog/Underdog*, Parks conflates references to Lincoln and Booth, minstrelsy (Lincoln's white face), and the speech genre of the three-card Monty hustler, within the realistic context of a contemporary flat shared by two struggling brothers.

4. Charles Mee's *Big Love* (and *The Trojan Women*) mixes farce, pop songs, slapstick, and physical comedy within the framework of a classical tragedy: Aeschylus's *Suppliant Women*, Euripides' *The Trojan Women*.

For more on hybridization see Chapter 3.

Interruption. Used to break continuity, impede the easy access of form and content. A character changes into another character, interrupting the previous character's "through line." Interruption causes the audience to refocus attention, to work at "getting it," in a sense. Related to the formalist device of impeded form. See Chapter 5.

Journey play. A common structural format in new playwriting, the journey play involves the passage of space and time, and usually includes a traveler figure who moves between narrative and dramatic functions. Often based on a quest or search. See Chapters 3 and 12.

Markers. Signals for the audience that suggest various phenomena: a change in direction or character; anticipation of forthcoming events; a key name or identifying characteristic. Markers are important structural components of a dramatic work. See Chapter 9.

Metadrama. A self-referential literary element or device that exposes the machinery of the play. Some examples include a play within a play, an interpolated story, or a prologue delivered by an emcee. Story forms like fables and parables call attention to form. Homage, through references to past plays, literary works, or playwrights, offers another example of a metadramatic device as does intertextuality—a play's relation to past or similar plays, or specific dramatic conventions.

Metatheater acknowledges the existence of the audience—through direct address, asides, song, eavesdropping, and so forth. Metatheater exposes the artifice of the representational world. It foils the so-called willing suspension of disbelief. Any element that calls attention to the theatrical event may be considered metatheatrical. The traditional metatheatrical devices are augmented in the new playwriting to include sound techniques such as voice-overs, miked narrators, and other effects. The performer who "drops the mask" and acknowledges self as actor during performance qualifies as metatheatrical.

Monologism. Monologic approaches tend to be more planned, or static; the play "knows where it's going." Thus, traditional approaches to writing dialogue are usually more monologic than dialogic. David Lindsay-Abaire's *Rabbit Hole* is discussed. See Chapter 11.

Monologic/dialogic continuum. Table 1.1 demonstrates the difference between monologic and dialogic playwriting, and how new playwriting differs in varying degrees from conventional approaches. While set in opposition, these terms operate in a continuum of more or less; some or all elements on the list may apply in a given context.

Table 1.1 Monologic versus dialogic plays

MONOLOGIC	DIALOGIC
Unity	Difference
Linearity	Juxtaposition
Consistent	Hybrid (multiple sources, genres)
Genre tracking	Turns
Integral character	Split or bifurcated characters
Created materials	Found, borrowed materials
Drama	Metadrama
Language reflects culture	Language is a counterpoint to culture

Multivocal character. The multivocal figure bulks multiple speech strategies in a single character. This character can change level or approach to language "on a dime." See Chapter 2.

Negative space. The space between speeches or dialogue; includes the use of ellipses, pauses, silences, and other breaks of dialogue or monologue to create tension and interest. See Chapter 9.

Nouning. Wellman's technique involving the linear stacking of nouns or phrases, which are read sequentially, usually in a monologue format. Wellman describes the cumulative effect as "radioactive," insofar as word collisions create a kind of fission. Has become a commonplace of new playwriting seen quite often in works by Parks and Mee. See Chapter 12.

Ostranenie. A term from Russian formalism, a "making strange," the dislocation in agreement, function, or context, such as that between word and object. Related to Brecht's concept of alienation. As examples:

1. Parks's *Topdog/Underdog* utilizes "white face" in Lincoln's carny portrayal of his namesake, thus reversing the traditional "black face" of minstrelsy.

2. In Overmyer's *On the Verge*, eggbeaters found by the characters, who are unaware of their traditional function, are transformed into pistols.

3. In Congdon's *Tales of the Lost Formicans*, a hole in the backrest of a chair is seen by aliens as "the ever present eye of God" (I:1).

4. Sheila Callaghan's *Crumble* opens inside the set of an apartment, with the apartment delivering a monologue as a "character" in the play.

Pivot monologue. A *tour de force* by a secondary character that rebalances the hegemony of the single protagonist or anchor character.

Point. The culminating moment of emphasis or action in the scene. Should reveal something that is of crucial significance in the script. See Chapter 10.

Pointing. The actor's process of underscoring and emphasizing key words in a speech.

Polyvocality. Multiple language strategies and sources coexist in the play. Characters and narratives within the script may contain diverse interests or objectives, expressed in different speech forms. Polyvocality resists the notion of a single or dominant point of view in a narrative, thereby supplanting the single or privileged authorial voice. See Chapter 3. As examples:

1. Multiple narrators in Jenkin's *My Uncle Sam* foil any sense of linear narrative or central character.

2. The shifting narrators in Jenkin's *Dark Ride* undercut any sense of TRACKING the narrative.

3. Contemporary adaptations of most classical plays conflate the original authorial voice with the adapting playwright's.

Riffing. Repetitions, embellishments, or variations derived from a word or phrase of dialogue. Shadow riffing is an extreme variant of this principle. See Chapter 9.

Role-playing. The character takes on a specific performative function, by assuming either a different character or a front specific to a profession. Fronts are typical behaviors associated with a given profession to manage an impression. See Chapter 2.

Scenario is a BEAT-BY-BEAT narrative description of what happens in the play. It represents a sketch outline of the play.

Skaz. A type of monologue in which the character's mode of language seems independent from the rest of the play, and possesses an improvisatory quality. Matilde's opening joke in Brazilian stands independently from Ruhl's play *The Clean House*. The term originates in Russian Formalism. See Chapter 12.

Speech acts. Words or phrases that anticipate immediate or deferred action. Speech acts can take a number of forms; some examples include threats, promises, vows, or commands. See Chapter 9.

Speech genres. Language specific to a given profession or cultural group. Defined by patterns of speech, rhythms, and commonplaces. Some examples: auctioneer, sportscaster, weather man, preacher, hustler.

Spinning. In a TURNS-ORIENTED approach, dialogue feeds off itself, developing an oblique momentum that quickens the scene; this vertiginous effect is called spinning. See Chapter 12.

Stage figures. Unlike a standard character, a stage figure is given identifiable form by the playwright and actors through gesture, movement, posture, and costume; these forms are recognized and given specific traits and characteristics by the audience. Once formulated, the image of the character speaks for itself. See Chapter 4.

Story forms, genres. The formalist device of reinventing old forms such as parables, fables, or detective novels can create a dialogic and metatheatrical tension between content and form. New subject matter is "framed" through recognizable or antique story forms. The adherence to the story form is somehow made strange, oblique, or parodic. See Chapter 3. As examples:

1. Several critics considered Wellman's *Harm's Way* to be a perverse parable based on the Jim Jones massacre in Guyana.
2. Len Jenkin's *Kid Twist* represents a bowdlerized version of the gangster legend.
3. Nottage's *Ruined* integrates African storytelling techniques, songs, and personal narrative accounts of the victims.

4. Charles Mee's *Big Love* frames his heightened language and *tour de force* exploration of marriage and love using the first extant classical play, Aeschylus's *Suppliant Women* to provide his narrative structure.

Telegraphing occurs when a thematic "message" or other information is stated or divulged gratuitously by the playwright. Telegraphing serves the convenience of the playwright. See Chapter 12.

Tracking. Plot-oriented approach structured toward intensification, with complications building to a climax. Adjusting the dialogue to a previously constructed scenario rather than a language-oriented approach.

Turns simulate the give-and-take of dialogue and may include digressions, hesitations, BACK CHANNELS, even blind alleys or dramaturgical non sequiturs. Spontaneous and exciting for the writer, the turns approach keeps action in the present moment. Characters respond to the flow of language and situation. The downside is that it may lead to more significant revision than the tracking method. Table 1.2 indicates the different outcomes between the tracking and turning approaches.

Table 1.2 The tracking approach versus the turns approach

TRACKING APPROACH: DIALOGUE DETERMINED BY PLOT	TURNS APPROACH: DIALOGUE AS FREE RADICAL
Monologic play	Dialogic play
Character-specific dialogue	Multivocal characterization
Genre (comedy, farce, tragedy)	Hybrid (mixed genres)
Theater	Metatheater
Definite historical period	Conflated or contrasting periods
World of the play	Clash of worlds
Actor becomes character	Actor performs character
One character per actor	Two or more characters per actor
Character's internal motivation	Device of language as motivation
One narrator privileged	Multiple narrators
Protagonist-driven	No central character necessary; may be ensemble

Writing "off the line." Characters speak obliquely; meaning is carried subtextually.

Writing "on the line." Characters state directly what they mean.

Examples and exercises

Most of the preceding terms are defined more thoroughly in the following chapters. The terms are supplemented with examples and exercises that encourage practice in a specific technique. Generally, exercises follow the narrative discussion or analysis of a given example. To reemphasize: your understanding of each example will be enhanced if you read the entire play. Read the plays primarily for technique and strategy. Even if you do not like the play, you should be able to glean pertinent data from it. The exercises that follow the examples have been classroom or workshop tested by undergraduate and graduate playwriting students. I have provided a "comment" at the end of each exercise to give you some particular insight into how it might be applied in a workshop setting. The exercises are designed to increase your playwriting skill and dramaturgical understanding and are a key component in your growth as a playwright. For playwriting instructors who want to expand their pedagogy, they provide a sense of structure that challenges the student while allowing for a wide breadth of individual expression. In my experience, the more closely the students adhere to the structure of the exercises the more successful and satisfying are the outcomes. Jargon is kept to a minimum, although certain "concept" words are necessary to accurately describe and categorize techniques.

WHAT IT MEANS TO WRITE DIALOGICALLY

For the language playwrights, there is never a case of reducing the character to an idea; rather, the playwright energizes the capacity of language to give the character freer reign in exploiting the linguistic possibilities present in the dramatic moment. The result is the creation of formidable character identities shaped and sculpted by language rather than predetermined by psychological profile. To write dialogically, the playwright must let the characters speak their turn—the characters share the spotlight, striving to be "first among equals."

From the playwright's standpoint, the creation of the dialogic play can be construed analogically as a way of governance through sharing. Some have sensed its political corollary in pure non-totalitarian Marxism, which argues that "sharing is not only an ethical or economic mandate, but a condition built into the structure of human perception, and thus a condition inherent in the very fact of being human" (Holquist 1990, 34). We see evidence of this "sharing" in the spread of Wikipedia as the major source of information now on the internet. The internet site Scripped.com offers playwrights and screenwriters the opportunity to collaborate on group projects and to freely discuss each other's work. In the collectives of Clubbed Thumb and 13P the formation of the text is often collaborative. Madelyn Kent and Lynn Nottage work with non-native speakers in establishing their plays. Young Jean Lee built her text for *The Shipment* through workshops with black actors. In these cases, the "actor/character as independent self" becomes the material of the play; put another way, the character imbued as self can assume "authorial" function, whereas the traditional character serves the function of the author. *NPS2* mandates that the "other" is always a factor in the creation of the play. In these examples from the playwrights Nottage, Lee, and Kent, the author may be considered an orchestrator or arranger as much as an originator. Here, we emphasize the writer as play maker.

The system that follows should never be seen as rigid dogma but as both a point of entry into new playwriting and a point of departure for your explorations in playwriting. The goal is to inspire your creativity as well as bolster your technique. Dialogize with what you find in the book. Some points will resonate with you, others may not. Be aware of your three centers as you intake information. The book is not intended as an intellectual exercise, so, like the skilled and smart actor, open your heart and lower body to unlock potential blocks. Ultimately, it is my hope as a playwright, coach, and developer that you will encounter the observations and examples to challenge your current writing practices. I wish you success!

PART I

Strategies of language and character

2

On multivocality and speech genres

A core characteristic of the new playwriting is its emphasis on the *multivocal* character and the *polyvocal* text. The principle of multivocality refers to a single character's speech strategies throughout the play's script. Polyvocality expands this scope to include the orchestration and juxtaposition of all voices present in the play. Generally, the polyvocal text combines or draws from various language-based source materials, although sources may vary from image or sound-oriented, to those drawn from different contextual constructs. Examples of the latter include the penetration of minstrelsy in Suzan-Lori Parks's *Topdog/Underdog* and Kabuki theater in Naomi Iizuka's *36 Views*. The next chapter explores polyvocal strategies in the creation of the hybrid play. Because multivocality bulks speech strategies within one performer, the term is associated with the development of character in new playwriting.

The multivocal character is primarily constructed from language, and written to speak with unlimited linguistic potential and range, from street slang to high-toned discourse, and across languages, dialects, and speech genres. As a product of language, the character assumes a carnivalesque capacity for conflation and juxtaposition—in other words, differing, even contradictory, speech styles and strategies coexist in a variety of combinations. The term *carnivalesque* also suggests some overturning of traditional norms governing dialogue and characterization. It is as though the language eclipses or transcends characterization as the playwright pursues some residual essence or defining moment. The writing of the play becomes an encounter with language; the playwright challenges character (and actor) to execute split-second changes in intention to effectively meet the language shifts. Ultimately in new playwriting, character emerges as a function of language.

In traditional dramaturgy, language is a subordinate ingredient—one factor among many in the creation of the character. A character exercise earmarked for beginning playwrights makes this fact readily apparent: the creation of the saturated biography. The "saturated bio" explores all elements of the major character's "back story," the fictional history of the character before the beginning of the play. The playwright concocts cultural, educational, and geographic data that combine to influence a character's patterns of speech, word choice, and linguistic bent. This fictional world that the author (sometimes in workshops with the actor) creates establishes a specific psychological profile emphasizing a subtextual approach to characterization. This subtextual probing precedes (and may supersede) the exploration of the real text. Inevitably, the actor will know a character's super objective before fully engaging what the playwright has written. Tangential factors outside of the play become increasingly important; actors may balk at readings, or in rehearsal, taking the position that "my character would never say this."

The goal in traditional character development is to achieve character-specific language for each character. Character-specific dialogue has become a canonized term for play developers, surrounding the formation of character like a hawk, swooping down to eliminate digressions or anomalies in an attempt to neaten the character's arc or progression across the play. Character-specific as a descriptor suggests that the writer has found a "voice" or sounds specific to each character in a play—one that simulates real life and promotes the exploration of subtext. The problem with character-specific dialogue is that in real life people change mode, style, and level of speech to fit each situation. Most of us change speech strategies and corresponding gestural indicators to fit a context or circumstance. Nonetheless, character-specific dialogue ensures a degree of consistency in characterization and as such still reigns as a benchmark of playwriting craft.

On the other hand, the new playwright approaches multivocal speech strategies as a restaurant customer approaches a smorgasbord: with variation and multiple combinations in mind. For the playwright, variation may be shaped by a circumstantial shift in the play, or self-directed, arbitrary, and impulsive. This impulsive aspect can offer the playwright a wide menu for developing the nuances of a character's voice. It may establish a more or less carnivalesque turn (like Jell-O on the roast beef at the smorgasbord), overturning self-censorial restrictors in the establishment of dialogue. It unlocks the character from the limitations of a speech that is class or ethnically determined. Some early examples from new playwriting progenitors make the point.

In Mac Wellman's *Harm's Way*, the character named By Way of Being Hidden oscillates between a pompous, distancing, high-toned level of speech and a brutal, "in your face" approach (Wellman 1984). The gangster figures in Eric Overmyer's *Dark Rapture* (1993) speak with an intellectual fervor that is at first shocking as it transcends their *film noir*-esque tough-guy talk. The multivocal approach offers the playwright the option to conflate or juxtapose formal patterns, rhetorical strategies or foreignisms—whether real or concocted, as in Nottage's *Ruined* (2009) that conflates English with moments of African dialect, or Washburn's *Apparition* (2005) that concocts a faux Latin language. The formal patterns may vary from single syllabic repetitions to the polysyllabic to simple articulatory sounds, as indicated by examples from Suzan-Lori Parks's *Imperceptible Mutabilities in the Third Kingdom;* as publisher Douglas Messerli notes, the character Kin-Seer's "'Gaw gaw gaw gaw eeee,' ... is representative of the monosyllabic utterance to the [character Us-Seer's] purely articulatory ... 'FFFFFFFFFF'" (Messerli 1998, 877). The trend continues. Reflecting their bestial desires, the characters in Alice Tuan's erotically charged *Ajax(Por Nobody)* juxtapose sheep-like utterances, "meh meh meh ... etc." with normative dialogue (Wellman and Lee 2006, 304). This non-semantic use of language recalls the futurists' penchant for transrational language, with its strictly auditory appeal.

The rhetorical style may switch instantly from the massively monologic to the transparent one-liner: Messerli notes that the character Ray's four-page *crise de coeur* in Wellman's *Hyacinth Macaw* is capped by Dora's laconic rejoinder, "As we burn so are we quenched" (Messerli 1998, 1098). Often in new playwriting there is fluctuation from the conversational to literary styles, as exhibited in the writer's speech in Len Jenkin's *Limbo Tales:*

> WRITER: ... Am I awake? I've dreamed poems before, but this is extraordinary. I remember every word of it. It may even be good. Good? Genius! Stately pleasure dome! Caves of ice! This one will hit the anthologies for sure! ... Uh ... or ... What if I forget it? What am I thinking? I'm a writer. I'll write it down. (*Sound of typing* ...) Sunless sea! Nicely turned ... decree, sea ... This is fabulous—I don't even have to think! ... Mazy motion ... ah! ... A miracle of rare device? I love it, and there's more.
>
> (Jenkin 1993, *Limbo Tales*, 43)

In this passage, Jenkin is exploring two common features of multivocality: the juxtaposition of language styles and a patently dialogic approach to monologue (see Chapter 12). Moreover, there is a playful self-satisfaction in the character's unfolding discovery of language at the moment of its creation. While Jenkin's multivocal strategies are often used to effect structural aspects of his dramaturgy, in many cases, they simply provide grace notes or a sense of delight in word choices and combinations. The playwright is refreshed by a discovery, and this uncovering triggers more pursuits. The journey through language becomes a curious search for essences and wonder.

In rapid succession from Scene 6 to Scene 8, Young Jean Lee's *The Appeal* reveals the romantic poet Wordsworth, first "masturbating furiously" after consuming opium; then reciting his "heightened" poetry "in the darkness," concluding with this exchange with his sister Dorothy:

> DOROTHY: You're a total and complete fucking moron.
> WORDSWORTH: What?
> DOROTHY: What.
> WORDSWORTH: You just said that I was a total and complete fucking moron.
>
> (Wellman and Lee, 2006, 164–5)

In this play, Young Jean Lee effectively dismantles the stilted codes and accepted protocols for correct early nineteenth-century speech, unabashedly imbuing it with the profane and accusatory tone and utter banality of present-day conversation. Wordsworth's contretemps with fellow poet Coleridge contrast perfunctory speech with high-toned rhetorical arguments or philosophical ruminations. Lee even uses intonation to create multivocal effects, as Coleridge alternates between "gruff" and "normal" voices in presenting his new poem to Wordsworth (Wellman and Lee 2006, 160).

A MULTIVOCAL MENU

An effective way to achieve multivocal characterization is to shift the core vocal strategy, to alter the code from the expected or stereotypical. These shifts can be gradual or extreme depending on the effect desired. The more expected codes are violated or subverted, the more powerful the effect. This multivocal menu will provide you with a range of possibilities as you begin a new play or plan a revision of an existing work:

- Alter the level code: high-toned to standard to primitive; colloquial to slang.
- Alter the mode/code of speech: rhetorical, political, technical, jargon laden, literary, poetic, and practical.
- Alter the language or dialect code: character has second language or uses multilingual foreignisms, broken English, regional dialects—some of which may be understood by other characters. Foreign words may carry articulatory interest.
- Alter the syntactical code: deviate from traditional sentence structure, tense agreement; unique word arrangements in the script (see nouning, Chapter 11).
- Alter semantic code: words, speech genres, and so on shift meanings throughout the play. Neologisms and obscure words replace mundane descriptors. Proper names become signposts, adding specificity to the speech.
- Alter the intonation or voicings of the words: this may involve pitch, vocal placement, or articulation of sounds.

COMMENT: Jumps within and across speech codes are most evident in new playwriting, and have permeated more or less mainstream dramaturgies. Case in point: Lynn Nottage's *Ruined* which uses African dialects juxtaposed to English to establish local color and authenticity. These leaps create color or "radiance" of speech and affect a kind of "aura" about the language. These qualities inspire confidence and interest in the "smart" playwright's craft. While some leaps may seem extreme, it is important to consider that the multivocal character is an inevitable outgrowth of our multicultural, global environment.

EXERCISE:
Shifting levels of speech and "topping"

1. Write a scene in which two characters utilize a particular level of speech. For example: Character A grunts, is inarticulate, or speaks in profanities. Character B delights in jargonized, highly elevated speech.
   - Give them an action: each one is trying to describe the same event, a physical object, or person using a speech strategy from the multivocal menu.
2. Bracket areas of the scene where you will insert multivocal speech.
   - This should vary from the character's primary mode of speaking.
3. Allow A to speak in fluid English with an enlarged vocabulary and sense of polish: Let the speech carry the same intention as in the initial draft, but note the difference in effect and interest. Find a different vocal range for B. For example, B might shift to lower level slang, profanities, etc.
4. Note how intention seemingly follows the shift in vocal mode, as the characters react to the shift. Try to have each character "top" the other. Change intonation to mock the other character.
5. Which language strategy dominates? In other words, which character wins the argument? Or do they reach an impasse; is the "action" resolved?

COMMENT: Experiment with multivocality, testing the limits of what characters can say, and how other characters respond. Allow a character's language choice to trigger responses in the other character. Focus on the listening skills of each character. Note the specific shifts in language during the scene. "Topping," in which one speaker attempts to outdo the other, will stretch the playwright's linguistic abilities.

MULTIVOCAL DRAMATURGY: A SENSE OF THE BAROQUE

Another way of understanding how multivocality works is to compare it to the baroque style. The baroque is a recipe for opposition and tension as opposed to harmony and balance. The baroque intertwines, juxtaposes, is serpentine, or swings between polarities of high and low, comic and serious. There is a sense of sweep, mass, grandeur, and an exploration of the passions. In art, consider the florid, sensual paintings of Peter Paul Rubens, or the tension between light and dark areas (chiaroscuro) in a Caravaggio painting; or, in sculpture, the serpentine movement that belies the mass of Giovanni Bernini's figures. In dramatic literature, the baroque describes the late-sixteenth-century Spanish Golden Age plays that explore the polarities of love versus duty, comic versus serious, and religious versus sensual. Baroque is always associated with the emergence of opera, which is grandiose in scale and features virtuoso singing and special effects. Baroque operas and plays contain heightened, overreaching characters. Their dramaturgies feature abrupt shifts or contrasts from scene to scene, double or multiple plotting, the contrast between the serious and the comic, and a sense of the ornamental or florid. Through its oppositional nature, the theatricalized baroque approach simulates a dialogic strategy in which carefully constructed tensions are held in taut balance.

A self-described baroque sensibility is evident throughout Eric Overmyer's oeuvre, whether for theater or television. For example, the plotting of both *Law and Order* and *Wired* relied on weaving multiple and often-divergent story lines toward a final conclusion. As executive producer (or chief writer) of these popular series, Overmyer innovated a baroque approach that forever changed the landscape of police dramas. On stage, through his heightened characters' aria-like speeches with their sudden twists and turns—as in Babcock's opening monologue in *Dark Rapture*, or in Hungry Mother's vocal tirades of dialogic circumlocution in *Native Speech*, which exhibits mass and dimension. Note the sharp turns of phrase and topic in the hyped-up disk jockey Hungry Mother's aria, late in the play:

> And now this hour's top short stories ... Dengue Fever raging out of control across Sub-Sahara Africa ... absolutely terminal, no, I repeat, no antidote ... Green Monkey Virus spreads from Germany to Georgia! If you gush black blood you've got it! And you're a goner! Isn't that something?! ... And ... the Pope is engaged! We'll be back later in the week with more on the Forty-Second Street sniper. These are this hour's top tales, brought to you by Ominous Acronyms Ominous Acronyms, dedicated to raising the ante no matter the pot. And now a spiritual word of advice from the pastor of the First ... Chinese Baptist ... Church of the Deaf! ("chinee") Leveland Bluce Ree here. Lememble! Don't wait for the hearse to take you to church! (Cheery) Thank you Leveland Bluce. Next hour, my impression of a JAP. And I don't mean Japanese. Don't miss it. But first? ...
>
> (Overmyer 1993, *Native Speech*, 39)

Overmyer's oppositional push and pulls within this speech reflect the baroque dynamic of creating form through dynamic tension. Rather than emphasizing the internal psychology of the character, Overmyer's multivocal shifts demand an external, hyperbolic acting approach that favors verbal and gestural exaggerations. Hungry Mother's mimicked Chinese dialect reflects not only its articulatory aspect but also the derisive edge in the intonation of the accent. Overmyer requires the actor playing Hungry Mother to make pinpoint shifts, challenging the actor to differentiate topics through intonation, rhythmical emphasis, or changes in rate. These juxtaposed turns are indicative of the extreme dialogism inherent within and across the speech strategies.

We can now examine multivocal strategies at closer range, dissecting individual components that make up the language-based approach to playwriting.

In his later writings, Mikhail Bakhtin stressed the importance of speech genres as a means to understand how certain utterances emanate style and meaning and provide a sense of intonation. By definition, a speech genre is coded language that is suggestive of a certain group, occupation, literary genre, cultural bias, and so on. As such, speech genres may include discourses, dialects, idioms, and slang; in everyday usage they typically function as a kind of linguistic shorthand. For this reason, speech genres offer a valuable language option to playwrights who seek to establish context quickly and avoid lengthy expository dialogue. In *Poor Folk's Pleasure* Len Jenkin establishes a sense of place and circumstance through the repetitive patterns and staccato rhythms typical of the game show host:

> GIRL: We have a winner, we have a winner! Number 18. Seven tickets, any prize, bottom row. Known from the rock-bound coast of Maine to the sun-kissed shores of California, it's Fascination. Time for another game of Fascination, Time for another game of Fascination! (rings bell) Roll 'em up! Roll 'em up! And the first ball is out.
>
> (Jenkin 1993, *Poor Folk's Pleasure*, 9, 286)

Because the speech genre of the game show host immediately establishes a sense of context, the playwright is open to explore nuances in texture, rhythms, and coloration. The structure of *Poor Folk's Pleasure* juxtaposes numerous speech genres (such as salesperson, newsperson, carnival barker) across the play to create a collage-like polyvocality.

Playwrights constructing a two-hander (a two-person play) are always faced with the problem of sustaining interest within a context of limited interaction. Suzan-Lori Parks effectively parodied the black dialect genre in *The Death of the Last Black Man in the Whole Entire World*. However, in *Topdog/Underdog*, her use of "speech genre" grounds the action of the play in a specific language strategy—unique in shaping the world of the play. By utilizing the palaver and patter of the "three-card Monty hustler," Parks moves our perceptual field from the apartment to the "street" as we become the audience for the hustle. The heightened presence and immediacy of the language suspend any sense of interiority we might experience in a traditional one-set environment. Thus, Parks's use of this speech genre creates both a performative and multivocal world of the characters, while it transcends the spatial limitations of the setting itself. Language in *Topdog/Underdog* is doing the heavy lifting, making the dramaturgy pliable and resilient.

Unlike most speech genres, the distinct and specific cadence of the hustle is to keep the viewer/player off balance. Moreover, the language is accented with the shuffling and dealing of cards, so both the eye and ear are engaged. Parks keeps our attention in the moment, because like Booth, we do not want to be duped as the cards are dealt. This juggling between the physical and verbal creates a heightened immediacy and groove that allow the monologues to move quickly yet rhythmically. The speech genre provides the structural underpinning of the play; it is the arc of this hustle that ties us to the characters' fate through the progression of the play. It provides the moment of Booth's final humiliation that triggers Lincoln's demise; it sets up the brother's master/apprentice dynamic as Booth struggles to gain the expertise of his world-weary brother.

> LINCOLN: Lean in close and watch me now: who see thuh black card who see thy black card I see the black card blackcards thuh winner pick thuh black card that's thuh winner pick thuh red card that's thuh loser pick thuh other red card that's thuh other loser pick thuh black card you pick thuh winner. Watch me as I throw thuh cards. Here we go.
>
> (Parks 2002, 4: 6–65)

Speech genres operate dialogically, functioning specifically within the play while referring back to the cultural or professional site of linguistic origin. David Mamet utilizes specific speech genres to establish power struggles but also rituals of male bonding in *Glengarry Glen Ross* (salesperson talk) and *Speed the Plow* (Hollywood movie lingo). As a strategy, the playwright can alter, or appropriate, the context of the speech genre to effect thematic resonance. Harold Pinter, for example, utilized the idiomatic "odd man out," taken from sports parlance, to describe the triadic dynamic underscoring the characters in his play *Old Times*. Once the genre is established it can be manipulated or "played with" as material in the text. This dialogic tension creates meaning and interest. For example, Hungry Mother's arias are based on the speech rhythms of a typical disc jockey whose patter is broken up with weather reports and on-mike advertisements. Throughout the play, Overmyer subverts or "makes strange" the standard hourly weather report by substituting Hungry Mother's "street drug reports." He parodically names the station's paid advertiser "Ominous Acronyms." For Overmyer, the deejay's linguistic bent provides the format and point of departure for this virtuosic defamiliarization.

In new playwriting, the use of speech genres is a core language strategy that is readily accessible to young playwrights who want to expand their dialogic skills. Examples are readily available: Mac Wellman's intergalactic vocabulary in *Whirligig* and *Albanian Softshoe*; Jenkin's proclivities toward the 1940s slang of detective novels and *film noir* in *Kid Twist* and *My Uncle Sam*; Overmyer's use of foreignisms and dialects throughout *In Perpetuity throughout the Universe*; Suzan-Lori Parks's parody of black dialect in *The Death of the Last Black Man in the Whole Entire World*. Establishing several speech genres across a play will effect polyvocal tension. Parks does this effectively in her *Red Letter Plays*, which feature a range of speech genres from the welfare case worker to the "official" speak of the doctor and reverend (Parks 2001).

Other examples include juxtaposing language from various eras: in Jenkin's *Gogol*, Pontius Pilate's arcane biblical phraseology clashes against the epigrammatic tendencies that identify the quack, Dr. Mesmer, with utterances like, "My motto is service" or "cop and blow."

EXERCISE:
Speech genres

The objective in this exercise is to become acquainted with the use of speech genres.
1. Tape an announcer of a sporting event, game show, auction, or carnival.
2. Transcribe the key phrases, repetitions, and transition points, attempting to grasp the rhythms and intonational subtleties of the speaker.
3. Write a monologue using the transcription as a point of departure.
4. Option: Recontextualize the genre along the lines of Overmyer's Hungry Mother's "take" on the traditional disc jockey.

COMMENT: This exercise runs the gamut, requiring the playwright to use technical means (taping, transcription) to achieve imaginative ends. The execution of step 4 will offer the potential for discovery by refitting the genre into a new context. Intonation, which determines how words and phrases are voiced by the actor, is embedded or coded within the speech genre. Intonation suggests the way of saying a phrase or speech style, whether from the carnival huckster, the gangster tough guy, or the sly femme fatale. In *Dark Rapture* Overmyer offers a Marlene Dietrich-like approach to stating sexual desire through the femme fatale Julia. Julia's breathy call for sex is "Pull my focus, cowboy."

DIALECTS AND FOREIGNISMS

How far can the playwright go with dialects and ethnic stereotyping without being offensive? New playwriting has largely refuted the move to politically correct orthodoxy, which it decries as a form of self-censoring. For example, Jenkin parodies the Charlie Chan type in several plays that feature a Chinese laundryman ("no tickee, no shirtee"); similarly, opium den denizens are found in Jenkin's *My Uncle Sam* and Overmyer's *The Heliotrope Bouquet*. Wellman's seminal article, "Theatre of good intentions," derides the politically correct model as voiding the theater of energy and risk. Indeed, the problem of properly identifying with the correct sociopolitical agenda has been a difficulty for the African-American playwright Suzan-Lori Parks. Her play *The Death of the Last Black Man in the Whole Entire World* (Mahone 1994, 239–80) conflates black American dialect with the conventional speech genre of the "stage Negro," a character type derived from minstrelsy. The character Queen Then Pharaoh Hatshepsut offers an example in the first scene:

Before Columbus thuh worl usta be roun they put uh /d/ on thuh end of roun makin roun. Thusly they set in motion thuh end. Without that

/d/ we coulda gone on spinnin forever. Thuh /d/ thing ended things ended.

(Mahone 1994, *The Death of the Last Black Man in the Entire World*, 251)

Parks's strategy of dialect, linguistic event, and typification of character diminishes the importance of the content-related issues concerning Christopher Columbus and the shape of the world. Through the speech, a phonetic, actually phonemic variable /d/, has significant repercussions suggesting that the inclusion of /d/ changed the course of history. Parks's focus on the phoneme /d/ further draws associations to the colonization of the New World, and by implication, its connection to slavery. At the same time, the /d/ draws our attention to the language-oriented nature of the play—here bracketed in its smallest phonemic sense. For new playwrights, interest extends beyond words to what can be verbalized or vocalized—it can be about syllables, sonic utterances, or phonemic variables. The bracketed /d/ dialogues between its formal capacity as a sound unit and its ideological ramifications.

Parks's typified character names establish a risky ideological context: Black Man with Watermelon; Black Woman with Fried Drumstick; Lots of Grease and Lots of Pork; and so on. Parks shapes their language into formal linguistic patterns using stereotyped inflections and accents. The result is a form of parodic metaspeech (speech that calls attention to itself). Parks's concern with creating a unique language for her plays, and for being absorbed in the formal or plastic quality of language, has led to criticism from members of the African-American community who define the need of the African-American theater to be consciousness-raising, thereby advancing social, cultural, and economic awareness.

The use of foreign utterances can certainly provide tension between formalist and sociocultural aspects of language. In Overmyer's play *In Perpetuity throughout the Universe*, the Chinese-American character Dennis Wu recounts a joke in Chinese:

DENNIS: New gee ng gee do Cock Robin mei yup ying yip gai gee chin hoy geo mut murn? Kurn jal hey geu jo Penis Rabinowitz! (*Laughs uproariously, Then tells the joke in English:*) What was Cock Robin's name before he changed it to go into show business? Penis Rabinowitz. (*Stone faced. Shrugs.*)

(Overmyer 1993, *In Perpetuity*, scene 23, 211)

Overmyer provides a multilingual example of dialogism, in which the real humor is disclosed through the articulatory aspect of the sound of the words rather than their meaning, which for American audiences would be unknowable. Dennis's deadpan shrug seems to acknowledge the tired mundanity of this old vaudeville joke, contrasting with his expressive response to the ersatz foreign version.

Combining dialects or foreignisms with other speech strategies will enhance the aural texturing of the playwrights' work. Madelyn Kent's *Sachiko* imposes Japanese syntax on American speech to create a distilled, yet strange sounding of language that embodies the sinister nature of the encounter between the Taxi Driver and the young woman, Sachiko.

> SACHIKO: It is sweet of you. What are you doing in midnight?
> TAXI DRIVER: I just taxi driver. But I found you. When my customer.
> Getting off before.
>
> (Wellman and Lee 2006, 119)

Kent, whose plays have been produced at Soho Rep and the Public Theater, developed this play through improvisations with Japanese wives in her theater workshop. The effect is to create a distinct "sound" to her dramatic language that remains in dialogic tension with normative syntax.

EXERCISES:
Multiple languages or dialects

1. Write a two-character scene that involves the beginnings of a committed relationship. One of the characters speaks a foreign language or relies on dialect; use dialect or ethnic expressions.

   - Have the other character react to these speech patterns to either provide a source of insight or conflict with the "other."

   - The characters work through obstacles of alienation, frustration, desire, and so on. Resolve scene as they either come together or pull apart.

2. Place several diverse characters in a situation or event where they cannot clearly understand each other, yet are thrown together: in a lifeboat, a room in a burning building, or a hostage takeover—the setting exerts pressure on the individuals.

   - Use language to create or motivate comic outcomes based on the situation. Allow language interactions to reflect cultural differences in customs or conventions, for example.

Here are three exercises to work into a play you are redrafting, or a new play you are conceiving:

1. Utilize a strong dialect or ethnic "take" on English, as a springboard for an apparently weaker character.

2. Give all the characters in your play a different dialect, language, or regionalism, attempting to use the speech as a comic handicap. In other words, there are misunderstandings, strange pronunciations, and ethnic idioms that must be interpreted and played off of by other characters.

3. Review several movies from the thirties and forties that feature the speech of recent immigrants; attempt to transcribe phrases and key words. Integrate these into the dialogue of a character you are currently revamping.

COMMENT: Utilize YouTube to upload examples of various accents and dialect patterns. This allows you to hear the intonation in speech, and the various placements of articulators that create sounds unique to a region or country.

FROM DISCOURSE TO SLANG

In Mac Wellman's *Three Americanisms* (Wellman 2001, 185), three characters without names are juxtaposed in a clash or collage of discourses and slang rearranged through Wellman's idiosyncratic syntax. Discourse, unlike normal dramatic or conversational language, is distinguished by coded words, "buzz-phrases," often with a reliance on technical terms or argot. Underlining the strategy of a discourse is an essential ideology and historicity. To this extent, discourse is time bound. Examples of discourses include the Marxist, academic, feminist, theory-based, technology-based, scientific, fascist, medical, religious Right, Tea Party, traditional liberal, Southern preacher, and environmental. Discourse gives a character an ideological front or façade that may be activated strategically to empower, intimidate, moralize, or to aid and inform. In new playwriting, however, discourse tends to be more ruminative than argumentative, more marginalized than mainstream. It moves along by association and incremental repetitions rather than by progressive trails of logic. In this sense it is more dialogic than dialectic, since new playwrights rarely advance politically committed positions. Its dialogic and ruminative bent tends to personalize the rendering of language; thus, a character emerges rather than a thematic cipher—telegraphing the playwright's message. Often, the character will reflect upon or work over the discourse being said. This passage from Jenkin's *Limbo Tales* illustrates that move, from the anthropology professor Driver's taped pedagogical discourse to his commentary on his lecture for Anthropology 201:

Once the Mayans constructed their grand pyramid at Uxmal, on top of it was stationed a man chosen by lot, called the Illum Kinnal, the Time Watcher. His job is to protect the sequence of orderly time, to keep it running smoothly from past to future. He does this by guarding it with his eyes. If his attention weakens for one moment, there is a subtle break in the time line. Past. Present and future mix. Work in the fields stops. People have visions, headaches, momentary hallucinations. The priests notice, and the Illum Kinnal is killed, his heart offered to the gods, and he's replaced by another time watcher... .

DRIVER: I don't think I'll mention it to Anthropology 201, but the truth is that the Mayans were nuts.

(Jenkin 1993, *Limbo Tales*, 21)

Invariably lively and entertaining, new playwrights often use historicized discourse to instruct, combining what the nineteenth century called "lay sermons" with the American tradition of tall tales. Jenkin's Mayor, in *American Notes*, is typical:

> This is amazing country. Sea to shining .... I'll tell you what it is. It's fertile. I was on my way out the door one day, little buddy of mine, about to take my mayoral constitutional, had a handful of pumpkin seeds to munch on the road. I turn around to wave goodbye to the wife and kids, and one seed fell outta my hand. Before I could turn back around that seed had taken root in the earth sprouted up and spread so high and wide that I was dangerously surrounded by enormous serpentine vines, caught in their green clutches. The volunteer fire department had to break out the axes and cut me loose …
>
> (Jenkin 1993, *American Notes*, 242)

Along these lines is the discourse that stems from a troubled consciousness, evident in the characters Hawthorne and Melville in Jenkin's *Kraken* (2008), and lurking ominously in the character Death. In the beginning speech of his *Dark Ride*, the Translator strives to find the meaning of an ancient text. His various interpretations provide the basic story line for the play. Interest in the character is created as he works over the possibilities in front of the audience. Depending upon its application, discourse provides the character with special knowledge about a person, object, place, event, worldview, and so forth. The Translator figure has special knowledge about interpreting nuances of arcane manuscripts. Special knowledge, which is borne in discourse, thus becomes a significant factor in the making of character.

EXERCISE:
Scene revision/special knowledge

This revision exercise gives a character in a scene special knowledge about something; this knowledge can be emphasized by raising or lowering the level of diction. Len Jenkin factors in special knowledge to "professionals" that show up in his plays: the tattooist, the mesmerist, the game show host, or the others who "have the goods on someone else."

1. Select a scene from something you have written that contains two or three characters of a specific social class.
2. Allow one character a heightened level of knowledge about another character. The disclosure of this knowledge should surprise others in the scene. The information revealed is crucial to the action of the scene. It may be a particular secret, something hidden that is revealed.
3. Utilize coded words, special jargon, foreignisms, and so on. To varying degrees, this framing of discourse establishes an ironic or self-parodying take on what is being said.

COMMENT: Wikipedia and YouTube will provide you with ready sources and examples of special knowledge enough to give your character the aura of authenticity.

Capability Brown's ruminations on gardening in Jenkin's *My Uncle Sam* demonstrate his special knowledge within the framework of eighteenth-century historicized discourse:

> The apple, poppies, pumpkins, and all melons come to fruit. HAVE FOLLOWING: IN THE EARTH: mounds, grotto crypts. ON THE EARTH: groves, labyrinths, fountains. IN THE AIR: aviaries, containing the ostrich, peacocks, swans, and cranes. Buzzy bees. A slew of automata among the rocks. Include my patented mechanism for the production of artificial echoes.
>
> (Jenkin 1993, *My Uncle Sam*, 181)

Lifting directly from Capability Brown's eighteenth-century journals on designing the English garden, Jenkin reframes Brown's discourse within a contemporary play. The "estranged" context and linguistic eccentricities (e.g. "Buzzy bees") create particular interest in this theatrical character. Rather than being built from a psychological model, the character emerges from a particularized discourse and sense of place. In new playwriting, the projection of discourse never seems arid or pretentious because the actor can sense an underlying earnestness, sincerity, or buoyancy in writing that is eminently playable.

EXERCISE:
Developing discourse

Character as discourse: Revise a scene you have written by introducing a character who serves as a narrator/commentator on the action. Multivocal characters might change the levels of discourse across the play or in a given speech. When several discourses are present in a play, they create an internal dialogism.

1. Make this narrator figure an expert—such as a doctor, psychologist, witch doctor, professor, biologist—of some arcane knowledge; the more extreme and 'marginal the better. Imbue the character with a particular discourse. Use coded phrases, vocabulary, and syntactical choices.
2. Write a monologue in which the character attempts to describe a discovery just made. This may involve an object, an experiment, a body, and so on.

COMMENT: Dramatic interest need not be tied to rising action, structures of causality, and strong protagonists. Within the dialogic scheme, more options appear for the playwright willing to experiment, opening the notion of what defines a play. In the above monologue, the character, through description is really attempting to gain control of the object. Nevertheless, the recontextualized discourse offers both juxtaposition and comic potential in action. Search

SLANG AS SPEECH GENRE

Slang is the flip side of formal discourse: operating as coded language: its usage is initially restricted to those "in the know." Identifiable through its subversive and often profane words and phrases, slang is a species of speech genre, and is introduced along the societal margins before it is accepted into mainstream usage. As it assimilates into general parlance, slang takes on broader applications and meanings depending on context. Eventually, slang dates itself, and is mediated out of contemporary speech. This state of flux makes its usage solvent for playwrights because historicized "lingo" is immediately identifiable to audiences, creating a specific sense of genre and period. Onstage slang becomes "framed" or foregrounded. Transplanted from its particular sociohistorical context, it is refrained in a theatrical context.

Moreover, slang operates dialogically, resonating between current and contemporaneous contexts. While the word "buzz" in the 1970s may have referred to the reaction to an illegal substance, now it more often connotes a level of interest or reaction by a particular group. Sometimes, gestures operate similarly to slang. For example, an actor making the peace sign (a V with his fingers) will be read differently by a Vietnam veteran, a war protester, or a twenty-year-old who has no personal associations with its historical origin. Other gestures provide shorthand corollaries to their more or less profane utterances.

Slang is usually made up of neologisms, or it may be recycled from a different context or era. An example of the former is Parks's *Fucking A* which uses the concocted slang called TALK; for example, die Abab-nazip is code for The Abortion. Parks uses TALK to artfully cloak vulgarities (references to female genitalia) that would otherwise be overly offensive to most audiences (Parks 2001, 223). Slang may range from impolite to profane, but should be colorful. In contemporary usage, discourse often combines with slang to create juxtapositions in sound and meaning. Slang encapsulates a specific action or takes in a short phrase, with language full of "pizzazz." To no small degree, the popularity of new writing can be attributed to this linguistic "aura," a by-product of the writing style and the sound of the spoken language.

EXERCISE:
Slang at the ultimate party

1. In the class or workshop, playwriting students should take a specific period and group to study with the goal of capturing slang, colloquial expressions, regionalisms, or foreignisms that define historicized or ethnicized Americana.

Consider the widest range, from pioneer, beatnik, or early immigrant to current New Yorker. Other eras rich in colloquialisms or slang were the swing era, the Roaring Twenties, the Old West, or the be-bop, surfer, hippie, yuppie, preppie; generation X, grunge, and valley girl eras. Consider using language-based dialects such as Cajun, Creole, Chicano (Spanglish), British, Irish, and Latino; also consider idioms from "the mob," the service (army, navy, etc.), the jailbird, or sports-related figures, and so on. (Overmyer frequently uses Spanish or Chinese speakers in his plays; he utilized Chinese effectively in *In Perpetuity throughout the Universe*. Wellman juxtaposes street language with various colloquial formats.)

2. Compile as many expressions, words, phrases, and gestures as possible, setting a time limit of about one month so that ample research can be conducted. Movies, books, and other contemporary references are appropriate.

3. Make a four- or five-columned list that might define the way a character speaks. The lists should be from opposing groups you have compiled. For example, one might be service-related, another generation X, another beatnik, and so on.

4. Construct a multicharacter scene that demonstrates the most incredible and extreme party you can imagine. Make certain that each figure you construct interacts at least once with each other figure. Vary the lingo according to character. Attempt to create a polyglot of speech. Don't be tame, really explore and explode the boundaries to the limit.

5. Allow the collision of lingo to somehow lead to a catastrophic event and pivotal moment.

COMMENT: The exercise above is a variation on the "Ultimate Party" exercise utilized by award-winning playwright Matthew Maguire. It challenges you to stretch your imagination and linguistic capacities. You will develop your ear and open your awareness to the richness of the American language. There are several questions to address: Why and how does language determine our perception of character? How does speech precede and predict events? In what ways does the context of the "ultimate party" allow for a release of the self-censor? In the workshop, you can Google any type of slang and get numerous examples and their meanings readily at hand. Divide the group into duos to execute the first three components of this exercise; then, everyone writes their own scene.

EXTREME RHETORICAL LEVELS

Language playwrights utilize rhetorical tropes and figures in their plays. Hyperbole, distortions, and diminutions stretch the boundaries or limits of language. They are most effective in determining a dominant language style for certain characters or types. The character Senator Armitage appears only once to deliver a monologue in Wellman's *Bad Infinity*, but his exaggerated, rhetorical style defines his pompous, overblown nature. Jenkin's oddball professors, like the "defrocked" scientist in *American Notes*, consistently try to persuade characters through exempla (examples). This persuasive tactic backfires when it reveals the twisted logic of the character's mind. Conflating the rhetorical with the grotesque can create stunning moments for the character (and the actor in performance). In Carson Kreitzer's

Freakshow, Judith (the dog lady) describes her debased act in the tent side-show in rhetorical flourishes:

> JUDITH: More rips than dress.
> Caged up, men starin' down at me.
> I'd see the sick thing swelling in their drawers. And me, and me down on all fours. I'd sniff over to him givin' the evil eye an' I'd set up a howlin
> AAAAOOOOOOOUUUUUU
> Then you'd see 'um shrink and quiver, yes
> Then you'd see a True Believer. Scared on back to wife and kinder.
> Never see her in her night-dress with the light on.
> Never see her down in the dirt.
> Gotta pay to see a woman debased. With'r ass in yer face. Licensed, like.
> It's all right. Gotta pay to see a woman down. In the dirt.
> Course you could just knock down the one you got. Many do. There's lots do that. Knock the one you got in the dirt.
> In front of God and Kinder.
> All in all, this's Easier. A woman so ugly you can't look her in the face.
> You can't help but look her in the face. Can't help but stare.
> GOD SHE'S UGLY and all that Beauty down Below.
> Swollen pink and white and muddy. What's that Glimpsed a bit through her nightie. Sure that's a nip. Godawmighty what an ugly. What a beauty.
> It starts stiffing in their pants and I come a howling. Dog girl can sniff out sin in yer pockets.
>
> (Striar and Detrick 2007, 294)

Kreitzer's Judith reverses standard norms on what is beautiful and what is ugly in the female body. While formatted as monologue the rhetoric is dialogic: from her howling as a dog to her directed interactions toward the sexually aroused men who ogle her. Kreitzer uses carnivalesque speech to juxtapose the sublime with the grotesque, the human lament with the bestial howls. References to "True believer," to God and Kinder, and "sniffin' out sin in yer pockets," are redolent of a reverend's homily. Kreitzer captures issues of objectification and abuse in a *tour de force* of sarcastic rant. While the dog lady's debasement is total, she seems morally inured to her audience's responses. The effect is problematic as Judith, despite the psychic humiliation, finds some palliative value in her performance.

Occasionally, Wellman explores a political matter in an estranged or oblique way. The following speech of Sam's, near the conclusion of *The Professional Frenchman*, follows the banal comments of the characters regarding a professional football game that Sam and Jacques have been watching and gambling on. Sam speaks:

> Take my advice Mevrouw. Never gamble
> Gamble against professionals.

They are merciless.

(*They laugh. Pause. Sam speaks in a strange demoniac, deep voice*)
You have to beat them
Into submission. Once you get a man down
In America, blessèd America,
You have to fucking pound
Him into the clay, you have
To finish him off. Destroy Him. Pulverize him. Be-Cause
if you show a man any mercy,
Any kindness. If you leave him with any
Small part of his self-respect He'll never forgive you, he'll
Make you bloody well pay
For every fucking thing you Ever did. For him.
Never give a man a second chance. When you get the opportunity
To eat a human being
Swallow him whole
Or grind him to
Pulp, but never NEVER
Leave the tiniest bit
Of living humanity left
Or you'll be sorry for it.
    You can bet your ass
Reagan won't. Reagan—Reagan the first …

(Wellman 1985, *The Professional Frenchman*)

Wellman's rhetorical strategy is made strange through *Grand Guignol* excesses of portrayal (the demoniac, low voice). He draws upon the genre of "coach speak," that is, the annihilation rhetoric of the football coach, the dog-eat-dog ethos that is this character's capitalistic mantra. Ideologically, through this rhetorical tirade, Wellman historicizes an essential element of the me-first Reagan years with a mocking, searing jest.

Language playwrights maximize the rhetorical proclivities and predispositions of their characters. To begin, I urge you to explore the comic potential of the rhetorical. You don't want a character to be pedantic and dull, as might be the case in reality. Pomposity, or the longwinded, can be handled in a humorous or ironic way if (1) the character delights in her wordsmithing; (2) other characters dissect the speech in a satirical mode; or (3) bizarre or peculiar linguistic relationships are posited and made palpable. The quintessential longwinded speech is Valere's from David Hirson's *La Bête*, recently revived on Broadway. His twenty-minute-plus monologue in rhymed couplets (no less) combines (1) and (3) above, although Valere himself provides the satirical bent (2) to the rant that motors it along.

In Jenkin's *Dark Ride*, Mrs. Lammle's rhetorical flights on the "world of coincidence" not only offer bizarre stories and a humorous characterization but also indicate that the worlds of this play are dialogically interrelated through happenstance. Mrs. Lammle's omniscience establishes a rhetorical or quasi-rhetorical stance, since the special knowledge of the omniscient character requires a degree of pontificating. Moreover, Mrs. Lammle's waxing about coincidences is reflected in the action of the play.

The playwright won't "hold the boards" with long speeches or philosophical debate unless these are somehow coded into the play. Kreitzer's example above, for instance, demonstrates an extreme take on character—it is theatrically coded and performative in giving a full range to Judith's vocal play and physicality. Mrs. Lammle's waxing about coincidences is reflected in the structure of the play as discoveries and revelations are the result of chance encounters.

MULTIVOCAL PROFANITY

American playwriting over the past thirty years probably contained more profanity than we find in current plays. The early plays of David Mamet and David Rabe had the power to shock audiences with profanity, but in the contemporary theater profanity has lost its capacity to surprise, shock, or advance fresh and daring subject matter. Religious-based or family audience members may find its excessive use offensive; nevertheless, the majority is inured to its effect. Indeed, our youth have grown up within a culture that finds it acceptable as a mode of social discourse. Sometimes profanity can be an effective means of characterizing an individual, particularly if contrasted with other linguistic styles in the play. Tony Kushner's rendition of the foul-mouthed Roy Cohn in *Angels in America* still rang true in its successful 2010 off-Broadway revival. Profanity works as character-specific speech in portraying the hardball style of Cohn. Unfortunately, young playwrights are prone to using profanity indiscriminately. In fledgling attempts to ape Mamet's macho, misogynistic style, they fail to match his nuances of rhythm and intonation. Young playwrights can avoid this trap by making more specific choices for insults or expletives.

Profanity can establish a level of multivocality when uttered impulsively by a character at an unexpected moment. In some cases, the "f word" is resplendent in its dialogic mutability. Note the various connotations of fuck in this selection from Jeffrey Jones's *Seventy Scenes of Halloween:*

JEFF: All right! I fucked her! Is that what you want to hear? Is it? You want to know, goddamn it, you're going to know: Three times I fucked her! One right after the other (which we never do). And the third time in the morning! And I can get hard right now just thinking about it. And yes—I feel guilty—okay? And, yes—I know it's fucking everything up—okay? And I'm not saying it's right or it's wrong except it's something I've wanted all my life and now I have the chance for it and I am not going to spend the rest of my life wishing I hadn't let it slip away! Does this mean anything to you or are you too fucked up with your own self-pity— I mean, look at you—look at you! Nine years! Nine fucking years, Joan, and none of it matters, does it? (The Twenty-Second Scene, 84-85)

(Wellman 1985, *Seventy Scenes of Halloween*, 84–5)

The poignancy of this cruel revelation notwithstanding, Jones is certainly "playing" with the meanings as he progressively alters the connotations of the word "fuck." Each meaning is contextually derived, its semantic range from denotation (intercourse) to emphasizing the ongoing futility in their marriage ("fucking years") to a descriptor of his wife's mental state ("fucked up") and the state of their marriage, how Jeff, the character's actions are "fucking everything up." Jones's strategic use of "fuck" makes a powerful statement that would not be as forceful or edgy otherwise. Moreover, he allows the actor significant latitude in terms of intonation, a factor the playwright must factor when profanities are sprinkled throughout the text.

The above example demonstrates how profanity/slang ranges from cursing and confrontation to more casual assessments ("fucking everything up"). Like all "lingo," profanity too can become dated. Profanity may underlie a speaking style that is irreverent, flip, and uninhibited, and this translates into a character that may seem more spontaneous and endearing than threatening to audiences. However, as the profane aspect is downplayed in most dialogue, its use can become superfluous and weighty. In Mikhail Bakhtin's scheme, profanity is defined as a form of grotesque speech offering strange juxtapositions or conflations that are colorfully scatological (such as "shithead" or "buttface"). These conflations have been staples of low comedy and farce since the Greek old comedy, but they may never exhaust their potential for new and more provocative configurations.

EXERCISE:
Playing profanities

This is a good exercise for working through or getting out the desire to see profanity in print. Indeed, for many young playwrights in the workshop, writing out this desire might serve as a rite of passage. Again, it's not a question of being censorial; rather, it's about the need to interest and surprise through the use of language. Sometimes profanity is the best or only way to get it done. For this exercise, use the example from Jeffrey Jones's play as a point of departure.

1. Write a moderate-length monologue in which a character either serves up, or receives bad news. Another character is addressed who may be present or absent.

2. Use one profane term four to six times, in various configurations. Consider the variety of meanings and intonations so that they are continually shifting.

3. Strive for some novel juxtapositions or conflations.

4. The character should make a transition from the beginning to the end of the speech; for example, from anger to resignation, indignation to humiliation, or ignorance to understanding.
5. Members of the workshop should read their monologues aloud, vocally indicating the changes in intonation.

COMMENT: In the workshop, upload video examples from Comedy Central and have members identify when profanity has a payoff and when it is simply gratuitous or shows a lack of imagination in the writing or delivery. Notice how the most effective monologists, like Lewis Black, always use profanity to create a build, a surprising juxtaposition, or even, a sense of pathos.

FACETING

Conceptualizing the multivocal character is similar to preparing a finely cut gem. The exploration in the early drafts is analogous to the jeweler's preparation of the roughly hewn gem—now to be realized in all of its refined facets: shaped, honed, and buffed to a fine finish. For the multivocal character, the facets of language create a network of dialogic relations that are held together in exquisite tension.

Multivocal faceting is evident in Wellman's one-person play, *Terminal Hip*. The re-formation of representational speech is accomplished through syntactical aberrations that try the seemingly familiar:

Your shoes are worth fifteen dollars a day, and buddy
we'll pay you hard cash money for them shoes
you got because we believe in giving hard cash money to people
such as yourself who as gots shoes on they feets sure you bet.

(Wellman 1995, *Terminal Hip*, 264)

While the first three lines establish or ground a kind of character-specific speech mode, Wellman quickly re-facets his intention in the final line with his disorienting syntactical choices.

Rather than reflect or imitate "conversation," Wellman arranges phrases and speech fragments to confront the context of representational meanings in language, echoing various speech rhythms and styles, while corrupting standard syntactical strategies. In recent works like *The Difficulty in Crossing a Field* and *Bitter Bierce* (Wellman 2008), Wellman celebrates the playwright's unique reformulation of historicized language as he confronts audiences' expectations of how language operates to fabricate the narrative. For example, faceting the multivocal Bierce includes juxtaposing discourse from his *Devil's Dictionary*, his short story "An occurrence at Owl Creek Bridge," various misanthropic diatribes, yellow journalist entries, and more normative biographical data. The arrangements of these "facets" not only marks the remarkable character of Ambrose Bierce, but provides the structure of Wellman's one-person play. In this sense, Wellman is the formalist, exercising the right of language to move beyond its representational capacity, to unleash the power of language as the modernist painters released painting from its need to represent objects. Faceting promotes a kind of formal arrangement of speech strategies, and marks the composite of the multivocal character.

EXERCISE:
Faceting and the multivocal character

(Read Wellman's *Bitter Bierce*.)

1. This exercise can be used to create the multivocal character from scratch, or to identify the multivocal components in an already constructed character.
2. Identify how many "facets" are in the composite character.
3. How do these component facets dialogize with each other.
4. What is the sequence of the various multivocal components?
5. Does each component have a shape or arc?
6. Hone and sharpen each part of the facet by paying careful attention to each transition in the characters language.
7. Come up with a "form" for your multivocal character in the terms of a shape (square, diamond, triangle, hexagonal, and polish each component accordingly. How many component parts can be identified in Bierce, for example.
8. This provides you with a good method to evolve the formal structure the multivocal character.

COMMENT: Ambrose Bierce was a writer and journalist, so Wellman had an array of materials available to create this multivocal character. As you consider writing a multivocal character the more source materials you can assemble the better the chance at an optimum composite characterization.

SPEECH STRATEGIES AND THE IMAGINATION

As this chapter demonstrates, the multivocal approach offers numerous strategic options to the playwright. Tactically, as a matter of craft, they can be combined, conflated, or juxtaposed. Nevertheless, it is up to the playwright's imagination to transform the patchwork into a satisfying quilt, one that holds interest and elicits wonder. So while you dutifully pour over these elements of craft and construction, never be afraid to let the imagination trigger your foray into language. Open all your senses to the possibilities— anticipate the wonder that is coming, as the character Tim does in Jenkin's *American Notes*:

> TIM: You are a man who can smell true love when it's coming down the street, you can smell it coming to you cross the rivers and seas, its odor mixing with the salt spray and the quick perfume of the flying fish ....
>
> (Jenkin 1993, *American Notes*, 234)

3

Polyvocality and the ascendancy of the hybrid play

The dialogic play is by definition polyvocal. Polyvocality suggests that a variety of language strategies, voices, and source materials may be used by the playwright to construct the play's text. Variable language strategies might include changing the level of language or speech style through slang, discourse, speech genres, or syntactical choices. Unlike a single "playwright's voice," a hallowed term in play development circles, the new playwright may orchestrate a polyphony of voices across an array of characters. For example, one character may speak with a dialect, while another utilizes foreign terms. Some voices are derived from transcriptions, others from arcane, popular, or historical sources. These myriad sources include film and literary genres that "frame" our perception of the written play. At times, the source might be an arbitrary word or neologism inserted into the dialogue to provoke the playwright and the play in a different direction.

The new playwright continually responds to the "other" in the shaping of the script. Quite simply, the playwright synthesizes, alters, and re-channels the component voices and sources, establishing, as the play is written, the nature of the juxtapositions, clashes, and conflations. To accomplish this effectively, the playwright must become a master strategist as well as an imaginative creator. Knowledge of various strategies will enhance creativity by providing more choices and reference points. Optimally, the playwright's voice will be stretched in different directions, expanding their range of possibilities in the writing of the play. While striving toward virtuosity, it is at first important to achieve competency in the basic principles involved. In this chapter, we will identify how polyvocality can be implemented into your play making.

Polyvocality mandates that different, diverse, and often clashing elements converge in the making of the playtext. The outcome of the polyvocal approach can be described as the *hybrid play*.

DEFINING THE HYBRID PLAY

What is the hybrid play? The hybrid play is a literary and theatrical cross-breed, a blending of genres and disparate sources both textual and performative. In many cases, the sources are unrelated and may appear to be random or arbitrary. The hybrid play may take on myriad forms and combinations: from literary pastiche to collage-like performance pieces. The collage is an apt corollary from the world of art, since collage transforms diverse found materials into a new, aesthetic whole. The collage artist gives over to the transformative potential of the raw material. The transformation in the function of the materials through juxtaposition and arrangement gives the collage its sense of wonder; new playwriting, which has been described as the "theater of wonders," shares this magical capacity with art.

The history of the hybrid play features the putative master, William Shakespeare. Most Shakespeare's plays are constructed hybrids; materials are drawn from diverse sources, genres, and historical accounts. Story lines or entire plays (such as *King John*) are reformulated to fit the author's scheme. Shakespeare was not beyond synthesizing well-known or commonplace materials in shaping his plays. *Cymbeline* embeds a popular story from a Giovanni Boccaccio novella with elements adapted from a *commedia dell'arte* pastoral scenario.

Shakespeare also adapted characters and traits from other idioms: the advising, meddling father Polonius, from *Hamlet*, is a descendant of Pantalone from the commedia dell'arte—a literary and performative source. Many of his royal characters are drawn from Elizabethan historical accounts documented in the *Holinshed Chronicles*. Early plays reflect the wit and badinage of early modern speech genres, and showcase Shakespeare's background in Latin. Historically, the measure of artistic genius in the late Renaissance was based on the success of the invention (*inventio*) the author applied to found materials, and the arrangement of parts (*dispositio*), rather than the creation of a work solely from the imagination or observation of real life. Then, the author would focus on the execution of language (*elocutio*), which included figures of speech, metaphors, and the degree of wit, for example. So while sources were lifted, the author impressed the audience with skills in language and characterization. This process is really quite similar to the making of the contemporary hybrid play.

Along the way, the hybrid has been difficult for some periods and authorities to accept. Theatrical hybrids, such as the opera, pantomime, and vaudeville, were extremely popular and successful with contemporary audiences. However, these forms have met with staunch resistance from authorities. French seventeenth-century academies declaimed the contamination of dramatic genres in an attempt to codify tragedy and regulate comedy. The Italian comedians, who relied on a polyglot of dialects and masks, were banished from France in 1698. English politicians in 1737 licensed out of existence a number of the successful companies performing pantomimes (harlequinades) and ballad operas. Until recently, scholars and academics have relegated the theatrical hybrid to inferior status or have simply ignored it as a subject of study. Preference is given to dramatic literature that can be categorized in terms of genre. Published anthologies privilege those dramas that fit into categories: realism, neoclassicism, classical tragedy, restoration comedies of manners, and so on. The irony is that these genres have become historicized whereas the prevailing trend is toward hybrid structures.

The twentieth century brought the advent of the living newspaper plays, and of course, Bertolt Brecht's epic theater. Hybrid structures welcomed innovations like multimedia that could be interpolated to serve political ends. Brecht recycled cabaret songs, elements from the folk theater, and story forms like the parable. His *The Caucasian Chalk Circle*, for example, includes an opening section reminiscent of the proletarian "socialist realism" plays common in East Germany at the time. To address a problem that arises on the collective farm, a Capo uses the Simon and Grusha folk-tale to make a didactic point. This inner story is presented as a kind of absurd parable with the entry of the corrupt Azdak, the paragon of arbitrary justice. Brecht's move from socialist realism to folktale represents a clash of literary genres. No effort is made to synthesize the two, although both "texts" inform each other. Brecht's socialist prologue in *The Caucasian Chalk Circle* framed the traditional folktale—that is, the journey of Simon and Grusha—toward a didactic outcome.

In 1978, I attended a performance of the late Spalding Gray's seminal *Rumstick Road*. I was struck by the juxtaposition of Gray's own character with the voice of his mother as it was heard through the theater's sound system. Gray recycled tapes his mother had made with her psychiatrist prior to her suicide, and integrated them into the performance text. As found objects the tapes were recontextualized within a performance mode. Gray's one-person, autobiographical hybrid was a seamless pastiche of found and created materials. Here the playwright serves as compiler, adapter, and arranger—more accurate a descriptor than playwright as creator. Lynn Nottage, Eric Bogosian, Peggy Shaw, Young Jean Lee, and Guillermo Gomez-Peña (among others) have continued this form of theatrical polyvo-cality: for example, both Nottage (*Ruined*) and Gomez-Peña (*New World Border*) juxtapose racial and cultural voices; Shaw (*Menopausal Gentleman*) expresses the multiple and contradictory voices of gender. These artists serve as the conduit or filter for plural voices they recycle and integrate into aesthetic form. At the borders or boundaries between "voices" meaning is determined. Similarly, the ensemble Wooster Group recycles and juxta-poses textual and found materials to create truly dialogic performance texts. In the hybrid form, narrative is often diminished in favor of aural landscapes and exciting spectacle. The trend toward the hybrid has perme-ated the musical genre with the successes of *Spring Awakening* and *Bloody, Bloody Andrew Jackson* rejecting the traditional book musical toward a mélange of rock-and-roll, full environmental settings that break the fourth-wall, and historical pastiche.

NEW PLAYWRITING AND THE HYBRID

A widely held belief among theatergoers is that great playwrights possess signature, distinctive voices that are immediately identifiable. As new playwrights trend away from the mainstream, their virtuosic use of language and theatricality sets them apart and becomes definitive. Indeed, they could be considered benchmarks of the individuated style. Their harshest critics laud their use of language, if not their unique dramaturgy. However, underlying the identifiable "sound" of each playwright are shared characteristics that can be explored and recapitulated.

New playwrights, whether by plan or intuition, embed diverse source materials, styles, formats, and approaches into their plays. The combinations may be integrated into the text, as is the approach in Charles Mee's adaptations, or stand side by side, as juxtapositions in the hybrid structure. Naomi Iizuka's *36 Views* accomplishes the latter, as Kabuki stagings complement a more or less conventional play. Len Jenkin's plays reflect a menu of hybrid options: in *Kid Twist*, the gangster idiom is integrated into sketches involving American icons like Babe Ruth and the Joker, from *Batman* comics, as well as the signature event of the Nazi dirigible the Hindenburg's burning; *Limbo Tales* is really two separate acts linked only by a narrating character, the Master of Ceremonies, who also provides an "intermezzo" bridge between the separate acts. The two acts of *Limbo Tales* stand in juxtaposition but are neither thematically nor dramatically similar. In *Like I Say*, Jenkin provides a trackable, sequential through line that is interpolated with puppet shows and intermezzo breaks. The intermezzi and puppetry are throwbacks to the Renaissance practice of offering variety entertainment during the act breaks. By its inclusion of these non-dramatic formats, the hybrid places emphasis on the theatrical. *Poor Folk's Pleasure* is a hybrid in its overall formation; a structure that is mirrored in a number of scenes. Scene 4 interpolates a "live" scene from the movie *Spartacus* into the ongoing action to create a kind of surrealistic effect:

SALESMAN: I believe I'm in a hotel. I'm sure of it. I've been in them before. Not exactly like this one. Similar. I have no conception of why my employers imagined I should be able to sell here. The planet's dead. I think I'll watch some local television. Uh oh. No television in my room. I'll go down to the TV viewing lounge in the hotel basement.

He moves to another area where a MAN watches television.

The TV is already on. Kirk Douglas in Spartacus. A man is watching ... I think it's the same man who welcomed me at the desk.... Hmmm ...

A portion of Spartacus is performed, live: noble Romans with British accents, Kirk, slaves etc. The MAN watching turns off the TV.

Now he's not looking at the TV any more, but at a picture that hangs on the wall nearby. It's of a young girl. [To MAN] Excuse me, I'd like to pester you with some sales talk if I may.

MAN: Look at her. Carefully. Tell me what you see.

SALESMAN: She looks very pretty ... and a little sad, Perhaps she lost her ...

MAN: She was a murderess ...

(Jenkin 1993, 274–5)

Later in the scene the "live" version of *Spartacus* returns. Hybrid elements are "made strange" as they are removed from their original contexts. Jenkin's scene clashes theater and film worlds, but also performance styles and historical genres. Rather than run a tape of the movie, which would not read theatrically, Jenkin "exploits" the theatricality of the *Spartacus* segment with its "gladiatoresque" costumes and Kirk Douglas impersonator. Jenkin derives humor and whimsy from the juxtapositions of real-time action and virtual time parody; contemporary dress versus "historical" costume; and dramatic versus performative values. Language dialogizes between spatial realities, and across narrative, dramatic, and theatrical elements to affect a kind of restless dramaturgy. The *Spartacus* segment, as a "send-up" of the film, primarily serves as a comic marker, although many of the male baby boomers in the audience have special attachment to the film as a cultural icon. Younger audiences will be familiar with the legend through the current television series. The embedding of American cultural icons in his plays is a standard of Jenkin's dramaturgy, continuing with *Kraken* (2008), which featured the 1856 meeting of troubled literary giants trying to reclaim past glories while skirting Death: Nathaniel Hawthorne and Herman Melville. In Sheila Callaghan's *Crumble (Lay Me Down, Justin Timberlake)*, a glib Justin Timberlake "flies" in to fulfill the eleven-year old Janice's dream; a few scenes later, her mother is visited by Harrison Ford, defined linguistically by his signature laconicism. These Hollywood send-ups, requiring an intonation shift in the actor who plays both, comment theatrically on a celebrity-crazed culture (Striar and Detrick 2007, 70–80).

CLASSICAL ADAPTATION AND HYBRID STRUCTURE

In creating the hybrid play, the playwright serves as conceptualizer/adapter as much as author of materials. While remaining authorial, the playwright is seldom the sole generator of textual materials. This is particularly true in the case of adaptations of classical works, in which elements of the source text are used, removed, or recycled as a point of departure for the playwright's re-creation. In adaptation, the writing only begins after an arduous process of selection, arrangement, and formulation. Often, multiple sources and translations provide the core materials. Many playwrights today view adaptation as the quintessential hybrid, as the overlayering and addition of various theatrical and contemporary components obscures or supplants the original source text. The adaptation process forces the playwright to change function from the sole creative source to the imaginative responder of plural elements.

Adaptation covers a continuum of approaches with a large degree of variance and techniques. For example, Charles Mee's adaptation of Euripides' *The Trojan Women* utilizes loud rock music, sounds of aircraft and bombs dropping, with video footage of the carnage of war to open the show. As the play continues, there are frequent breaks for rock songs representing a variety of styles and eras, and some will appear tangential to the original narrative. Mee's hybrid approach consistently favors the theatrical over the dramatic. On the other hand, Karen Hartman's *Troy Women* contemporizes Euripides' play while remaining faithful to its structure and characters, with the notable exceptions of Cassandra and the chorus. Rinde Eckert's Pulitzer finalist musical (2007) *Orpheus X* contemporizes the Orpheus/Eurydice legend, with the titular character played as a brooding and blocked rock star who has lost his muse. Alice Tuan's eroticized *Ajax (Por Nobody)* sends up the Sophoclean original with references to Ajax cleanser and the character's sexual interactions with sheep. The original becomes fodder for the adaptation, rather than a serious retelling of Sophocles' original, in which Ajax slays (rather than lays) the sheep. In Tuan's take on Ajax, Alexander describes his sister's erotic interaction with the sheep she called Z:

> ALEXANDER: That one would lick her all over, she'd giggle and giggle, try to catch its tongue in her mouth. Meh. She start poking at his wool, he'd lick even harder. Z'd even go down to her sacred spot and when and when his wand'd get lit, Id' have to break them apart. She'd go mad trying to get back with Z. At night Z'd meh and meh, you know that sound, meh meh meh meh, like he was calling for her. And from her bed she'd meh back to him. Meh meh, all night long. I'd try to calm Z, meh meh, want her to come out. It'd drive Pops mad, knowing this star creature was mehing for his girl. And so, and so, one day it stopped.
>
> *Pause*
>
> Pops had taken his sword to Z.
>
> *Pause*
>
> Z's smell through the house, the folds of his flesh tucked with garlic. My sis never came down to dinner from that day on. She never forgave him. And she refused ever to wear clothes again. We wouldn't let her leave the house 'cuz of it. She ran away, became part of another family's business. So I'd have to do all the sheep myself.
>
> (Wellman and Lee 2006, 264)

Tuan integrates the sheep more as a digressionary analogue to her sex romp, than as the central feature in Ajax's demise per the Sophoclean original; that is, Ajax's humiliation at discovering the enemy Achaeans he had thought he annihilated were actually a herd of sheep. Tuan uses the transformative grotesque, converting the bestial lust into the family meal. Further the "meh" sound becomes integrated sonically as an articulatory element that provides comic, ironic relief. At his demise near the end of the play, Alexander, in enormous pain after having his testicle plucked from his body by his cohort Jessie, is bleeding to death. Tuan trivializes his classically staged death by having the immolation come from an award show statue. The stage directions read:

> *ALEXANDER paints with his blood on the tiles, screaming. All run from him like sheep and huddle together in a corner. ALEXANDER places the American Music Award on the long black. It shimmers red. He staggers, holding his crotch blood in.*
>
> ALEXANDER: meh meh meh weep, meh meh meh leap, meh meh meh sleep
>
> *He falls and impales himself on the American Music Award. He ends mouth open with a taxidermed stare.*
>
> (Wellman and Lee 2006, 306)

Displays of eroticism, extreme violence, and unabashed lust are standard fare in a many contemporary adaptations; Matthew Maguire's brilliant rendition of Racine's *Phaedra* (and the Euripidean original, *Hippolytus*) presents the "titular" character modernized as Faye, not in the sublimely repressed manner mandated by neoclassical decorum, but as a woman with a phallocentric obsession. The language of sexual lust and power dynamics provides the fuel of Maguire's *tour de force*. New playwrights are unleashing the Dionysian forces that lurked beneath the surfaces of these original classics.

WIKIPEDIA AND THE NEW HYBRID ADAPTATION

In *A Joyful Noise: "The Metamorphosis of Ajax" as Spiritual Tract*, John Leland explores John Harington's 1596 treatise on the invention of the flush toilet as a metaphor for the cleansing of man's baser instincts. Indeed, Tuan's stage set which consists of a tile surface with hoses and other "gurgling" sounds echoes a kind of open bathroom, in which blood and other body fluids are washed away during the play, as if to purify or purge the lust and desire from their lives. Tuan's play is draped in various ironies and references to original source materials that are not readily decipherable. This is an important aspect of how hybridism conflates various antecedents in creating novel, and often shocking, transformations. This is what I would describe as the Wikipedia-based adaptation. Any playwright wishing to approach an adaptation quickly will find myriad source materials readily available online. The hybrid adaptation thrives on connection and conflation, and a most convenient (and increasingly reliable) place to start (after reading the source play text) is Wikipedia. In this sense, the adaptation opens itself to various "associations" that the playwright wishes to explore in the remaking of the original source. The text becomes the simulacrum of the hyperlink as the playwright picks and chooses among various connecting threads to realign the narrative.

EXERCISE:

The Wikipedia-based adaptation

1. Assign the workshop members a classical playscript(s) to read and adapt.
2. Depending on time, encourage the students to read more than one translation/adaptation.
3. Using Charles Mee's approach, have the students identify the bare bones structure of the play in the form of a schematic.
5. Consider their corollaries in contemporary culture.
6. Research Wikipedia beginning with the title, then ancillary sites that are linked. For example, for *Electra*, you would get Electra complex, Elektra the Marvel comic, the movie with Jennifer Garner, and so on.
7. Find iconographic links as to vase paintings, graphic representations, and so on.
8. Have the students come up with a content bundle that they can attach to the core structure.
9. Playwrights can then consider what to keep, how to alter the structure, and scope of the project.
10. The outcome can vary from a scene to a one-act play, length dependant on pragmatic or aesthetic variables and contingent upon your time flexibility.

COMMENT: This exercise combines dramaturgical and playwriting components. It is an excellent antidote for addressing the young playwright's tendency to write only from an autobiographical perspective.

Caridad Svitch's *Divine Fire: Eight Contemporary Plays inspired by the Greeks* (2005) offers a stunning collection of contemporary classical adaptations along these lines. In the modern adaptation, the paradigm has become the hybrid, because its essential core involves a dialogic exchange between the original author and the playwright. Mee favors the classical adaptation as a great exercise for the playwright because the basis of the story and the structure are right in front of you. It's a way for the playwrights to work through the voice of "the other" in shaping a new and vital play. After creating a huge impact at the 2000 Humana Festival, Mee's *Big Love* became one of the most widely produced plays in regional theaters and universities over the past decade. Although it owes its narrative framework to Aeschylus's first play, *Suppliant Women*, Mee's *Big Love* references works by tenth-century Japanese author Sei Shonagon, would-be Warhol assassin Valerie Solanas, and self-help gurus Leo Buscaglia and Gerald G. Jampolsky, among many others. *Big Love* is unabashedly theatrical, with helicopter landings, raucous physicalizations of heightened language, and mergings of dance and multiple sources of music and sound. While an element of tragedy is maintained in the death scene at the end of the play, the overall approach is a conflation of theatrical styles and approaches. Mee's personal website offers a complete selection of his plays and commentary regarding his creative approach.

HYBRID STUFF

As another approach to creating the hybrid, Mac Wellman and Len Jenkin require their students to build plays from "stuff." During one of his residencies at the University of Alabama, Jenkin assigned students a basic checklist of items that would provide the genesis of a new work: a picture/work of art; a piece of music (to inspire, not underscore, the work); several tangible items that a character could hold or use; a caption; and a short piece of writing. Some of these items could be utilized in the play, while others served as creative spurs or points of departure. Wellman cajoles students to observe beyond their own interests, to "see what's in the newspaper," noting bizarre or interesting events that might prod the imagination. Wellman's fetish-like fascination with the phenomenon of fur balls in *Sincerity Forever* stemmed from an article that demonstrated their potential to shut down a major city's sewage system. Wellman took delight in the serious ramifications of something as benign and innocuous as a fur ball. Moreover, he notes the strong associational and visual values emanating from the term.

Wellman patches random words, phrases, and quotations into his plays, with openness to the direction in which they will take the play. Excerpts from *The Devil's Dictionary* by Ambrose Bierce became a major structural component of his play, *Bitter Bierce*. He will also work a tag line throughout a play until he exhausts its potential (such as "chails of cats" in *The Invention of Tragedy*). Wellman's process is both ecological and dialogic: he is not only a recycler of language, but thrives on the clash or frisson brought on by the juxtapositions of varied dramaturgical elements (his use of the chorus in several plays is indicative). Rather than strive for unity, Wellman creates dramaturgical interest through difference and surprise, energizing the gaps between disparate, albeit contiguous elements.

In new playwriting, sometimes the frisson between scenes can energize an entire play. The assassination scene at the Armenian-American car dealer's lot in Eric Overmyer's *Dark Rapture* is in its political force and violence unrelated to anything else in the play. Embedded within the structure of the first act and drawn from a real-life account, the scene frames the violence and menace that informs the rest of the play. Dramaturgically anomalous, it places the play's most intense scene away from the major character, Babcock. Moreover, it raises a thematic, political question that remains unresolved throughout the rest of the play. Interestingly, audiences have found this scene to be the play's most compelling. Its ineluctable immediacy and gratuitous force are magnetic, functioning to pull the audience into the thematic core of the text.

EXERCISE:

Conceptualizing the hybrid play

The following examples offer several strategies for beginning the hybrid play. The list is open-ended and intended to prompt your imagination to further exploration.

1. Google several quotations from a celebrity or political figure, enough to create an overall profile of the character.

   a. Establish a well-known historical figure that has some resonance with your main character. (An obvious example is Lincoln in *Topdog/Underdog* playing the assassinated president, in white face.)

   b. Consider two periods of history in the play: perhaps the present and the period of your historical figure. (Stoppard's *Arcadia*, Young Jean Lee's *The Appeal*, and the recent musical, *Bloody, Bloody Andrew Jackson* offer good models.) Scenes may conflate, exist side by side, or be sequential.

   c. Locate specific objects or props that can be used across historical periods.

   d. Designate some music that somehow informs the piece.

   e. Find a piece of writing that "says" something about the material (for example, quoted material, famous sayings, wise aphorisms, etc.)

COMMENT: Found materials offer convenient sources for the hybrid play. A corollary in the world of art is the assemblage. The Wooster Group used this method of assemblage to revisit and reexamine Tennessee Williams's later play, *Vieux Carre*. The playwright can integrate hybrid structure in various ways. For example, the play may juxtapose characters from film or literary genres against more normative types. (For example, *Dark Rapture* attempts to execute the *film noir* genre, theatrically). Or several historical periods may be juxtaposed in successive scenes, then converge into one story line. The hybrid is a good vehicle for satire or parody because the formal values inherent in a given genre may themselves comment on the material or subject at hand. The appropriation of well-known fairy-tale characters such as the three little pigs or the big bad wolf has obvious implication when positioned against a political troika or fundamentalist preacher, for example. Interpolating songs from different eras can be most successful. In her adaptation *Eurydice*, Sarah Ruhl culminates a sense of the lovers' Orpheus and Eurydice bond and innocence through their singing of the 1940s American song later popularized by the Andrew's sisters: "Don't sit under the apple tree." Although the song is a joyous marker of their wedding, the final words "'til I come marching home" (a reference to the soldiers in the Second World War) presage Eurydice's death two scenes later (Ruhl 2006, 347–8).

JEFFREY JONES AND GRAFTING CONTEXT

While Jeffrey Jones is now best known for his advocacy of new playwrights at venues like the Toxic and Flea theaters in New York City, his earlier playwriting was widely influential. His play *Der Inka von Peru* is representative of his "contexting" approach. As a dramaturgical strategy, contexting explores how meaning in language is determined. Mikhail Bakhtin used the term *heteroglossia* to describe how meaning is factored only in the moment of utterance; it is reliant on circumstances, intonation, and past histories. In other words, meaning is mediated through shifting contexts. The meaning of words like "surfing" and "texting" has been coopted by technology. Now, of course, the word "surfing" has been mediated by its mainstream connotation with the internet, and its original aquatic referent has been moved to the background. The word "wired" may even have contradictory meanings depending upon context. The variance in connotations, whether from a historical or contemporary perspective, gives words dialogic bounce.

To create this exemplar of contexting, with regard to *Der Inka von Peru*, Jones became a contemporary palimpsest, scraping, lifting, and recycling what had already been spoken. In the play Jones combines soap opera dialogue, quotes uttered by celebrities in popular magazines like *People*, and historical accounts detailing Francesco Pizarro's conquering of the Inca in Peru. Jones grafted sections of found text as a given character's dialogue. These grafted entries offer counterpoint to the author-created dialogue of the other characters; in some cases, the grafted dialogue is the exclusive language spoken by the character. The clash of language sources—banal television dialogue, celebrity "strips," historicized "lingo" relating to Pizarro, and Jones's self-generated choices—provides the interest and "meaning" of the play, although meaning itself is indeterminate. Traditional dramaturgical phenomena such as the through line or unity are superseded by the polyvocal clash that propels this hybrid.

While the lifted passages bear no relation to their original context, they are still ensconced within the larger cultural milieu. Dialogism occurs in several ways:

- Jones establishes an internal dialogism in the script, in which two language systems operate codependently. Neither is privileged, yet both interact and inform each other. The texturing activates a surface frisson. New playwriting acknowledges that the surface and external form is the site of meaning.

- Jones allows the "other" to enter into a dialogue with his own creative process of producing language. In traditional playwriting, the playwright feels he has "ownership" of all written materials. New playwriting opens the playwright to how language can be generated in the creation of the script.

- The "strips of language" operate inside and outside of the play; they are intermittently within and outside the frame of the play. This linguistic phenomenon allows Jones more flexibility in dialogizing between the "found strip" and the actors' interpretation of and response to it.

The beat poet William Burroughs had worked with a similar process in constructing his poems. Burroughs would cut out words from various written sources then rearrange them in random fashion; this collage effect abstracted the arrangement of words on the page. With Jones, more conscious planning is used to fabricate the script, although the grafting process remains similar.

BUILDING THE JOURNAL/SCRAPBOOK FROM PASTICHE TO HOMAGE

Some playwriting instructors require students to maintain journals, sourcebooks, or scrapbooks to use as the fodder for the creative process; however, most playwrights have a difficulty maintaining the discipline over time. Mac Wellman keeps a journal or scrapbook, not in a soul-searching way, but as a compilation of useful materials that can be practically applied. Many of his strange references (his interest in fur balls, or funny words like "wiggly"), have arisen from the scrapbook. Len Jenkin, on the other hand, finds the discipline of keeping a journal taxing or tedious, and too diverting from the limited time he can spend on his playwriting.

To be effective, the journal should be utilized as the *commedia dell'arte* actor used the *zibaldone*—a sourcebook collection of found or created materials that provides fodder for creative and imaginative expression. Consider play building as pastiche, allowing a wide array of sources to enter your journal, and later, your work. This "resourcing" or recycling of found materials into your play is a dialogic strategy, when the "other" is mediated by your own creative and imaginative talents.

You can focus your journal to increase the polyvocal level in your plays. Include foreign literary and conversational references; foreign idioms with interesting sounds; maxims and quotes; peculiarities in regional syntax; wise sayings and rubrics from religions and primitives; "technospeak" from various professions; strange etymologies; proper names of businesses, people, towns, and so on. Graft these appropriately into your plays. At other times, the journal will provide the inspiration to begin a play, or answer the riddle to the revision in a play you have shelved. As you build the journal, you are consciously developing your "ear" for language. Moreover, just as *zibaldoni* gave strength and endurance to the *commedia* actor, they provide you, the playwright, with the resources to complete more ambitious projects.

The following exercises should be undertaken at the beginning of the term to allow for the compilation of materials. The journal should be integrated as much as possible into the student work, or it will become a tiresome appendage.

EXERCISE:
Billboarding: figure, ground and landscape solutions

This technique is useful in a monologue to establish the dialogic relation between figure and ground. The figure is the character, the ground the contextual landscape provided by the passing imagery of the billboards. The spatial/temporal signification is totally created by language. The figure is contextually situated and mediated within the shifting landscape.

The billboarding exercise is an effective way to begin building a journal.

1. Note the billboard and advertising signs between your home and a destination that you frequent regularly, as in a daily commute. Usually billboards are contracted monthly, so changes occur, particularly around seasonal events. Also, consider digital billboards, and church signage that changes seasonally. In the journal, jot down slogans, terms, and proper names, dating the entries.

2. You should observe several repeating motifs: the scraping off of the old, the plastering over with the new, the relation between them; when the old begins showing through torn or faded sections. (Note, if possible, the ecotauge, when billboards are defaced by environmental groups protesting their negative physical and aesthetic effect on the environment.)

3. How does each sign suggest a different thought or action, impose an outside force on your reality, or suggests you change your life in some way? Note specific phrases.

4. Pay particular attention to proper names and key phrases that crystallize a certain phenomenon, or characterize a profession, for example.

5. In the workshop have each participant contribute several slogans, then mix them up and draw them out of a hat, randomly.

6. Brainstorm collectively about play ideas, using other shared slogans and materials, from the participants' lists.

7. Now write a scene or monologue. Utilize phrases, proper names, and conflations to stimulate, augment, or direct a character's internal journey or realization, about some change in their life.

COMMENT: In the workshop, allow this exercise to run over several months as playwrights compile a list of items in the journal. Proper names, mottoes, and product tag lines lend specificity to time and place as they resonate within a cultural milieu. In the Bible-Belt South, the landscape is laced with "voice-of-god" conflations, directing you to save your soul as you enjoy your Dreamland barbecue. When staggered sequentially, the billboard device can serve as a marker for space and time passages. Read Jenkin's *Dark Ride* or Wellman's *Whirligig* for exemplars of this technique.

GRAFTING DIALOGUE (FROM FRONT TO FAÇADE)

A related exercise requires accessing quotable material from various sources. Comments from celebrity or political figures are available in magazine interviews, other print media, and online sources. You might graft the language of celebrities and politicians because, to a great extent, their language is already "framed," or calculated by publicists toward a particular public reception. The celebrity is "fronting" a certain persona for public consumption: a rapper will front a gangsta persona; but even when a "bad" image seems authentic (Keith Richard as drug addict) the press is framing out particular elements that don't fit the public image. In Richard's autobiography *Life* (2010) he points out that he's been "clean" (from addiction) for 30 years; far from the image the media continues to project. In creating the hybrid play, this framed language is then reframed within the new context of the play. This doubling strategy foregrounds the language itself, and leads to its further exteriorization and sense of façade.

Fronts, a term coined by sociologist linguist Erving Goffman, describe how the self performs in public, particularly in work or social situations. Language is a major component in presenting a front, as are fashion, grooming, and behavior. The end result is what Goffman termed "impression management," the degree to which the individual controls the signals they are sending. Those signals that are controlled are "given," while others (often more important) are "given off." Probably no politician in history controlled the "givens" as well as Barack Obama in his successful campaign for the presidency in 2008. However, after the "disastrous" midterm elections of 2010 both supporters and detractors lambasted Obama for presenting a façade that has not jibed with reality—that is, what is "given off." Thus, rhetoric that was at once inspirational and charismatic was recast as hollow and misguided—at least for the near term. With the proliferation of reality-based television we now witness how media can manufacture "fronts" for performers who have no talent or training to anchor them. Packaged and hyped, television producers establish conditions for "given off" behaviors that, while catty, self-serving, and petty, provide an appealing selling card to audiences.

ROLE-PLAYING

An examination of fronts and impression management will sharpen the playwright's awareness of the relationship between language and behavior, essential components in constructing characters. The playwright can then manipulate performative levels throughout the play to achieve variety and surprise. In the hybrid play, some characters will be their front; others will offer variance, or be constructed from other strategies. When the front persists as the dominant mode of behavior, it can more accurately be described as a *role*. Role-playing requires a performative, externalized approach to characterization. Linguistically, role-playing relies on the coded speech strategies discussed in the previous chapter. Role-playing has varied applications in the new playwriting. Len Jenkin describes his conception for *Poor Folk's Pleasure* as a "theater piece for five to seven performers. These performers take on a variety of roles" (author's interview with Jenkin at Actor's Conservatory Theater, 1996, San Francisco). In *Poor Folk's Pleasure*, the concept begins with the actor as performer, rather than the notion of a assigns numbers to members of the ensemble. Suzan-Lori Parks's *Venus* ensemble orientation bulks roles to fit the strengths and interests of the performers complementing the singular actor playing Venus. Sheila Callaghan's *Crumble* requires the actor playing the Father to also "impersonate" pop icon Justin Timberlake and Harrison Ford.

Another example of role-playing occurs when a character assumes a different front depending upon the circumstances in the play. The character may assume a part in an acted-out sequence in the play (a play within the play) or perform a given role as the script demands. Jenkin's *Pilgrims of the Night* and Washburn's *Apparition* are examples of the latter. Playwrights can utilize role-playing and its essential theatricality to explore options that are performative rather than psychological. This fuller palette can be particularly effective in comedy, where characters are forced to perform unlikely or awkward roles. In the new playwriting, role-playing is usually a facet of the multivocal character. For examples, the charlatans Crowsfoot and Mr. Flip, in Wellman's *Harm's Way* and Carson Kreitzer's *Freakshow* respectively, drop in and out of their roles as a carnival pitchmen. The tension between the character's and the role's level of language creates a significant level of interest, as it layers several voices and performance approaches for the actor.

Playwrights should begin by exploring fronts or façades in terms of speech and behavior. As you become more confident in delineating these levels, you can integrate role-playing as a strategy. The difference between a front and a role is one of degree. A role may occur over one or several beats, while a front persists as a dominant strategy across beat segments or entire scenes. A façade usually suggests a false impression, whereas a front is the expected behavior of a particular profession, for example. A good example of the former is the character Jean in Sarah Ruhl's *Dead Man's Cell Phone* (discussed later in this book: see page 127), who assumes the façade of the dead man's confidant. David Mamet's characters in *Glengarry Glen Ross* (real estate agents) and *Speed the Plow* (film executives) provide excellent examples of fronts. These explorations will increase your dialogic, multivocal instincts as they afford you new techniques. As you begin to sense the layering possibilities you can experiment with scenes within scenes, or the play within a play.

EXERCISE:
Fronts and façade

(Read and familiarize yourself with the Ruhl and Mamet plays mentioned above.)

Fronts and façades can be differentiated by intention. A front represents playing the role well: dressing appropriately for a profession, or behavior apropos to protocol. On the other hand, the façade is a misrepresentation of self, usually intending to deceive for some gain, or to further one's interest. This exercise works best when one character is dominant, the other subordinate, or where a character gains status through an effective front or façade:

1. Character A uses language and certain front behaviors to create an impression for Character B. Language is used to intimidate, manipulate, make a sale, and so on.

2. Graft strips of language from your journal that work, appropriately.

3. Character B attempts to crack the façade or front of A.

4. Character A goes to extreme lengths to maintain their front. Graft in quotes from your journal that are effective.

5. Conclude the scene with a clear idea of who wins and loses.

Journal: To start, incorporate media clippings into the building of a character. There are some issues this process raises:

• language as front or façade, versus language that discloses the heart

• the playwright as collector of language. In a manner similar to visual artists who keep examples of other artists' fragments (a hand, a tree, a piece of fruit, and so on).

COMMENT: Consult Chapter 8 for more information on creating fronts and facades.

FABLE AND STORY FORMS

Story forms such as the fable, parable, fairy tale, folk tale, tall tale, and legend foreground plot devices that are familiar to audiences. A fable or parable can be condensed structurally, either in part or whole, then adapted to whatever setting the playwright desires. The recognizable structure informs the material and affects the audience's perception in some way. A dialogic interaction is engaged between the original and the adaptation. This self-reflexive quality is metadramatic, whether the story form is used partially (as with the play within a play) or wholly, providing the structural format for the entire play. As a metadramatic tool, story forms can enhance the polyvocal potential of the play's script. As such, they offer the playwright a range of options in manufacturing the hybrid play. Len Jenkin's *Country Doctor* is derived from a story by Franz Kafka that the original author had adapted from a common folktale. The former adaptation is used as a play within a play, whereas the latter (Kafka by way of a folktale) provides the basic format and storyline of Jenkin's play. Erin Courtney's *Demon Baby* draws on the gnome fables of Romantic literature, and the common statuary of nineteenth-century gardens, to create the titular character.

The young playwright gains technique by studying and then adhering to a given structural format. Poring over story forms, which tend to be brief (and often didactic), enables the playwright to quicken and facilitate their sense of plot, since most short forms feature a taut story line without extraneous materials. Contemporizing the story line will bring about a dialogic tension between the original and the updated version. The treatment of the materials can range from parodic to straightforward, particularly, since the teleology of the fable, parable, etc. is some moral lesson or dictum.

CONDENSING STRUCTURE: THE QUEST ("JOURNEY PLAY")

Certain story forms are repeated often enough that their structures suggest a model or paradigm. One such model is applied in the following exercise. The quest has its origins in Greek myths, medieval romances, and the Spanish picaresque novel. It's a commonplace in cinema storytelling, as indicated by the popular success of the *Lord of the Rings* series. The quest provides a strong structural basis that includes a central character with an unwavering desire to achieve a goal; a journey that includes an increasingly forbidding series of obstacles or tests that need to be overcome; a definite and desirable destination that is earmarked at the beginning of the quest; a love interest who may be the "destination," serve as "guide," or create the sense of romantic longing (the girl or boy back home); a guide, or omniscient character who unlocks secrets along the way; and characters who provide comic or anecdotal relief. Once the quest is achieved, harmony and balance are restored.

Examples of embedded quest structures in new playwriting include, among others, Jenkin's *My Uncle Sam, Margo Veil,* and *Dark Ride* (discussed at length later in this book: see pages 213–16). The motif of traveling to seek fortune or to change one's lot is at the heart of the American psyche. It is personified in numerous character types, from the historic Yankee and "go-westering" pioneer types to the con men and salesman that frequent Jenkin's plays.

EXERCISE:
The ten-minute play (the quest)

The objective is to write a ten-minute play utilizing the quest format. The configuration of the quest encompasses three stages. The tripartite structure closely mirrors the rites of passage sequence established by the cultural anthropologist Arnold van Gennep. Since the goal of any quest is to achieve some change in your character(s) lot, the rite of passage becomes a solvent descriptor for the process. In the ten-minute play, the separation phase may be referred to in the middle or transitional phase, with the separation occurring prior to the play's point of attack.

1. Separation: Some separation from family, homeland, or familiar moorings is required.
   a. The separation can be relatively brief in duration.
   b. The main character senses some dilemma that must be addressed. This requires a journey of some sort. Typically, the character is a "fish out of water."
   c. Consider a polyvocal landscape with varied ecologies (see below).

2. Transition: This is the most dramatic of the three stages: a goal is sought, obstacles are dealt with, and so on. It is marked by uncertainty, negativity, the strange or bizarre; the character's addressing not only the goal but also the self as character.

   a. Consider omniscient characters, guides, and fellow travelers. Each has a specific front or façade. Use your scrapbook to define characters in language.

   b. There is an increasing level of obstacles and frustrations for the major character. Develop adversaries from literary or visual sources. Consider icons.

   c. Alter the dimension of time at some point in this phase.

   d. This is the rite of passage phase and must culminated in some status change for the character.

3. Reintegration: The goal of the quest is achieved, a new status for the character results, and there may be a celebration, betrothal, award, etc.

   a. Restoration of (or establishment of a new sense of) balance and equilibrium.

To begin, playwrights should complete this exercise in a ten-minute-play format (an increasingly popular format for play contests). In the ten-minute format, the tests or obstacles appear quickly and are dealt with in as few beats as possible. The quest can be compressed successfully if the playwright first sketches out the desired end, goal, or destination. In the ten-minute play, I advise writing the ending first, condensing the separation phase, and allowing maximum flexibility during the transitional phase. The strict parameters of this format can be realized by firming up the end at the beginning. Since the final phase in this tripartite structure is reintegration, the nature of the ending is more easily resolved.

Along the journey, explore the nature of the major character through the series of obstacles that confront her; vary the obstacles to keep pressure on the character. Strive for a unique theatrical landscape, and consider alterations in time as crucial. The ten-minute format provides an advantage for students who can read aloud many of the plays within the time constraints of the workshop. The playwright gains skill in condensing and distilling essential story elements. If time constraints are not a factor, this exercise can be suited to a variety of play formats from one-acts to short plays to full-lengths.

COMMENT: Playwrights at all levels have difficulty resolving their plays. Perhaps the most public acknowledgment of this phenomenon is by the producers of the musical *Spiderman*, which at the time of writing was lingering in previews, in search of a satisfying end. Ironically, the most expensive theatrical endeavor in history doesn't know how it wants to conclude! Writing the end is a pragmatic strategy, and can free the playwright from worrying about closure. I remind the playwright that the end can always be adjusted; think of the end as a flexible target that can be moved or removed. Writing the end several times will prove to be a useful focusing strategy. As a rule of thumb: the end should encapsulate the overall thematic statement of the play.

EXERCISE:
Writing the end

- If you consider the thematic values inherent in the script, you should be able to wrap a conclusion that jibes with the action of your play.

- If it is the case that the character achieves the quest, the ending can recapitulate selected values of the given character.

- If you desire an ironic ending, track the ending back to the final plot point and simply reverse expectations.

- If you desire wonder or the "strange," resolve a specific character marker or beat from the script in which a character is confronted with "special knowledge"; or, bring to light an object that has been imbued with some talismanic power.

- Finally, consider whether you want a *coup de théâtre* ending that is highly theatrical, or a resolution of marker beats that relate to character, theme, or story form.

COMMENT: In the workshop, this exercise can be particularly helpful as participants conclude early drafts of their final plays; as such, it can be incorporated into the final project assignment as a separate component.

HYBRID VARIATIONS: SPACE, TIME, AND DIALOGIC CLASH

The hybrid allows significant latitude in establishing spatial/temporal parameters. No longer locked into the fixed rules determined by period and convention, the new playwright is flexible to juxtapose, deconstruct, or reassemble space and time. Paula Vogel's *How I Learned to Drive* fragments the sense of a linear time narrative by moving back and forth from "present" to "past." The clash between time periods and characters in this play energizes a dynamic that propels the action forward in a way that disorients the viewer. This disorientation structurally mirrors and enhances the problematic relationship of the character Lil' Bit with her abusive uncle.

Playwrights can open themselves to this new dramaturgy by shifting the spatial/temporal context of the characters. When language alters space and time, established moorings are loosened, as conventions are interrupted or displaced. The characters are decentered (as is the audience) in a vertiginous environment. This decentering forces the character to make sense of an ever-changing theatrical landscape (See Chapter 8, on Sarah Ruhl's *The Clean House*). The changing environmental factors create an interactive spatial/temporal field that is a dynamic contrast to conventional dramaturgy. It's a different way of "taking your characters to the wall"—the core of good playwriting, according to the late Romulus Linney. Linney implored student playwrights to make their characters struggle, to confront dangerous, fantastic, or outrageous circumstances.

Spatial and temporal options are often overlooked in the conceptualization of the play. Allow the imagination to explore the possibilities. For example, what does a shifting spatial/historical context suggest about language? The idea is that contexting allows environmental or historical circumstances to weigh heavily on the action. Some British playwrights have exploited this ground successfully: Howard Brenton's controversial *Romans in Britain* juxtaposes the Roman Empire's occupation of the British Isles with the British occupation of Ireland. Tom Stoppard's often produced *Arcadia* utilizes an early-nineteenth-century country manor to juxtapose scenes set in the period with those featuring present-day occupants of the house.

Expanding the spatial/temporal fields also engages the question of scale. Wellman has experimented with juxtaposing our world with other worlds in several plays. Constance Congdon conflated alien/human characters in *Tales of the Lost Formicans*. Young Jean Lee's *The Appeal* reduces the scale of the famous Romantic poets Wordsworth, Coleridge, and Byron by having them speak in trivialized contemporary American speech patterns. Erik Ehn's *The Saint Plays* conflate liturgical icons or canonized figures within contemporary settings and characterizations. The use of multiple landscapes, of bridging cultures and worlds, opts for varying the concept of scale. Bonnie Marranca's *Ecologies of Theater* (1996a) posits that the future of theater lies in its ability to incorporate this multilandscaped, globalized presence of cultures and theatrical systems on stage.

On a purely theatrical level, Robert Wilson's "theater of images" has realized this view to an extent, and his hybrid model, which focuses on the *mise-en-scène* rather than the script, has its corollary in the new playwriting. Wilson's polyvocal theatrical vocabulary blends American, European, and Asian stage traditions, a performative strategy utilized in Naomi Iizuka's play *36 Views*. Iizuka integrates elements of the Kabuki theater into her dramaturgy. Wilson agonizes over his storyboard sequences, while Len Jenkin reshuffles blocks of text in his revision process. Whereas Wilson emphasizes gesture and movement, the new playwrights place a stronger formal emphasis on language. Both experiment with formal qualities of juxtaposition, repetition, and patterning. This underlying thrust of theatricality supersedes dramatic procedures. Seen in this light of the external, the plastic, and the theatrical, the new playwright is more like an auteur/director than a traditional dramatist. A comparison between Wilson and new playwrights demonstrates the shared aesthetic principles at work:

- the juxtaposition of opposites
- the fragmentation, dissolving, or deconstruction of linear time
- the recontextualizing of historical systems
- the dynamics of scale.

Wilson has been successful at realizing his experiments on a grand scale.
Generally, the avant-garde has been relegated to the lofts and small theaters, and this fate has dogged the language playwrights as well. Perhaps Wilson's large-scale productions (consider *Einstein on the Beach, Ka Mountain, CIVIL WarS, The Forest*) offer a more ambitious paradigm to the language playwright in search of the larger venue and audience. Marranca states it rather eloquently in discussing the virtues of Wilson's *The Forest* when she writes:

> The biodiversity of Wilson's theater lyricizes both space and time. All species—flora, fauna, human—enliven narrative in this advance stage of theatrical evolution. He frames their adaptability and process of hybridization in scenes that visualize the insistent nature/culture theme as a structural feature of the work. If Wilson loves the city, he needs woods. What is a theatrical landscape but a species of desire?
>
> (Marranca 1996a, 38)

EXERCISE:
Spatial/temporal juxtaposition integrating globalization

The work of Robert Wilson opens up the potential to create plays on a grander scale—through globalized theatrical and dramaturgical forms. Wilson's polyvocal principles and strategies can be adapted by the playwright in the conceptualization of the play. After brainstorming about an entire piece, write several scenes. It may be helpful to work with images or thumbnail sketches. You can even consider elements of language and narrative as large component blocks.

1. Consider some broad cultural/historical event (in the mode of Wilson).

   • What figures from other eras can be juxtaposed?

2. Articulate a diverse sense of landscapes: city, country, forest, oceans, and so on.

   • Consider how the shifting landscape alters context of character and language.

3. Establish a narrative center for the piece.

   • For example, Andre Serban, Suzuki, and a litany of theater artists have reinterpreted classics like *The Trojan Women*. The text is a point of departure.

4. Embrace a variety of languages, dialects, or speech genres in your consideration of character.

   • The character may have a performative basis: Noh drama, *commedia dell'arte*, circus performing, and so on. Compare Suzuki, Mee, and Serban's versions of *The Trojan Women*.

5. Consider in this conceptualizing stage the possibilities for clash, contrast, and interaction among the various elements.

6. Rough out a pattern of progression that relies on serial juxtaposition, direct opposition, simultaneity, and/or repetitions.

* Consider single, dual, or multifocus scenes.

7. Write three or four scenes altering the sequence in order to explore the various configurative possibilities.

8. Have participants in the workshop construct a visual collage if they are having difficulty conceptualizing these juxtapositions.

COMMENT: Internet sources make finding historical and cultural information relatively convenient. Also, seek out local archives that contain historically-based and often intimate, detailed personal narratives. These offer fantastic resources for plays in developing closely observed characters and are often overlooked.

The consideration of the spatial/temporal dynamic opens the playwright to thematic concerns that can bring politics into the mix. It is a potential strategy for the committed playwright, who wants to address ideological concerns on a large scale. Lynn Nottage's 2009 Pulitzer Prize winning play *Ruined* explored the horrors of the Congolese rebel wars on a group of refugee African women forced into prostitution after being raped; then, as a direct result, ostracized from their native villages. Combining "strips of language" from interviews with the victims within a mixture of Western and African storytelling forms, including dance, drumming, and chants, Nottage fashions a hybrid of awesome stature and resonance. In this sense, the hybrid becomes the artistic corollary to globalization whereby multiple languages, discourses and modes of communication combine to create an artistic whole.

THE TRIUMPH OF THE HYBRID

As we can see, the hybrid suits the cultural move toward globalization in the arts, and a broader more democratized network of communication made possible by You Tube, Facebook, Wikipedia, Twitter and so on. Traditional playwriting has been penetrated by hybrid aesthetics, as playwrights become increasingly anxious about the artifice and limitations of the linear narrative. New playwriting, with its conflation of the performative and the polyvocal, offers the playwright excellent models of hybridization. As the hybrid becomes more and more the norm in contemporary theater, it assumes super-genre status over-arching its own subcategories and headings.

4

The theatricality of character

ESTABLISHING NEW APPROACHES TO CHARACTER

A non-psychological, external basis for character distinguishes the new dramaturgy from conventional approaches. Traditionally, American playwrights have conceived characters based on realistic, psychologically oriented models. There are two primary reasons:

- Since actors are trained in method-based or Stanislavskian approaches suited to the realistic style, playwrights have responded pragmatically by writing plays for this idiom, thus privileging the internal over the external style.

- Television and film continue to have a pervasive influence on dramatic styles and approaches.

Prevailing conditions necessitate communicating ideas effectively and quickly, and as a result, the shorthand code of the actors' studio has been established as the dominant language in American theater. Playwrights and play developers have adopted the terms of the actor: through line, arc, subtext, fleshing-out, intention, obstacle, and conflict are as solvent for the actor as they are for the playwright. Because the central character-driven play still reigns as the model (if not in reality), the often heard "Whose play is it?" is a familiar criticism of new work. Fleshing out a character works for the playwright whose characterization is too thin, but also for the actor who must manufacture "back story" to create more resonance in the "moment." A playwright sharpens a character's intention by eliminating digressions in the script, while the actor focuses on clearer choices in behavior. This shared shorthand is effective in the development of a traditional character, whether for stage or screen. However, an entrenched code is resistant to change and innovation. Moreover, because creating theater involves multiple collaborators, change comes slowly. To a significant extent, theater jargon, or "play speak," has stymied further growth and exploration in playwriting approaches.

Problems emerge when traditional terms are applied to new approaches. Because the old terms do not quite fit, we assume something is wrong with the play. Thus, in play development or rehearsal there is a dilution of the new into old familiar bottles. "Talk back" sessions after a reading almost always bear this out, particularly when the discussion turns to matters of character. When playwrights achieve the stature and publication history of Mac Wellman, Len Jenkin, or Suzan-Lori Parks, they may have directors who "know what they're getting into," but what about other collaborators, from designers to business managers and, of course, the ultimate collaborator, the critic? New playwriting is at a disadvantage because until the first edition of this book, no vocabulary existed for discussing multivocal, carnivalesque, or equivocal characters. To assess the character Hare in Mac Wellman's *Invention of Tragedy* based on the traditionalist Sam Smiley's six crucial qualities of character—volition, stature, interrelation, attractiveness, credibility, and clarity (Smiley 1971, 92)—is impossible and irrelevant. In his revolt against established norms, Wellman's characters blatantly contradict the notions of an integral character with "core" essentials. Does the playwright simply sprinkle in a bit of interrelation or volition? How organic is that? In striving for clarity of character, many playwrights overboil expository material and the character suffers rigor mortis in the process. The playwright who is exploring Smiley's text needs to know that his dramaturgical aesthetic is based on the representational or classical premise that character must be considered as an integral whole. With such widespread entrenchment of terms and constructs now being challenged, it is important to construct a new idiom that will accurately or persuasively represent a different premise of character.

An extensive checklist can numb the creative process as readily as focus it. Moreover, outside of the workshop, not many playwrights are disposed to revising characterizations according to checklists. Experienced playwrights know that revising, or "building-in," character traits creates a domino effect that alters other factors and relationships in a play.

BEYOND THE PROTAGONIST-CENTERED PLAY

The protagonist tradition solves a basic problem of playwrights. Unlike some literary forms, such as the novel, a play happens before a live audience. With a single character at the center of the play, the playwright provides the audience with a clear identity to root for or against, and a journey that can be followed easily. This maintains interest and dispels confusion. The action of the play is more tautly compressed if a clear structural network of relations is established from the top character down. On the other hand, the playwright who establishes several characters at the core of the play continually faces the problem of focus. Multiple protagonists may blur the central action of the play. A strong central figure focuses a play, as the instrumental soloist focuses a concerto. We may admire the supporting players, but only insofar as they support and enhance the efforts of the soloist/protagonist. A limited scope facilitates a unified vision. Quite simply, by linking the central action to the agency of one major character, the playwright achieves a measure of coherence.

Most playwriting instructors and manuals recommend a strong protagonist at the center of the play, which answers the frequently raised question of play developers, "Whose play is it?" Yet it is not the appropriate question to ask about Mac Wellman's recent *Jennie Ritchie*, that presents characters constructed as variable discourses rather than psychologically rounded individuals. Further, the canon of Len Jenkin, with the possible exceptions of his adaptations of *Candide* and *The Country Doctor*, resists the strictly protagonist-centered play. Even *Margo Veil*, named after the central character, contains divergent twists that veer the play in several directions. The dialogic move to polyvocality works against the unilateral focus of the protagonist-centered play. The most notable oppositions to the protagonist model are provided by women playwrights; women members of Clubbed Thumb and 13P offering the most recent examples. If the exception makes the rule, only Erin Courtney's *Demon Baby*'s character, Wren, provides a clearly focused arc as the spine of the play. In the anthology *Funny, Strange, Provocative: Seven Plays from Clubbed Thumb* (Striar and Detrick 2007), Sheila Callaghan and Lisa D'Amour feature mother–daughter dualities in which their "bundle" creates parallel protagonists. For example, in Callaghan's *Crumble (Lay Me Down, Justin Timberlake)* the characters have age-specific parallel relationships: Janice, the daughter, with Justin Timberlake, and the mother with Harrison Ford.

Nevertheless, there are several protagonist-based plays that combine elements of the new playwriting with the unifying principle of the single character. Len Jenkin's *The Country Doctor*, adapted from Kafka's novel, situates the Doctor as the center of focus. Suzan-Lori Parks's *Venus* unequivocally focuses our attention on the journey of the titular character. While the protagonist-centered play affords unity, it seems to be in disfavor with women playwrights. Recent plays by Sarah Ruhl, Young Jean Lee, Naomi Iizuka, Lyn Nottage, and Alice Tuan have proven successful without the central character model. While the protagonist model has its advantages, it is time to loosen the tyranny of this format that had long been considered the standard, particularly, as the baseline criteria of new work.

MOVING FROM THE ARISTOTELIAN MODEL

Although Aristotle was writing about tragic form, his *Poetics* still remains the putative criterion for most dramatic forms. Aristotle's focus on the dramatic rather than the theatrical privileged the literary dimension. Of the six elements, he relegated spectacle to the lowest rung on the hierarchical ladder, below plot, character, thought, diction or language, and music. Indeed, the inclusion of "theatrical" stage directions rendered the literariness of dramatic literature problematic. Historically, for dramatic works to be accepted into the canon, literary values needed to be emphasized while theatricality was diminished in importance. There was an emphasis on character decorum and verisimilitude. Then the advent of psychology and psychoanalysis in the nineteenth century revolutionized notions of the personality.

The "inner life" of the character became the focal point. Over time, the parameters of the well-constructed character have been established as a manifestation of these nontheatrical rubrics.

However, this trend is undergoing a major shift. The popular panto-mimic and comedic traditions of European theater and the physicality drawn from Asian theatrical forms, that have emphasized an external approach to character, are now transforming American dramaturgy. Recent plays, such as Naomi Iizuka's *36 Views*, which interpolates Kabuki theatrics, and Parks's *Topdog/Underdog*'s salvo to minstrelsy, conflate external and internal dramaturgies. This expands the putative profile of a dramatic char-acter that blends Aristotelian agency (or choice), psychological protocols, and thematic considerations that arise from given cultural conditions into an organic whole.

Even a strict Aristotelian such as David Mamet laments the speculative nature of dramatic character:

> How equally foolish to wonder where Oedipus went to college, or if Big Daddy is the Kind of Guy Who Might Play Golf, or, finally, to vitiate any of the carefully constructed problems of the play by unconsciously posit-ing and then accepting the existence of THE CHARACTER, as if the character were something other than a series of actions delineated by the playwright.
>
> (Mamet 1990, 38)

In the play development process, playwrights are importuned by directors or actors to provide "back story" to characters they have written. In public staged readings of their work, playwrights are pressured by traditional "staged-reading" protocols to justify every intention, motivation, and "what-if?" whether it is in the play or not. Rarely is the character's theatricality considered, despite current trends that emphasize it. In reaction, the mission of playwrights' collectives like 13P and Clubbed Thumb is to produce the work of its members, bypassing the well-intentioned but often deadly process of new play development. Further, that many of these play-wrights are women, is opening the theater to a litany of new voices who otherwise would not be heard.

Theatrical forms such as vaudeville, melodrama, the musical, Kabuki, *commedia dell'arte*, and pantomime, have historically proven that core theat-ricality can provide the root of character. New playwrights, in a variety of styles and formats, build upon a theatrical construct of character that is shaped externally through language, gesture, movement, physicality, and costume. In brief, language playwriting facilitates a broadening of theatrical conventions to shape character.

Mikhail Bakhtin's dialogism is related to his influential construction of the carnivalesque—and its qualities of transformation and overturning of societal norms. Bakhtin described carnival, traditionally the period between Epiphany and Ash Wednesday, as a time when normative functions were suspended, and serious culture was turned upside down—anything was possible.

Carnival promotes the strange juxtaposition of events and characters, and delights in the unexpected and the magical. As such, the carnivalesque offers a metaphor for character in the new playwriting. The carnivalesque character uses the gestural body, delights in vivid and sometimes ambiguous speech, and is often at the margins of the mainstream. The carnivalesque allows for sudden turns and identity transformations. In Len Jenkin's *Margo Veil*, Margo's sequence of identity transformations is actually played by different actors, pushing this technique to the extreme. More commonly, the carnivalesque character is part of an ensemble playing roles in the larger scheme of the play. Carson Kreitzer's *Freakshow* provides an excellent example of the latter with a group of characters that conflate the bestial with the human: featuring the Human Salamander and Judith, the dog-faced girl, along with Amalia, the Woman with no Arms or Legs, and the Pinhead. Case in point: The Human Salamander, relegated to years in a fish tank, has grown "gills" overtime, and a major part of his character's arc is the reinstatement of the ability to breathe through his lungs, and thus, resume human status. The terms carnivalesque and grotesque are often used interchangeably; the latter specifically refers to the conflation of animal and beast, and references to body parts, excretory functions, and sexuality, all at the heart of Kreitzer's *Freakshow*.

CONTINUUMS OF CHARACTERIZATION

Most playwrights following prescribed methods of characterization will establish characters along psychological lines based on need, desire, or goals. As a result, playwrights avoid conceptualizing along the lines of a showing, gestural character, deeming the thinking or emoting character more worthy of attention. Playwrights write these characters "off the line" (as indirect, oblique, implied), allowing the actor significant latitude in forming a subtextual approach. The more the subtextual level of character interiority is featured, the stronger the matrix—the actor has become the character (see Chapter 12 for more on matrixing and dematrixing). On the other hand, language in new playwriting tends to be "on the line" (as in, say what you mean), and when it isn't, the formulation is more often an ironic "take" rather than internalized subtextuality. As a result, the matrix between actor and character flips, since the writing style demands a more externalized performance approach. Plays like Len Jenkin's *Poor Folk's Pleasure* and Kreitzer's *Freakshow* encourage a broader gestural and visceral performance style than the method-based norm. Table 4.1 delineates several differences between the traditional and new writing approach from the actor's view.

Table 4.1 Traditional versus new approaches to character	
ACTOR BECOMES CHARACTER	ACTOR PERFORMS CHARACTER
Emotional, psychological identification	External, performative projection
Integral traits; one character	Contradictory traits; one actor may play several characters
Matrixed (actor hidden)	Dematrixed (actor exposed)
Subtextual	Surface textuality
Off the line	On the line
Interiority	Virtuosity

While this table is by no means exhaustive, it illustrates differences that establish what the new playwriting is all about. Any poetic or language-oriented style will demand a heightened performance style. The playwright needs to understand that the demands on the actor will differ in new writing, albeit there is a range or swing in this continuum, so that the actors playing in Wellman's *Bitter Bierce* might opt for a more externalized approach than those approaching Jenkin's recently published historical play *Kraken*, or his Chekhovian homage, *Like I Say*. For example, in Jenkin's *Kraken*, the two major characters are Herman Melville and Nathaniel Hawthorne. An actor approaching these icons might be first drawn to the external forms through images and photographs, supplemented with research of personal correspondence and written documents that disclose internal states of mind. In this regard, several current-generation playwrights like Sarah Ruhl and Erin Courtney (spawned from the mentorship of language playwriting venerables Paula Vogel and Mac Wellman respectively), sinuously bridge internal and external approaches in the same play.

THEMATIC-BASED CHARACTERIZATION

Situated in the gap between traditional approaches to character and external theatrical approaches (discussed below) is the thematic character. In *Angels in America* (successfully revived in repertory at the Signature Theatre in New York City in Fall 2010) playwright Tony Kushner blends a fairly traditional aesthetic of characterization with thematic ideas by shifting the balance between the character's emotions and rhetorical impulses that purport an ideological message. Kushner describes himself as a committed playwright—by definition, one who advances a political message. The playwright committed to a cause walks the tightrope between advancing the action and advancing the agenda. In *Angels* (parts 1 and 2), the line between what a character thinks and what Kushner feels about an issue is blurred. Indeed, there are moments in *Perestroika* (the angel monologue) and in *Millennium Approaches* where rhetorical monologuing overwhelms (or at least stresses) the dramaturgy. These speeches cause a caesura in the pull or forward dynamic of the play, foregrounding theme over the agency of character. Curiously, even supportive critics of the recent revival have remarked upon this detriment to the flow of the play. Speechifying has to be handled deftly, or results will appear heavy-handed, as if coming directly from the playwright versus the character.

In general, American audiences prefer political opinions dosed with comic satire and irony rather than earnest or heartfelt. The popularity of *The Colbert Report,* John Stewart and Lewis Black attests to this recent reality. A recent Nielsen rating during election season showed more viewers watching John Stewart on the Comedy Channel than the regular nightly news! Even theaters that have an audience constituency with shared values or representing a specific cultural, racial, or ethnic group want the politics packed in theatricality. For example, New York City's WOW Café serves up fare with a feminist perspective for an intended female audience (the acronym WOW stands for World of Women), often using cross-dressing or various "theatrical" types from lesbian culture. Recent works at WOW by the Giddy Multiple Vaudeville Co. probe lesbian culture through circus acts, and nineteenth-century theatrical forms such as burlesque.

In Great Britain, the tradition of political playwriting has been transformed by Martin McDonagh with a far broader emphasis on the grotesque or carnivalesque. *Lieutenant of Inishmore* centers around the murder of the Irish independence leader, Padraic's black cat, and the carnage that follows. "What's most remarkable about the writing is the way it captures in comic terms a particular kind of madness that has infected Ireland for most of the 20th century" (*LA Times,* July 13, 2010). McDonagh's newest play, *A Behanding in Spokane,* trumped Mamet's *Race* for its more provocative and bold irreverence regarding the use of the "n" word. Carmichael (played by Christopher Walken on Broadway in 2010) is both psychopathic and racist, a trait he "inherited" from his mother. McDonagh ironically presents a debate on racial slurs while the one-handed Carmichael douses his antagonists with gasoline. McDonagh attempts to shock us with a bizarre and entertaining subversion of the "issue play" genre. Conversely, critic Ben Brantley accused Mamet of treading familiar ground: "these might once have shocked, but by now most have been thoroughly excavated by black stand-up comics, from Richard Pryor to Chris Rock" (*New York Times,* December 7, 2009). The upshot is that playwrights now consider the entertainment value of the "issue" and address it with novelty, wit, theatricality and most importantly, eccentric characterization. If Kushner's grand opus rang the bell of political correctness in the late 1980s, McDonagh's and Mamet's recent work seemed to have rung its death knell. I had the sense in viewing McDonagh's *A Behanding in Spokane,* that the playwright was relishing the brazenness of using the "n" word more as a ploy than a political statement. Coming from the offbeat cadence of celebrity performer Christopher Walken, its use seemed more bizarre than taunting.

Aristotle discussed the tragic play without character—what we would call melodrama. If character represents agency, or choice, the play without character is like a nineteenth-century melodrama in which evil versus good is personified in the villain and hero. Thematic-based characterization "telegraphs" a certain thematic message or point of view from the playwright without fully integrating it in the aesthetic construct. This creates a distancing effect between audience and character that affords the comic treatment of extreme violence, for example. McDonagh's lead characters are primarily theatrical constructs. Thus, plays with seemingly heavy thematic material like *Inishmore* and *Behanding* (or *Pillowman*) that feature crazed, sociopathic villains, Padraic and Carmichael respectively, never seem close enough to reality to be taken seriously. McDonagh encases his message within a framework of the grotesque and bizarre, and has built his reputation on this technique. This may explain McDonagh's broader appeal than say, Sarah Kane, whose stark brutality in the play *Blasted* stands without relief. Of course, Bertolt Brecht remains the original ideologue as showman because he knew that, for the message to be effective, it had to be theatricalized through music, poetry, or well-known forms like the fable and allegory.

DIALOGIC VERSUS DIALECTIC

Should playwrights disguise thematic concerns so as to avoid "telegraphing" a message? Perhaps this is one dilemma of so-called serious theater. If the play or major character represents an ideology or belief system, discovery becomes less interesting or aesthetically challenging since it is a given circumstance. The early plays of Heiner Müller, a force in the European avant-garde of the 1970s and 1980s, represent a move from a post-Brechtian epic theater to a dialectical theater in which character represents a given ideological point of view. Müller's early plays, written within the strictures of East German censorship codes, contain proletarian characters drawn along ideological lines, representations of the dialectical forces at work within the communist system. These committed plays serviced common societal ends, similar to the socialist realism plays of the 1920s Soviet Union. In his later works, Müller evinces the mature synthesis of thought with theatricality, and these works invite the director to explore a broader landscape of character. Müller collides place, genre, and era in the dialogic, rather than dialectical sense. In Müller's signature plays, like *Hamletmachine*, he leaves it to the audience to glean a difficult or conflicting message—one that resists telegraphing.

Charles Mee's adaptations of Greek classical drama demonstrate how "arguments" can be addressed in a dramaturgy that still provides theatrical values. *Big Love* targets difficult or contradictory perspectives within the carnivalesque range of characters: can force be justified as simply an extension of natural law? Do we place too much value on human choice? Is compromise necessary to retain humanity? Is the relationship between *eros* (sexual or romantic love) and *thanatos* (death) inextricable? Mee's dialogic dramaturgy establishes the opposing forces with ends that are less determinate than those of dialectical theater. Dialectical theater attempts to arrive at a specific determined end as the result of conflict between forces, one of which is both privileged and predetermined. This strategy leads to a didactic theater, and is related to a committed political or social praxis. Probably the most effective and successful venue for didactic theater today is children's theater: we want our children to hear positive messages and develop caring, humanistic values. Moreover, children's theater allows for the most innovative flights of imagination. Small wonder that Jenkin, Wellman, Congdon, and other new playwrights have been commissioned to write for children's theater.

Two British plays that are still widely produced reflect thematic/character dialogism. Characters in Tom Stoppard's *Arcadia* "instruct" the audience how to interpret what the play is doing. The rhetorical mode of character, which emphasizes teaching or persuasion, takes over. Yet, as embedded in its dialogic structure, *Arcadia* reflects the juxtaposition of historical eras and discourses. David Edgar's polyvocal play *Pentecost* explores the tumult around a Giotto fresco found in a medieval church. The church has just been reconverted within a post-communist Eastern European country, which is overrun with foreign entrepreneurs, prostitutes, and displaced individuals. The dialogism between language, cultures, and political forces creates a multilayered, thematic landscape that is reflected in the dramaturgical structure. If Edgar's play presaged Bonnie Marranca's prophecy that this multilayered, theatricalized relationship between cultures, voices, and themes is the future of drama, the success of Lynn Nottage's 2009 Pulitzer-Prize winning play *Ruined*, which explored the devastating effects of rape in war-torn Uganda, confirmed it.

SATIRICAL APPROACHES

Some plays advance a politically unpopular message through an eccentric character. We have noted that Martin McDonagh's risky decision to place the "n" word in the mouth of the white protagonist, Carmichael (in *A Behanding in Spokane*), provoked audiences and blogged some outrage. The thematic interest in the play was its eerily ironic treatment of race relations. Was this satire? Did the playwright support these positions? How did the celebrity actor playing Carmichael, Christopher Walken, feel about these questions, and about uttering "nigger" so often and blatantly? Sarah Ruhl, in *Dead Man's Cell Phone*, deals with the problems of the black market for human body parts in a manner that is more blatantly satirical—through the "living" character of the dead man, Gordon. Satire embodies thematic intent within genre. It can be more theatrical than seriously committed plays, because it relies upon exaggeration and typification of characters. In *Sincerity Forever*, Wellman ridicules the Ku Klux Klan through repetition and silly wordplay. Wellman's *7 Blowjobs* offers an incisive satire on scandal cover-ups at the senatorial level. Wellman mocks the tragic enterprise in his recent *The Invention of Tragedy*, with choruses of cats, for example. Wellman often cloaks serious issues in bizarre humor or silliness, using comic strategies to veil his political beliefs.

EXERCISE:
Theatricalizing the thematic

Read and familiarize yourself with McDonagh's plays (*Behanding, Pillowman, Inishmore*).

1. Consider some "politically correct" topics in the workshop.
2. Try to achieve a balance of outcomes by assigning each topic to more than one playwright.
3. Devise a construct of an appropriate villainous character that is grotesque, extreme, depraved, and so on.
4. Consider handicapping the character in some physical way (as in missing limbs, speech impediment, or blindness).
5. Establish a twisted rationale for the character's behavior (Carmichael blames his racism on his mother).
6. Write a three-character scene (three to five pages) that pits two characters against the "villain."
7. Have the "villain" take radical action to ensure control of the scene. (Check the shootout scene in *Inishmore*.)
8. Allow the "PC" material to fuel the antagonism and outrage of the other characters.
9. Conclude with decisive violent action against one or both antagonists.

COMMENT: The challenge for playwrights, then, is to position the thematic character within the theatrical aesthetic. Consider the use of the carnivalesque or grotesque in creating satirical treatments. Rather than foreground a sociocultural message that a character posits or volunteers, playwrights must establish characters along theatrical or external lines whereby the core theatricality of the character balances or juxtaposes the ideological framework that the playwright wishes to establish. As Brecht said, theater *theaters* everything, so explore that which is inherently theatrical for its potential to transform the theater. What appears strikingly new in ways reformulates solid theatrical practices of the past.

TOWARD A THEATRICAL CONSTRUCTION OF CHARACTER

PREMISE: Theatricality supersedes the dramatic function as the root of characterization in the new dramaturgy.

Theatricality defines a self-evident condition of the theater that distinguishes it from literature: the live actor who inhabits character, the actor–audience dynamic, the living gesture, and the visceral and evanescent engagement with the collective audience. Theatricality is about what "works" as theater: the plasticity of language, the immediacy of action, the spatial/temporal imagination, and the virtuosic performance. It is about surprise, wonder, and daring, the reckless, the strange, the visually arresting, and the erotic. The playwright integrates or juxtaposes these elements, constructing character as an aesthetic—not representational or thematic—construct. Developing characters from a theatrical aesthetic rather than a psychological base represents a fundamental shift in the assumptions behind good playwriting.

As playwrights, dramaturgs, and critics now recognize, there has been a root shift in defining dramaturgical standards; terms like conflict, through line, arc, and subtext may be subordinated or less viable. Indeed, the increased recognition of the theatrical dimension as an essential component of characterization has revitalized the art of playwriting.

THE THIRTEEN TENETS OF THEATRICAL CHARACTERS

1. Characters are larger than life, often exaggerated, extreme or heightened beyond the normative. As such, they rip the reader/audience out of the comfort zone of predictability. Consider, for example, the character Gogol in the opening scene of Len Jenkin's eponymous play from the 1980s:

GOGOL: Welcome, I am Gogol. I am not lights and shadow. I am not the mountain or the lake below. I am not a stick, not the ashes, I am not an ape. I am not a hummingbird. I was born a man, and that has not changed, no matter what I do.

I am not mother, I am not teacher, I am not a hero or a thief. I do not make paper snowflakes or count stars. I am not funny, I am not poisonous. I am not joking. I am Gogol, cloud and mud. I am extinct. I run the roller-coaster at night. I am a go-go dancer and a fool.

I have an excellent notion of why you've come here. Let me assure you that each thing you expect to happen will happen. And less. And more. I am Gogol. Believe that, and I will tell you another one.

(Wellman 1985, *Gogol,* 5)

In this opening monologue, Jenkin establishes an obviously heightened character based in negatives and absences (what he is not, and what he does not do) before he identifies himself. Even Gogol's identity is problematic ("Believe that, and I will tell you another one"). Gogol, in fact, is not actually based on the Russian playwright. He becomes a loose cannon, a self-deprecating oddball who if nothing else is unpredictable. As the playwright, Jenkin demonstrates a confidence in his directness and clarity of purpose. While unpredictable, the character is risky, edgy, and sharply drawn.

2. Characters are formed externally rather than internally. External form suggests that there is no subtextual basis of character. There is the concomitant obsession with doing something. An analogy could be made to the masked character, whereby the subjective and the psychological are de-emphasized and the gestural is heightened.

3. Characters can be inserted for texture or strange juxtaposition, or to create a counter-dynamic in the play. For example, an eighteenth-century character, Capability Brown, is inserted in Len Jenkin's *My Uncle Sam*, presenting an iconic strangeness juxtaposed to the central action. Capability Brown serves a dramaturgic rather than dramatic function. In Lisa D'Amour's *16 Spells to Charm the Beast*, the character of the Beast does not enter until one-third of the play has been performed. From that point the Beast creates a counter-dynamic to the action and character of Lillian.

4. Characters are drawn from a number of source materials, not simply imitations of life, or to service familiar roles (fathers, wayward sons, and so on). As such, they are given the capacity for heightened language. Often marginalized, these characters find their lot through, and in, language, as if language in new playwriting substitutes for traditional character traits and subtextual concerns. Beyond his characters with lost dreams (see Chapter 6), Len Jenkin draws characters from pop icons like comic books, hack detective novels of the 1940s, and carnival hucksters; Young Jean Lee forms a contemporary play that utilizes romantic poets Wordsworth, Coleridge and Byron as characters in *The Appeal*; Erin Courtney based her eponymous character from the play *Demon Baby* on garden gnome statuary.

5. Characters are seldom built along thematic concerns or to forward an agenda in a play. The first generation of new playwrights suffered during the "politically correct" era by not allowing their work to be appropriated by any special interest groups. Critics, as well as theater insiders, jumped in on this bandwagon: for many years, Suzan-Lori Parks had been criticized for not supporting traditional black themes, until her crossover hit *Topdog/Underdog* got the critics off her back. Historically, critics, dramaturgs, and literary managers have preferred characters to represent thematic values that mirror or resonate with popular culture. Potential producers are wary of offending corporate sponsors, while the political left has been keenly sensitive to not offend any marginalized group through racist language or sexist characters. We have seen a relaxing of the latter, evidenced in the overt racist language in McDonagh's *A Behanding in Spokane*, and the raw, insistent sexuality of the women in Alice Tuan's *Ajax (Por Nobody)*.

6. Characters transform, change, fragment, or deconstruct. There is often a tension between the performer and character in these plays. In Naomi Iizuka's *36 Views* the westernized, contemporary character Setzuko Hearn transforms back and forth from a Kabuki figure to Hearn, later from a woman of the Heian era to herself defining the equivocal character (that is, one actor transforms to and from multiple identities). Here, a character dynamically serves as the theatrical corollary to the various ancient Asian art periods and customs pertinent to the play's subject matter. Iizuka demonstrates how an antique and non-Western theatrical stage form like Kabuki can uncover a deeper thematic that informs both the play, and the character of Setzuko Hearn. By actually showing the change through an unveiling of costume, Iizuka makes the actor (and costumer) work to achieve a memorable theatrical "moment." Margo, in Len Jenkin's *Margo Veil*, continually transforms her physical appearance using a magical transforming device, as other actors stand-in for the mutable character.

7. Characters may be unnamed or nonhuman. In Wellman's most recent monologue plays, such as *Bitter Bierce* and *Jennie Ritchie*, there are no character titles presented; rather, the audience formulates an image of the character based on the language and performance choices of the performer. The late Mel Gussow's *New York Times* review of one of Wellman's earlier experiments, *Three Americanisms*, described three very individualized characters that in the script are blandly listed as Man 1, Man 2, and Woman. Gussow "created" the individuals through their use of language, and by their presence and dress onstage (fronts). Wellman has used actors to portray aliens, crows, dogs, cats, hares—even shadows. Jenkin's use of props and animals adds a sense of charm and whimsy to the beginning of *Gogol*. The stage directions read, "*A giant turtle enters, moving very slowly. It has a small saddle on its back. As it passes behind Gogol, he mounts it, facing the audience. The turtle never varying its pace carries him off*" (Wellman 1985, *Gogol*, 7).

8. Grotesque and/or grossly satiric portrayals define characters that advance causes or serve as representatives of maligned groups. Or they are given an extreme physical handicap. There is no attempt to cure societal ills through the characters serving as moral agents. Nor does new writing draw sympathy directly to any of these characters, whatever their handicap. For example, in Kreitzer's *Freakshow*, Judith, the hideous, dog-faced lady rants about her degradation in developing the sideshow attraction of a sexualized, groveling dog, conversely feeling a sense of pride and worth at the financial success gained from her performance. Wellman's political satire *7 Blowjobs* presents Senator Armitage as a feckless, grotesque politician.

A recent trend in playwriting is to present characters with missing body parts, or who have been dismembered. The loss of a visible limb or appendage becomes a marker for a characters' motivation, anxiety, or pain, while providing the audience with an external focus point. Carson's *Freakshow* (Amelia, all limbs); McDonagh's *Pillowman* (toes) and *A Behanding in Spokane* (hand); Ruhl's *The Clean House* (breast) and *Dead Man's Cell Phone* (kidneys); Alice Tuan's *Ajax (Por Nobody)* (testicle) represent a few examples of this startling choices for creating the externally based character.

9. Characters are archetypes. Characters are larger than life, represent the ideal of their type, or assume an aspect of American mythos.

They stake out territory that suggests specific actions and traits. In some cases, this is evident in the naming of characters: in Jenkin's *Dark Ride*, the Translator, Deep Sea Ed, and the Thief could be considered archetypal characters. In Lee's *The Appeal*, Wordsworth, Coleridge, and Byron arrive as archetypical romantic poets, only to have the playwright refocus on their petty bickerings and debunk their mythos.

10. Characters are stage figures. A stage figure is a formation in which the actor creates a certain shape, pattern of movement, or gestural sense that the audience recognizes as a definite identity and imbues with traits that would not otherwise be evident. The audience builds the character by projecting its image of the ideal upon the stage figure. For example, an actor who mimics the gait and dress of Charlie Chaplin is seen as Chaplin or as Chaplinesque, and as such, the audience endows the figure with other traits. Stage figures can be created by costume (Dracula, Superman, other pop icons) or physical attitude (carnival showman, disoriented professor). This too is like the *commedia dell'arte*, whereby a character like Harlequin was imprinted upon the audience through mask, dress, and physical attitude. The audience anticipated and expected his preordained physical and psychological predilections for food, thievery, and laziness. The figures of Babe Ruth and the Joker from Jenkin's *Kid Twist* represent American versions of the stage figure. Babe Ruth is an icon from America's pastime (baseball), but eclipsed the sport as an American hero representing power and consumption— embodied in the epithet "the Sultan of Swat." The iconic Joker is immortalized in his bouts with Batman in comic books and in recent movie adaptations. Jenkin's *Kitty Hawk* includes the James brothers, the Wright brothers, and the Smith brothers (of cough drop lore) as characters. Sometimes the stage figure is rendered as a symbol or emblem. For example, Man with a Scythe in Wellman's *Bodacious Flapdoodle* is the standard iconographic symbol for the grim reaper. The character Demon Baby is recognizable as the statuary of the garden gnome seen in many nurseries and garden shops.

11. Characters may be dematrixed. New playwrights use dematrixing techniques. The actor/character is dematrixed when they fracture the mold of a specific character; directly acknowledge or address the presence of the audience, or foregrounds the presence of the actor over the character. Dematrixing utilizes some level of metatheatricality by self-consciously calling attention to the artifice of the stage. In Wellman's *Energumen*, Megan is rehearsing a story while prompted by Jacques, who cajoles her, "Remember how it was in acting class?" He is calling attention to the dynamic between actor and character. Here the effect is doubled: Megan within the matrix of character rehearsing a role; Megan the character as actor in training, in "acting class."

12. Music and sound act as character motivators. Jenkin uses music as a prod to character formation in the early stages of the writing process. In production, Jenkin and Wellman utilize *leitmotifs* to define an absent or approaching character, often to a comic end. Notable is Wellman's use of the chorus of cats in *The Invention of Tragedy* (see Chapter 12). Playwrights may rely on highly amplified sound and music in production as determinants to a character's choice of action, or to shift the direction in a character's speech. The eerily haunting repetitive melody of "Who put the Y in YBOR" in Wellman's *Fnu Lnu* serves as a choral interlude and tag line that marks the structure of the play, a device we see repeated in *The Invention of Tragedy.* Jenkin uses nightclub singers to create ambiance and define characters in *My Uncle Sam,* and the club duo in his recently revived *Dream Express* weave music in and out of the action of the play. Music or sound can be seen in its structural or textural function rather than as primarily supportive or evocative. Sound can be used in rehearsals or workshops to "get at" character, or establish the basis of a character. Characters may be urged to sing, even if not well, in a number of plays. Jenkin experiments in rehearsal with sections of text that may be sung (although these sections may not be indicated in published versions of the script).

13. Characters are construed erotically. Presenting the erotic on stage provides an external stimulation for the audience that suspends or enhances the dramatic moment. Alice Tuan's play *Ajax (Por Nobody)* features double penetration, insertions, castration, lesbian sexuality, and unbridled desire that verges on pornography. Barbara Cassidy's drug-addicted character Joy in *Interim* removes her blouse, makes out, indulges in self-arousal, and describes herself as "horny" and "wanting to fuck." The limbless Amalia in Kreitzer's *Freakshow* is obsessed with her sexuality, and describes the positions she uses in sexual intercourse in her opening monologue. Iizuka makes references to the pornographic Eastern *shunga* as a means of triggering the sexual liaison of the main characters. Female orgasms, male anal orgasm, and frontal male nudity are graphically displayed in Sarah Ruhl's *In the Next Room, or the Vibrator Play.*

The erotic is a generally a marker for transgression. It can be used to create arousal in the audience, or provide an effect of "making strange," as in the male nudity near the conclusion of Ruhl's aforementioned play. Curiously, all of the above examples are from women playwrights, who are now writing the most erotic or sexually explicit scripts. References include both genders, as a number of plays contain phallocentric images and allusions. Since sexuality involves displays of the body, the focus is on the external form of the character, with a momentary suspension of the emotional or rhetorical. Nevertheless, this physicality creates a vital human connection to the material, as sexuality provides the shorthand to a character's values and identity. A good example is the male nudity in *The Vibrator Play* which presents the irony of Dr. Givings, who facilitates female orgasm, yet is unable to experience his own needs for intimacy and sexual contact with his wife. As such, the erotic is not gratuitous but an arc to the character's discovery of a deeper relationship with his wife. Since writing the erotic involves risk for all involved, especially the playwright, it remains a frontier that challenges further exploration.

These thirteen tenets are useful descriptors that demonstrate how the playwright can build theatrical characterizations. The key link is usually between theatricality and language. This poetics (or artistic making) need not be tied to strict imitation (*mimesis*). But it may cause those in the dramatic process to ponder the origins of the word *mimesis*, which Aristotle sought as his basis of action. Characters in classical tragedies were masked, usually with features extraordinarily exaggerated or typified. We think of Antigone and Oedipus now as fully realized individuals who can be analyzed psychologically, but in antiquity their masks, costumes, and even footwear inculcated them with a magical theatricality. And like the Japanese Kabuki theater, and Shakespeare's as well, all the actors were male.

HISTORICAL COROLLARY: THE MASKS OF THE COMMEDIA DELL'ARTE

A useful analogy links the characters of the new playwriting to the masks of the *commedia dell'arte*. The *commedia dell'arte* used fixed character types determined externally by masks, physical traits, dialect, and function. While the language focus of the new playwriting differs from the unscripted scenario sketch of the improvisatory *commedia*, the new dramaturgy contemporizes *commedia*'s rhetorical strategies such as tirades (in Wellman's haranguing monologues, for example), or *sproposito*, which means "nonsense speech" (Wellman's or Parks's transrational monologues could also be related to the *spropositi*, which were usually given when the character was overcome with madness brought on by grief or inebriation). Wellman's blustering, pompous Senator Armitage simulates the self-aggrandizing Dottore type. The Ruzante-like characters who talk to themselves in Jenkin's *American Notes* are all marginalized, displaced, and in an ongoing stream of self-talk, like Gordon in Ruhl's *DMCP*. *Commedia* and new playwriting monologues exemplify the role of the virtuosic performer, who orchestrates sharp turns in intention, or dialect, with gestural thrusts and parries that leave audiences astonished—and breathless. This freeing of language from psychological implications or thematic intentions makes for the vivid moment-to-moment excitement that represents theater at its optimum.

What does a sixteenth-century Venetian Pantalone or Arlecchino from Bergamo have to do with contemporary characterization? The external, iconic, and sometimes comic-book approach to character in Len Jenkin's plays simulates the *commedia* tradition of charlatans, con men, and hucksters of various ilks, usually with a full bag of props. Case in point: Jenkin's eponymous character from *My Uncle Sam* is a novelty salesman with props like goozeleum glasses, poop cushions, and illuminating crucifixes. Jenkin's characters bulk actions of deceit, chicanery, and thievery, with colorful slang-laden lingo, laced with double-entendre and innuendo. Similarly, in Wellman's early play *Harm's Way*, the character Crowsfoot is the quintessential mountebank, selling quack cures and paraphernalia to whoever is gullible enough to pay. This rascal-dupe dynamic is the essence of street comedy, circus (recalling P. T. Barnum's "a sucker is born every minute"), and the topical style of the *commedia*. The snake-oil peddling charlatan on a makeshift platform with the sexy "inamorata sidekick" (contemporized in *Harm's Way* as the character Isle of Mercy) is at the heart of the first commercial theater. Marginalized salesmen and ersatz clergy abound in Jenkin plays, nowhere more evident than in the Lightning Rod Salesman figure in *Limbo Tales* or the Reverend in *Margo Veil*.

In Wellman's production of *Murder of Crows* at Primary Stages, the central character, played by Stephen Mellor, used macabre *Grand Guignol* makeup in such an exaggerated way as to suggest a mask. The use of the face and body to indicate heightened states is typically seen in performances of works of the new playwriting. The chorus of crows (in crow costumes) or cats in *The Invention of Tragedy* harkens back to the bestial tradition of the *commedia* pastorals. New playwrights utilize animal-like costumes to achieve comic ends in a carnivalesque vein. *Seventy Scenes of Halloween*, the most produced play by Jeffrey Jones, who is now active in promoting new playwrights, orchestrates scenes of the unraveling marriage with the intrusive silly masked figure that moves the play toward a farcical romp. The argumentative beats between the husband and wife skew into a reflection of the lover's quarrels (*contrasti*) of the early *commedia dell'arte*. Indeed, the director and actor who are exploring new playwriting for the first time should consider the *commedia* approach of performance as a more effective playing style than traditional internalized methods.

The *commedia* tradition has several premises that find their corollaries in the new playwriting, as the following list indicates.

1 The creation of a theatrical antiworld:
   - a world usually in between a simulated reality and a kind of "otherness" (science fiction, as in Wellman's *Albanian Softshoe* and *Whirligig* or Alice Tuan's non-referential sexualized universe in *Ajax (Por Nobody);* Ruhl's plays often begin in reality then devolve into otherness)
   - a world of man and beast, aliens, and so on (D'Amour's *16 Spells to Charm the Beast*)

2 A sense of artifice rather than a representation of real life:
   - external rather than internal or psychological form (surface, stylized dimension, textural)
   - characters derived from genres, tradition, icons, and pop culture. Madelyn Kent's work is synthesized from Japanese women

learning to speak English. The result is a highly formalized and unique cadence.

3 Fixed types and normative parts in the same play:
  • cameo-like roles, types from various genres or periods in history
  • a dissonant ensemble of characters, marginalized rather than mainstream (broken dreams, economic fringe)
  • a task-oriented and moment-to-moment existence rather than one that is arc-oriented and changed by circumstance.

4 The use of carnival-like language to create a sense of the bizarre, strange, or comic:
  • a mixture of high and low levels of language (colorful, playful)
  • words as attractors and shapers of character and destinations.

5 Gesture- and movement-specific work; an aspect of gesture related to function:
  • the relationship between man and beast; iconographic configurations (the part-man part-beast Human Salamander in Kreitzer's *Freakshow*, or action derived from Asian iconography, as in Iizuka's *36 Views*).

6 The work often requires a virtuoso, expressionistic interpretation by the performer. See Chapter 12.

This list represents a paradigm for characterization, the cartography from which an entire character ensemble might be constructed. Many of Jenkin's ensembles are built with a *commedia*-like company of specific types that are fundamentally interchangeable. These types are defined by role, as specific character names change from play to play. As *commedia* drew its fixed characters as much from the culture as from literary antecedents, so too are Jenkin's characters heavily drawn from pop culture, B movies, and private-eye fiction. Yet, filled with spirit and brio, they are neither flat nor two-dimensional in realization.

THE STOCK COMPANY OF LEN JENKIN

A Jenkin "stock" company would have the following fixed types (with their *commedia* counterpart in parentheses):

  • professor (Dottore)
  • reporter
  • artist
  • salesman (Pantalone)
  • master of ceremonies or showman
  • shadow (Brighella)
  • detective
  • shaman (Charlatan)

- thief (Harlequin)
- clergyman.

Notwithstanding the absence of detectives or reporters in the *commedia* tradition, it is nevertheless compelling to note the similarities. These stock types weave into the action with normative figures; travelers, or journeymen with destinations, and a variety of narrators or storytellers who clue us in to the story. In Chapter 6, we will probe this matter further.

INTERTEXTUAL DIALOGISM

This comparative reference to the *commedia dell'arte* should be taken either as a point of contact or a point of departure. For those who seek a solid historical link and theatrical formulation, *commedia* is one persuasive benchmark. Other less familiar external traditions with historical implications are applicable here: for example, Iizuka's Japanese characters in *36 Views* reflect the tradition of Kabuki in movement and formulation. Mellor's approach to Wellman's work, whether in *Terminal Hip* or *Murder of Crows*, derives partly from the macabre style of *Grand Guignol*. Susan-Lori Parks pays homage to minstrelsy in *The American Play* and *Topdog/Underdog*. The new playwrights' penchant for rebottling old forms has lent historical credibility and theatricality to a different way of making theater.

CREATING MASK AND SHADOW

Italian theater historian Roberto Tessari demonstrated that the *commedia dell'arte* mask carried with it many associations, including the devil, the notion of an antiworld, death, and the afterlife (1989). The external form of the mask is imbued with powers that create fascination and wonder. The mask relates to an audience on a primitive level, stirring the imagination in various ways. Tessari recognized that the mask's association with carnival meant that it signifies the overturning of norms, a kind of "anything goes" frame of mind. Moreover, the mask functions as a leveler of status, class, and even gender as it removes or effaces the individuality of the person wearing it. The mask neutralizes the distinguishing features of the face and eyes—the soul of the personality. It presents us with the "other," elements part man but also part beast. The mask forces the site of engagement with the audience away from the visage, to the gestural body in motion. Thus, the mask removes the psychology from the character, replacing it with an immanent theatricality that is edgy and immediate.

A playwright inexperienced with mask work can quickly recognize its potential for theatricality in the exercise that follows. The mask serves as a point of entry for the playwright interested in exploring external characterization.

EXERCISE:
Masks

This exercise is an excellent way to introduce playwrights to the notions of the external character. Typically, *commedia dell'arte* masks should be used for this exercise, although you can use whatever masks are available. *Commedia* masks are useful because they define a specific shape, color, and set of corresponding traits. For example, the curvilinear Harlequin masks suggest a circular sense of movement and gesture, as opposed to the angularity of Pantalone's. The green color of Brighella's mask is related to deceit and scheming. This exercise requires pairs of playwrights.

1. Approach the mask with great care. Study it carefully; sense its texture, form, and attitude. Hold it out at arm's length, then bring it toward your face, attempting to feel its power or energy transfer itself to you. Apply the mask slowly, feeling your way into it; let it "work" on you, directing you toward movements and gesture. Stand and walk about, then proceed to the next step.
2. One playwright wears the mask while the other jots down associations. The wearer of the mask should move about, play with gesture, sense the attitudes of the mask. As the other jots down associations, she should attempt to come up with an idea of character.
3. Reverse the roles and repeat the first two steps.
4. Based on experiencing and observing the mask, both playwrights should write a monologue together about a character who applies the mask. We should sense a transformation or transference that takes place at the moment the mask touches the face. Work your way to the transformation by-exploring the various associations you came up with in step 2.

COMMENT: After some character work with the mask, you will have a more confident approach to an exploration of theatrical character in the new playwriting.

CHARACTER CLASH

In formulating a character, most playwrights work from the basis of key relationships and the forces that are in conflict within a character's life. Typical in American dramaturgy is the dysfunctional American family, a continuing *topoi* in the plays of Eugene O'Neill, Arthur Miller, Tennessee Williams, and Lorraine Hansberry, through to Sam Shepard, August Wilson, Donald Margulies, Jon Robin Baitz, and so on. The family provides a shared language and interactional system in which the playwright can operate on terms "familiar as family" to an audience. The family is dramatically efficient because histories (and therefore subtexts) are shared, lessening the need for expository material. Moreover, the family provides an underlying structure, a "given" in which typical roles are played out, gauged, and tabulated. Dramatic interest emerges when this integral structure is threatened with upheaval or disruption through internal conflicts, power struggles, or external violation.

New playwriting, on the other hand, tends to look at non-familial subject matter, exploding the site of the play out of the living room. Even when a play concerns a family structure, as in Parks's *In the Blood*, the setting is marginalized—the underside of a bridge. The recognizable system in which the play operates as an integral whole can be altered significantly by the intrusion of semiotic elements outside of the expected norm. For example, in Constance Congdon's *Tales of the Lost Formicans*, seemingly normative, integral characters become aliens when they don sunglasses. This splitting of the integral character is a hallmark or new playwriting. *In the Next Room, or the Vibrator Play* riffs off the nineteenth-century parlor play in the style of Henrik Ibsen, but the discussion and displays of sexuality are contemporized.

Traditional playwriting establishes the through-line convention of character to ensure consistency throughout the piece. In the new playwriting, the terrain of character is shifting. In Wellman's *Albanian Softshoe*, normative characters become marionettes by act 2. In Jenkin's *Kid Twist*, scenes from the Hindenburg disaster collide against the surreal projections of the main character who is detained in a motel as part of the witness protection program. These manifestations of Kid Twist's dreams demonstrate new writing's affinity with surrealism, drawing sharp, satiric, and comic connections between the living and the dead. Further, the iconic characters of Babe Ruth, the Joker, and Kid Twist are juxtaposed in a visual, living collage that replaces traditional narrative. This clash of characters draws from American and German history, pop culture, and *film noir* gangster lore. The term character clash describes this collision of history, culture, or typology of character within play.

Over the years, playwrights have experimented with character clash to achieve thematic ends. The spectrum is diverse, from Adrienne Kennedy's early work *The Owl Answers*, which juxtaposed characters from various historical eras, to Young Jean Lee's *The Appeal*, which clashes current American speech with "historicized" romantic poets from the nineteenth century. In new writing, character clash involves the insertion of historical characters, pop icons, equivocal characters, aliens, and the like, juxtaposed to more or less normative characters. (Normative characters may be defined as reality-based.) This creates a polyvocality in the text, since neither "voice" is privileged. The result may be a hybrid, in which characters from opposing genres, cultures, or histories create a frisson in the text. Caridad Svitch's anthology of recent classical adaptations, *Divine Fire* (2005), offers many examples of the clash between ancient and modern as playwrights impose the modern on antiquity to address a particular theme or character of interest. John Jesuron's reworking of Sophocles' *Philoctetes* never allows the titular character to achieve the redemption of the original, rather focusing upon the character's struggles with isolation and illness through establishing multiple identities. This frisson between the antique and modern sparks tension and forward movement that propels the play along, substituting for the traditional through line or arc. Len Jenkin's first play, *Kitty Hawk*, established a dramaturgy of frisson by contrasting the great brother acts in history (see page 86). Each new entrance creates a clash among contexts, voices, and histories in which a shared language had to be found and then re-formed as each new fraternal duo was introduced. The term clash is accurate in describing a conflict of worlds and histories that these dual characters embody.

Character clash provides a nonlinear dynamic that interrupts or aborts a trackable, traditional narrative. The creation of an antiworld parallel to our own world is central to new writing, insofar as it establishes a uniquely theatrical environment. The play becomes a heterogeneous landscape of figures, cultures, and histories. These figural polarities churn the action of the play into unexpected directions and outcomes as they reveal the wonder of theater. Ironically, this polarized topography is more representative of current culture than the traditionally homogenous world-of-the-play. Indeed, Wellman and other language playwrights have argued for years that their plays are more reflective of our lives than the traditional fare that marks the dominant dramaturgy of the regional and Broadway theaters.

Character clash raises the aesthetic principle of *interruption*. Interruption occurs at the point at which one theatrical world or one voice is eclipsed by another. An example is the equivocal character construct in which the actor transforms from one character to another, as in Iizuka's *36 Views*, Overmyer's *Heliotrope Bouquet*, Jenkin's *Margo Veil* (see the next chapter), or Jesuron's *Philoctetes*, in which the lead character transforms across genders.

At the moment of interruption, the spectator or reader is forced to consider the work in its entirety and is in effect thrown into a closer relationship with the text. Len Jenkin utilizes interruption through the character of Capability Brown, the eighteenth-century botanist who invades the "present" in *My Uncle Sam*. The insertion of Capability Brown impedes the sense of linearity or representational objectivity. In his recent play, *Margo Veil*, the lead character Margo changes identity serially throughout the play, each time inhabited by a different actor. Jenkin forces the audience to track the character, subsequently played by a sequence of different actors. Mac Wellman utilizes another form of interruption in *Antigone*, when actors arbitrarily change characters throughout the play. In the gap, or moment of transition between Asian antiquity and modern dress in Iizuka's *36 Views*, the audience is made to experience or discover something about the character and the play. Sarah Ruhl's *Dead Man's Cell Phone* begins Act II with a *tour de force* monologue from the dead man, Gordon, thus interrupting both the narrative flow and established world of the play. For playwrights, this beat of interruption is one of the most powerful dramaturgic tools, because it defines a point of entry during which the audience completes its relation to the text.

As audiences now become more inured to the fractures in narrative that define contemporary playwriting, they are compelled to focus upon interruption as a means toward greater theatricality and wonder.

The principles of character clash are as follows:

- It creates a unique theatrical environment in which normative relationships are altered or skewed through the use of:
  - characters from different historical periods;
  - characters from different genres of literature, film, television;
  - characters with diverse sexual identities or peccadilloes.
  - characters that are living interacting with "dead" characters
  - equivocal character
- Characters are defined in relation to an "other" rather than in the traditional protagonist/antagonist sense. The self is continually reshaped in relationship to the "other" rather than existing as a self-integrated entity.
- Characters may be nonhuman, partially human, or dead.
- Characters clash on the level of language, attitudes, goals, discourses, and worlds.

EXERCISE:

Character clash

Exercise A

1. Select two characters, one from a foreign or exotic locale, the other a comic-book figure.

2. Establish one character as a traveler, the second as an expert or guide of some sort who has needed advice or information. A variant of the expert or guide is the omniscient character, such as a shaman, priest, or seer.

3. Create clash through shifting language levels and patterns:
   - How well do the characters understand or misapprehend each other?
   - Establish some common ground in language, or through visual properties.

4. Write a scene that marks a transition in the traveler's self-perception. At the same time, the traveler's interaction with the guide or expert embodies an external change in the action.

COMMENT: Consult Wikipedia to provide you with enough information to create an effective "expert, shaman, or seer."

Exercise B

The next exercise is popular with playwriting students. It involves a rewrite of the above exercise. Here, you add a new character.

1. Write a short scene with two characters in a conflict or win–lose situation. The outcome is that one character will win, the other lose.

2. During the scene, establish one character's interest or obsession with some dead historical character, or choose a character from a particular genre of literature or film. Use visually identifiable means, such as clothing, hats, and accoutrements to theatricalize this character.

3. Find a point of entry for the historical character to come into the action.

4. Rewrite the scene with the inserted "genre" character taking the side of one character against the other.

COMMENT: It can be helpful if each participant establishes the "historical or fictional" character as the initial part of this exercise. Again, Wikipedia provides ready source materials for this scene work. The recent Broadway musical *Bloody, Bloody Andrew Jackson* was actually created along these lines.

Exercise C: Utilizing visual modes

1. Students should download portraits of characters then construct the above-described scenes with these visual models for inspiration. This step can be a preliminary to exercise B, above, but take full advantage of its use in the workshop, where it will stimulate all the students. Visual sources promote a theatrical mindset--at the heart of the externally constructed character.

COMMENT: Experiment with character clash to get a feel for a theatrical mix that creates immediate surface and dynamic interest. The interaction itself can stimulate a dynamic that is immediate and potentially comic. Students with broader theatrical training can muse on the notions of characters wearing masks, or on the old *commedia* troupes that clashed dialects, masks, costume, and gestures to create an intensely popular form.

Let us now turn our attention to several different formulations of character transformation in new playwriting. Premises and modes of conceptualization will be targeted. Then, specific applications and exercises will follow.

5

The transformation of character

One of the most fascinating and challenging of the multivocal strategies is character transformation. This chapter provides various models and examples of some sophisticated approaches to creating the multivocal character.

As he turned his creative energies to television, Eric Overmyer's theatrical characters became more drawn from psychological or biographical profiles than archetypes. *The Heliotrope Bouquet* is based around the historical figure Scott Joplin and his sole collaboration with the unheralded yet enormously gifted pianist Louis Chauvin. The play captures a poetic rendition of the peregrinations in Joplin's mind as he recalls the past, particularly his heartbreaking relationship with Belle, mother of their deceased child. These moments are vividly realized as the transformations of his current wife Lottie into the "image" of his former lover, Belle. The transformations in Joplin's mind—the resultant agonies of tertiary syphilis—theatricalize his failing mental state. Lottie resents these ineluctable shifts in Joplin's mind which devalue her status as the most important woman in his life. The merging or juxtaposition of reality and consciousness provides the essential structure of the play. It allows different historical periods to fluidly dialogize in Overmyer's typically baroque style.

INTERRUPTION AND THE EQUIVOCAL CHARACTER

Overmyer presents a paradigm of the equivocal character in his rendering of the Spanish Mary, Belle, and Lottie character troika. If the equivocal character can be defined as one actor shifting between two or more characters, *The Heliotrope Bouquet* presents three. Spanish Mary in the first scene becomes Lottie; Lottie then switches back and forth with Belle. The equivocal character has the capacity to transform by switching from one character to another, or back and forth between two or three characters. Unlike a true transformation, Lottie neither transforms entirely into Belle nor vice versa. In this case, the switching mirrors the structural dynamic of the play—the movement back and forth across time periods. The characters Belle and Spanish Mary are deceased in Joplin's "real time" existence. His wife Lottie represents his current relationship. The device serves to capture the elusive past with its ambient sense of hope and promise, contrasted against a tone of bittersweet resignation in the present.

The effectiveness of the equivocal character is reliant upon the trigger mechanism, the device that motivates the transition from one character into another. Overmyer establishes the following transformation with a carefully disguised bundle. The transformation of the bundle from his former child with Belle back to the mess of spilled plums echoes the transformation from Belle to Lottie in Joplin's mind. The expressionistic projection of Joplin's mind is fully theatricalized by Overmyer:

> (*BELLE appears behind JOPLIN. She is holding a bundle.*)

BELLE: Oh Joplin.

JOPLIN: Belle. I'm so sorry.

BELLE: Coughed herself right out of this world and into the next. Poor creature. Tiny thing. Never knew a word:

JOPLIN: I'm so sorry. If I could find my work. If I could just find my work.

BELLE: What work? What are you talking about?

JOPLIN: *The Guest of Honor.* My opera. My ragtime opera. Mislaid. Misplaced. Where's it gone? Help me find it. If I could find that work, if I could just find that work, I could bring our baby back.

BELLE: Don't talk foolish.

JOPLIN: We could start over.

BELLE: I can't stay here.

JOPLIN: We'll go away to Chicago.

BELLE: You'll go.

> (*JOPLIN grabs her*)

JOPLIN: Don't go. Don't go. Don't go.

BELLE: I'm sore Joplin. A walking bruise. A lame dog and a broken wheel. Singing never saved a soul. Singing never brought nobody back. Once you're dead you're done. I'm done. I'm done, Joplin. Dead on my feet. I got no love for you or any man. Love died with my baby.

JOPLIN: Don't go. Don't go. Don't go.

> (*He shakes her. She drops the bundle and screams.*)

BELLE: Joplin.

> (*The bundle hits the floor and scatters: plums roll across the floor. Lights change. Belle becomes LOTTIE and stands before JOPLIN.*)

LOTTIE: Joplin. Look what you made me do.

(*She scurries about and picks up the plums.*)

LOTTIE: They were perfect. And now they're bruised. Ruined. Just like life. Like getting old. You make me tired. Old man, you called me Belle again. Damn you.

JOPLIN: Sorry.

LOTTIE: Now sit.

JOPLIN: So sorry, Lottie. So sorry.

> (*He sits at the piano. LOTTIE puts the plums in a bowl and sets them before him. SPICE enters with coffee.*)
>
> (Overmyer 1993, *The Heliotrope Bouquet*, 246–7)

Lottie's existential plight of a fractured identity is established through equivocal characterization. She can never achieve a stable identity in this marriage, and her frustration is palpable: "Old man, you called me Belle again. Damn you" clearly marks the volatile passive/aggressive dynamic at the core of the marriage, as do "You make me tired," and later, "Now sit." The plum bundle provides a semiotic doubling of this transference. By utilizing the bundle as the image of the baby, the playwright sets the audience up for a surprise discovery. The spilling of the plums provides the perfect sound and visual metaphors (small, vulnerable ripe fruit of a red purplish hue)—representing and exposing Joplin's denial of the infant's death, but also Belle's fecundity, and of course female genitalia, elements that Joplin gropes for longingly. For Lottie, the action of picking up the scattered fruit is the corollary to her picking up the pieces of Joplin's life, and marks her inability to capture a sense of wholeness about her life with Joplin.

Once the audience catches on to the back-and-forth shifts in the play, we come to expect, or at least anticipate, points of interruption. In the final moments of the play, Overmyer weaves between the two characters as each vies competitively for a stake in Joplin's world. Lottie's dilemma is that she is trapped by history and circumstance, whereas Belle is the actualization of memory, and not held to Lottie's spatial/temporal constraints:

JOPLIN: Belle.

LOTTIE: Oh, Joplin. No, not Belle.

JOPLIN: She was here.

LOTTIE: This is Lottie. The second one. The one saved your sorry life, remember?

> (Overmyer 1993, *The Heliotrope Bouquet*, 255)

The paradox of interruption is that it enhances the emotional involvement rather than aborts it. When Belle takes over the Lottie character; the emotional connection to the character persists, or is immediately heightened, especially at the moments of transference. This gap of interruption or "between-ness" causes the audience to examine where it is at that given moment. Rather than drawing us away, it causes us to affectively enter into the phenomenon more deeply. The equivocal character is experienced dialogically, as a theatrical conflation/divergence between two characters. Neither character achieves full absence or presence, and at the point of interruption the actor may suddenly be foregrounded over either character. Ultimately, meaning is determined at the point of interruption and deferral.

This example of the equivocal character theatricalizes the universal tendency to project the other on a present character—a particularly common component of love relationships—and in dramaturgical terms, a unique strategy of embedding dramatic conflict.

NAOMI IIZUKA: ICONOGRAPHY AND THE EQUIVOCAL CHARACTER

The equivocal character has been adopted by a number of playwrights within a variety of contexts. Naomi Iizuka's *36 Views* ensconces a modern realistic story about the art business within the iconography of ancient oriental art and theater, underscored by the soundings of ancient musical instruments. The director of the play's first production, Alan Macvey, describes the essence of the play's magical theatricality:

> The idea at the play's center are not just discussed by the characters, as they might be in a play by Shaw. They are also embodied by its theatrical elements. In the opening scene when a medieval woman is transformed to become a university professor, we are already forced to question our assumptions about what is real.
>
> (Iizuka 2003, 5–6)

If Overmyer uses the borderline waverings of Joplin's mind to initiate Belle's imposition on Lottie, Iizuka uses the iconography and artifacts of the art world to trigger character transformation. To effectively execute these transformations, the trigger device should seemingly emerge from the material at hand.

The play opens in a darkened art gallery described with focus drawn to a single hanging scroll: "On the scroll is a painting of a Japanese woman in a formal pose." From shadow, emerges the main character, Darius Wheeler, who begins his scene-long monologue, a narrative of pertinent backstory (Iizuka 2003, I:1, 11). Wheeler's utterance "cause he thinks you're a white devil, or a ghost" (2003, I:1, 11) triggers the revelation of a character dressed in a Heian Era (medieval) kimono, wig, and white face paint to the sound of the *shakuhachi* flute. Stage direction: "She begins to remove her makeup and her wig" (2003, I:1,11). As Wheeler's monologue progresses, the character turns while removing layers of the kimono to the sound of the flute— her actions accelerate to the beat of drums. The volume of Wheeler's monologue grows faint, as the percussion grows more intense. We are experiencing the embodied scroll as described by Wheeler. As Wheeler concludes, Iizuka writes in her stage directions: "Hikinuki, a Kabuki costume change in which threads are pulled and the outer kimono falls away, revealing a new costume underneath. The icon transforms into Setsuko Hearn the urbane, woman professor of East Asian Studies. The sound of wooden clappers." The clappers mark the transition to Scene 2, a party in Wheeler's gallery.

Throughout the play, Iizuka brings us directly into experiencing the art and cultural milieu of the subject matter. The clappers mark beat transitions, but also punctuate the modern with Kabuki stylizations. The result is dialogue and narrative sequencing that is familiar and accessible, juxtaposed with ancient Asian iconography, tableau, and musicality. Through juxtaposition and polyvocality, we perceive the thematic threads of truth and authenticity without commentary or rhetorical bias. By theatricalizing the thematic through conflated East and West dramaturgies, Iizuka unlocks the mystical energies of the narrative, and by so doing, the soul of the play. She makes her audience work to find meaning, but like Overmyer's use of the plums, reinforces the point of interruption and transition with sound and visual triggers, to mark Setsuko as an equivocal character. As Iizuka steers the conventional plot of her mystery cum romance, she elevates the dramaturgy by embedding the iconic artifacts within the character of Setsuko.

FROM CRITICAL EXPLANATION TO CREATIVE IMAGINING

For playwrights, the above analysis explains what's going on in the text. The question is, how can these techniques be used creatively? Three familiar aspects of contemporary playwriting involve memory, dreams, and historicity. These constitute an important facet of characterization because they target the soul or truth of an individual. Moreover, any manipulation of the character's relation to historical time should add depth to characterization. Memories of experiences provide the foundation for narrative, while dreams and the historical past have been fundamental components of the drama since the classical era. The equivocal character provides the playwright a key to unlock these elements dialogically through theatrical means. Otherwise, we become absorbed in self-indulgent ruminating or extrapolating—neither "holds the boards" very well.

There are several ways to approach writing the equivocal character, but it may better to consider some prior scenework, or, more ambitiously, in the revision of a drafted play.

EXERCISE:
Equivocal character and interruption

1. Write or revise a short three-to-four-scene piece that involves equivocal characterization.

2. Start from a likely premise: rebound situations are viable, where one character (A) recently lost a romantic interest (C) through death, divorce, to another, and so on.

3. Begin with the projection of (C) on character (B). Then move to the "real" time relationship between (A) and (B).

4. Target the points of interruption, where (C) become (B) and vice versa. What visual signifiers can pass from one character to the other? (The plums offer a good example.)

5. Strive to differentiate traits (C) from (B) and differ the responses of (A) to each character. For example, Joplin seems far more enraptured with Belle than he now is with the dutiful and pragmatic choice of Lottie.

6. What does it all add up to? Is it about winning and losing? The inherent possibilities at closure are multiple, from (A) overcoming his manifestation of (C) to (B) accepting (C) as a component of the relationship, even if the portrayal is relegated to a role-played distancing. How you work the scene determines the relative strength or weakness in each character.

COMMENT: Step 3 is important. Establishing a convention early, then reintroducing it at points throughout the play, makes the technique less gratuitous. The points of interruption in step 4 are major moments in the play. In production, we witness the actor work this magic to create great interest. Dramatically, the playwright provides the contour that will govern the ebb and flow of the scene.

SOME VARIATIONS

Len Jenkin's *Margo Veil* puts a 180-degree twist on the notion of an equivocal character. Through Big Betty's and Dwayne's Translation Machine, the character of Margo undergoes a series of transformations. Jenkin plays with our "willing suspension of disbelief" since the machine "magically" produces a different actor who plays the character of Margo. Thus, we are faced with the paradoxical illusion that a different actor is the same character.

In Wellman's *Albanian Softshoe*, included in his anthology *Cellophane* (2001), characters arbitrarily transform their identities as the scenes in act I progress. In scene 4, the setting remains the same while the characters change: Susan becomes Rachel as Harry becomes Fred. Wellman subverts the convention of a consistent character matrix in an ostensibly expositional monologue, utilizing the commonplace phone device to introduce the transformations:

RACHEL: Nell. This is Rachel. Rachel? Your neighbor. Used to be Susan. Right. There's a dead swan in your swimming pool. Oh, it's a nun? Fred it's a nun. I thought I'd tell you because I think Jill has been eating part

of it. No, tomorrow is garbage day. Fred is my husband. The same one.
Different name. I know it's a little confusing. Done wonders for our sex
life. Fred is no longer a homosexual. How about that? So long (Hangs
up). (I,14)

(Wellman 2001, 30)

Wellman's monologue focuses on the area between character and actor;
accepting the transformation of actors into various characters becomes a
source of dialogism among the various roles the same actor plays. In
Albanian Softshoe Wellman parodies the convention of a unified character by
bulking role changes in a manner that confounded audiences' expectations
at its world premiere at the San Diego Repertory Theatre. This device theatrically emphasizes the homogeneity of suburban "sitcomia," where character types are interchangeable and lifestyles imitate familiar actions.
Neither actor nor syntactical strategies have changed, yet the shifting characterizations bring about dramaturgical estrangement. The estrangement is
furthered as Wellman begins act 2 on a distant planet inhabited by space
warriors. The shifting characters from act 1 are now seen to have been
nothing more than an entertaining miniaturized "puppet show" for these
alien characters.

In her breakthrough play, *Tales of the Lost Formicans*, Constance Congdon
splits some characters into humans/aliens. This bifurcation allows the audience to discover the absurdity of human objects as seen through the aliens'
fresh eyes. Through this double-identity bifurcation, Congdon focuses our
attention on the "strangeness" we take for granted in our everyday lives:

CATHY/ALIEN: …The cushions of the chair are covered in a substance
made to mimic the epidermis of the sitter, but treated to hold a sheen
which is kept polished by friction of the buttocks against the surface. The
significance of the hole in the backrest is unknown to us at this time. It
was perhaps, symbolic: a breathing hole for the spirit of the sitter, or
even the ever-present eye of God.

(Congdon 1994, *Tales of the Lost Formicans*, 1)

The alien "other" allows us to "see" the chair beyond its limited function.
This foregrounding is an example of theater's capacity to transform a
mundane object into an object of fascination and wonder. By splitting the
characters, Congdon has established this essentially monologic speech in a
kind of dialogue with the human half of the character, who is continually
present.

The alien's awestruck way of seeing is part of the delight of *Tales of the Lost
Formicans*, and trademark of Congdon's distinctive theatrical voice. The following exercise is helpful in opening the semiotic and imaginative possibilities inherent in transformational objects.

EXERCISE:
Transforming the object

1. Write a monologue in which a character describes a common object as if for the first time. (Note for example, Mrs. Givings's response to the vibrator in Ruhl's *In the Next Room, or the Vibrator Play,* set in 1880"How extraordinary, it looks like a farming tool." (Ruhl 2010, 40) The character could be an alien, foreigner, child, and one suffering from loss of memory, or simply responding to a novel invention.
2. The character might arrive from another historical period, as a time traveler.
3. Imbue the common object with talismanic qualities.
4. Create an opposite to what is generally recognized as the object's value or function.
5. Describe the negative space created by the shape of the object.
6. Attempt to address the "why-ness" of the design in imaginative and transcendent language.

COMMENT: In a classroom or workshop setting it may be helpful for the playwright to conceal the identity of the "described" object. Only after the monologue is read do other participants attempt to identify the object described. The student's imaginative resources are focused or stretched. Since the responses are "right-sided" rather than critical, this exercise can work wonders in bringing a positive, relaxed atmosphere to a workshop or classroom situation.

PERFORMATIVE TECHNIQUES

A performative example of equivocal character occurs in the shift between the characters Dennis Wu and Tai-Tung Trahn in Overmyer's *In Perpetuity throughout the Universe.* Tai-Tung Trahn establishes the exoticism of the piece with his pantomimic opening—a hodgepodge of a *tai chi* master meets Fu Manchu type meets Peking opera type while dressed in a business suit. The movement patterns and apparel allow him to nonchalantly transform into the acculturated Asian-American writer Dennis Wu. Tai-Tung represents a common topos of American films from the Fu Manchu series to Chinatown—the Asian character as a subject of intrigue and dangerous cunning. In this conflation between the somewhat normative Dennis and the exotically theatrical Tia-Tung Trahn, the actor is challenged to meet a virtuosic turn that contrasts a normative, realistic style with a heightened and physicalized external approach. By allotting Trahn the traits of a businessman, Overmyer maintains a link and moment of ambiguity between the two characters, and this "interruption" in clarity draws our attention as an audience. Tai-Tung becomes the objectification of the thematic, subject matter at the center of the play. A third-tier publishing enterprise that employs Dennis Wu is built upon its publications of Orient-based conspiracies.

While the equivocal character and the notion of interruption are powerful dramaturgic components of characterization strategy, there are situations where it may be more effective to simply double characters. Character doubling should be indicated by the playwright on the character page, and should have a dramaturgic payoff. In a multi-character play, doubling is always a pragmatic concern: the fewer actors involved in production, the better the chance that the play will be produced. Generally, actors appreciate the challenge and financial bonus of doubling; directors and producers benefit by the savings in time and money. Overmyer achieves a dramaturgic payoff through the Babcock/Nizam double in *Dark Rapture*. Babcock is present throughout the piece; Nizam appears in one strikingly powerful scene where he is assassinated for his supposed connection (as a Turk) to the slaughter of Armenians early in this century. In a dramaturgic sense, Nizam provides the ironic and cynical Babcock character with a sympathetic resonance that carries over in production. On the other hand, there is no device of transformation or visible moment of "between-ness" since Nizam appears once in the play out of Babcock's range.

In Sarah Ruhl's *The Clean House*, the lover figures of Ana and Charles double as the parents of the Brazilian maid, Matilde. This doubling becomes most powerful at the end of the play, after Ana has died from cancer. In the final scene of the play she reappears with her husband (played by Charles) at the point in which she is giving birth to Matilde. Ruhl wraps death then life in this "doubled" character, thereby leaving the play with a hopeful and cheerful message.

Suzan Lori-Parks's *In the Blood* (2000 Pulitzer Award finalist) doubles Hester's five illegitimate children with adult characters in the play. This effects a dialogic tension in that the adult actor is "performing" the role of the child. Curiously, Parks begins her play with a chorus of these adult actors "dissing" the welfare mom, Hester, for not even knowing the identity of the children's' different fathers. By this use of doubling, Parks is embedding her thematic in the dramaturgy of character transformation. What seems like the solution (Doctor/Trouble; Reverend D/Baby) is also part of the problem, as both Doctor and Reverend D exploit Hester for sexual satisfaction. *In the Blood* utilizes the phenomenon of doubling to theatricalize the dramatic tension between adult/child, higher-up/downtrodden, medical care/forced sterilization—and thus embeds conflict within and among the ensemble of characters. Further, the character doubling renders a provocative contrast between characters' fronts and "given off" actual behaviors. There are no traditional "saviors" in experiencing this chilling play. (Parks 2001)

It is best practice for playwrights to duly hesitate before writing a character that appears in only one scene. The trend in the profession is to bulk parts whenever possible. This applies to functional characters. A current remedy is to have one actor play a serial array of functional characters, giving each a distinct flavor through movement patterns, dialect, and degree of gestural activity. Audiences enjoy the theatrical dialogism that emerges as the actor gives life to various cameo-like roles. The notion of doubling in its various modes has become a staple of contemporary playwriting technique. If your functional character appears once, however, consider writing them out of the play. See the first scene of Ruhl's *Dead Man's Cell Phone* which strongly implies there is a waiter, but never establishes her presence on stage.

EXERCISE:
Bulking parts

1. Revise a play so that one actor plays a sequence of functional roles (for example: taxi driver, waiter, bellhop, masseur.).
2. Revise a play, considering how doubling a character in the play would increase the impact of an offstage character (one we are told about but never see in the play), by integrating that character into the action.

COMMENT: This exercise is particularly useful for beginning playwrights who tend to proliferate functional characters without considering more viable alternatives. Unlike film, in which one hires a day actor to fulfill a functional role, the theater demands that the actor return every night—so there are pragmatic as well as aesthetic considerations. By having one actor play a sequence of functional roles, the playwright presents the actor with a great challenge, and also demonstrates a level of dramaturgical savvy to producers, directors, and literary managers. Never underestimate how your level of craft may give you an edge in getting your work produced.

IDENTITY AND GENDER POLITICS

Doubling characters may be related to the politics of identity, including the relation between sex and gender. In the early 1990s, Craig Lucas won a Pulitzer Prize for his play *Prelude to a Kiss*, which explored the switching of souls from Peter's wife to an Old Man who arbitrarily crashed their wedding. After this point, the play turns from a whirlwind boy-meets-girl romance to an exploration and search of recapturing past identities. That the piece was far more interesting as a play than in its unsuccessful film version bears testimony that theatrical immediacy makes this doubling device viable.

In Barbara Cassidy's *Interim*, two characters Tam and Kin are first witnessed in the background working on a problem with the telephone wiring. (Wellman, Lee 2006) Then, later they become party members flirting with Joya, the lead character. Throughout, their gender is equivocal, and, although cast originally as women, they move fluidly between male and female constructs.

In Brechtian terms, Cassidy is creating an alienation effect insofar as once the human characters are dissembled as functional workers they then force the audience to see or experience them in a different, more objective way. Doubling, in this case, precludes a high level of empathic involvement from the audience, a detachment that reflects Joya's ambivalent characterization. Conversely, in *Prelude to a Kiss*, the switching of inner souls creates a sense of pity and loss, as Peter recognizes the futility of continuing a marriage in which the "other" or Old Man character has taken over the identity of his wife. The poignancy of the play is that its implications extend beyond its story, so that audience members can reflect on the forces that change the people in their lives, and how relationships are continually challenged and reshaped.

The gendering extremes of character doubling are found in the one-person show. Performed in male drag, Peggy Shaw's *Menopausal Gentleman* is a *tour de force* that probes the tumult of a women going through menopause. Not only does Shaw explore dynamics across sexes (and within her own gender as a role-playing lesbian), she also effects a dialogic tension between ages: in drag, the fifty-four-year-old woman comments on her identity as a thirty-something man. The gaps and conflations between sexes, genders, and ages offer numerous opportunities for commentary and humor. Doug Wright's *tour de force* one-person play, *I Am My Own Wife* (Pulitzer Prize 2004) featured a male performer, Jefferson Mays, playing not only the lead role of the transvestite, Charlotte Von Mahlsdorf, but also over thirty other roles, in a constant shift of gender and class. John Jesuron deconstructs *Philoktetes'* ten-year isolation on an abandoned, forsaken island, by embedding female identities within the eponymous, afflicted character.

These gender crossings rely on a sophisticated dramaturgical technique or the playwright will overly confuse audiences and the structure of the play. In working toward the execution of the transformative character, begin by writing single gender monologues through the voice of the "other" that are closely observed in regard to traits, eccentricities, and specific behaviors.

EXERCISE:
Playing with gender and/or identity doubling

1. Begin by reading *Prelude to a Kiss, Interim*, and the first half of *Philoktetes* to achieve an understanding of this principle. If you Google Peggy Shaw, *Menopausal Gentleman*, you can upload a video of the production and see her performance.

2. Write a monologue in which you establish a primary character in a major dilemma: whether or not to leave a lover, to go on the lam, to undergo an operation, and so forth.

3. Now write another monologue from the standpoint of a double: alien, lover, opposite sex—whatever provides a level of contrast. This character must have a definite "take" on the primary character's monologue.

4. Allow the character in step 3 to inject, insert, or embody the primary character established in step 2. Weave together and edit the monologues into a scene in which the doubled characters interact. The shift in the primary character should be noted on a physical, psychological, and spiritual plane. The style or mood can shift, but comic aspects should be exploited.

COMMENT: It can be helpful in the workshop to provide contrasting portraits of the characters (as images, photographs, etc.) to aid in the visualization process that identity doubling demands.

The doubling technique can be central to a dialogic dramaturgy. Nevertheless, the playwright must consider each choice carefully: strive to gain a dramatic edge through doubling characters rather than bulking them to meet bottom-line expectations. Transformation is the essence of the dramatic, so these powerful techniques are natural extensions of this indigenously theatrical phenomena which goes back to the classical Greeks, who were never allotted more than three primary actors to play all the principal roles.

6

Len Jenkin's dramaturgy of character: from stage figures to archetypes

Stage figure is a term first coined by the Prague semiotician Jindrich Honzl. He used it to distinguish the function and operation of the fixed characters of the *commedia dell'arte* from the traditional idea of character. Honzl asserted that "stage figures like Harlequin or Pantalone were transferred from one scenario or play to another, and exhibited traits that conditioned—even dominated—the events of the plot" (Quinn 1988, 330–1). Honzl suggested that since stage figures could be identified by specific codes of gestures and dress, they could be instantly recognized in the "intertextual" sense. The intertextual figure is a hallmark of the plays of Len Jenkin, and an effective determinant of his dramaturgy.

Typically, the portrayal of the stage figure is iconic; in other words, the image of the figure "speaks for itself." For example, if we see a performer in a Superman outfit we automatically associate distinctive traits (flying, invulnerability) based upon our recognition of, and past experience with, the figure. An actor can readily simulate the figure of Superman, who is the archetype for invincibility and heroism. The huge interest behind *Spiderman: The Musical* has been based on the well-known comic book and film icon magnified by the extraordinary challenge of executing these superhuman traits on stage. However, in Jenkin's plays the stage figure is not usually as locked-in as Superman, Spiderman, the Lone Ranger, or Harlequin, with their specific costumes and prescribed traits. Rather, they evolve from the fractured archetypes at the seamy margins of the American mythos: the fast-talking carnival showman, the fried-out cantankerous professor in search of UFOs, or the failed salesman of lightning rods and dime-store novelties. In *American Notes*, the reporter figure does not work for the *New York Times* or even the local paper; rather, it's the less reputable tabloid *Flying Saucer News*.

Across Jenkin's plays we find recurring figures: the thief, the con-man, the showman or master of ceremonies, the cop, the professor, the artist, and the reporter. Jenkin may change their proper names and specific actions in each play, but like the masks of *commedia dell'arte*, their actions and traits are to a significant extent predetermined. As intertextual figures they express a resemblance to precursors in American popular culture found in genres like pulp detective fiction, comic book lore, and the

B-movie *film noir* fare of the 1940s and 1950s. Jenkin formulates his stage figures by skewing the archetypal image that exists for the audience—Kid Twist is a member of the Jewish, not Italian, Mafia, for example. As part of his process, he personalizes each character through careful attention to eccentricities, particularly in the use of language. Despite their pathetic, dated, or alienated core, the figures are humanized as each develops a distinct identity. The characters emerge without commentary, as Jenkin never uses his figures for blatant social commentary or to telegraph the message of the play.

While allowing for the variations and deviations in a given play, Jenkin's figures proffer an innate theatricality that guarantees appeal as well as audience recognition. As stage figures, their juxtaposition and interaction establishes pretexts and possibilities that determine the plot. In this sense, his plays are character driven, often with several figures at the wheel—like the ensemble performances of *commedia dell'arte*. The archetypal nature of the characters channels their actions, but gives latitude to the range of language. Language overwhelms the mold, never allowing it to consume or demean the unique individuality of the figure. If they appear at a distance like cartoon figures or cutouts, upon closer scrutiny the figures are fully dimensionalized. Jenkin dialogizes his characters to create a multiplicity of voices and figurations within his polyvocal theatrical landscape. We can now examine how Jenkin makes this work.

JENKIN'S STAGE FIGURES

The stage figures in Jenkin's work present iconic and linguistic variations of well-known archetypes:

- The professor usually specializes in some exotic subject, often "whacked-out," and of suspicious intent or legitimacy. The character Driver in *Limbo Tales* is a lecturer on Ancient Mayan culture. Botany professor Finley in *American Notes* feeds young female students to the man-eating Amazonian plant that he has cultivated. See also *Gogol* and *Pilgrims of the Night*.

- The reporter is on the margins of the reputable. Mrs. Lammle in *Dark Ride* is a finder of coincidences and has recorded them from all over the world. In *Kid Twist*, the Reporter recalls the hard-bitten 1940s style of reporter cum gumshoe. In *American Notes*, the reporter is affiliated with the *Flying Saucer News*.

- The artist or writer is often a struggling character within the various arts, sometimes a "wannabe," or someone who is given to selling out for a buck: Mark in *5 of Us* writes porn; Viva is an ex-dancer in *Pilgrims of the Night*; the club duo in *Dream Express*, playwright Arthur Vine and the magician Mortmain in *Margo Veil*. The character based on the real-life author Nathaniel Hawthorne in *Kraken* questions his "lot" as a diplomat in England.

- The salesman: there is a novelties salesman in *My Uncle Sam*; the Resurrection Man in *Gogol*, a gravedigger who sells stiffs to researchers; and the Lightning Rod Salesman in *Limbo Tales*.

- The emcee, pitchman, or showman is a charlatan-like character who nevertheless believes in what they are pitching. In *Country Doctor* the Pitchman opens the play with a strange optical device that allows one to see around or behind oneself. The Pitchman in *American Notes* is a carnival barker who sells tickets to see Bonecrusher, the Monster of the Nile, actually a dead American alligator. Crab Boy, in *Poor Folk's Pleasure*, is a legless man who has two digits on each hand that simulate claws. He exhibits himself to pay off a private eye who is tracking his daughter.

- The detective. This character is right out of the pulp novels of the 1940s, or the film noir hard-boiled variety. See Sarge in *Kid Twist*, the Plainclothesman in *My Uncle Sam*.

- The thief or criminal. Jenkin seems fond of his crooks. See *Kid Twist*, and the Thief character in *Dark Ride*. The act of stealing a jewel becomes the object of a search in *Dark Ride*.

- The cleric. The Reverend in *Margo Veil* offers an example of the marginalized, itinerant, or bogus reverend.

Together, and in their multiple variations, Jenkin's figures make up the playwright's "stock company." Indeed, his plays would have fit well within the nineteenth-century format of the "lines-of-business" repertory company.

ARCHETYPE VERSUS STEREOTYPE

The archetypal character can be distinguished from its negative counterpart, the stereotype. Stereotypical characters are uninteresting because they lack variation or individuality. Familiar traits or responses are repeated or represented without any distinguishing flair. The stereotypical character functions as a thematic extension of the playwright's bias. It conforms to a standardized mental picture shared by a specific interest group. In traditional dramaturgical terms, the playwright is telegraphing their message—speaking directly through the character's voice. While this is a transparent error, it is a common shortcoming in conceptualization. The flaw is evident in television writing, particularly in formats where characters must be quickly identified as victims, villains, persecutors, or saviors. The audience knows who to root for and against; the plot seems to drive the character, rather than the reverse. As television writing becomes more sophisticated, stereotyping can be disguised through emphasis on technological advances in the medium.

EXERCISE:

Playing with stage figures

Jenkin starts his scenes off with a narrator figure who simply begins to tell a story. As the story unfolds other characters begin to enter into it, often with the narrator figure also entering into the story in some role. Jenkin often uses writers: reporters, or translators, language specialists, who may be describing something they are writing or translating.

1. Using several of the above figures as models, create a sequence of scenes that involve an action suitable to the particular eccentricities of the characters.

    a. Use their archetypal actions as points of departure. For example, show your professor/teacher in the lecturing or professorial mode.

    b. Select a narrator figure from this group to begin the scene, allowing the other characters to enter as manifestations of the narrative.

    c. Allow these figures to frame subsequent scenes toward creating the sequence.

2. Using Jenkin's archetypal model, adapt the notion to create your own archetypal variations (for example, athletes, models, nuns, politicians, announcers).

    a. Marginalize the character by making them a "has-been" or "wannabe," for example. The character should project angst, be preoccupied, or in the throes of bad conscience.

    b. Imbue the character with apt eccentricities or bizarre behaviors.

    c. Create a monologue for each character that explores these sensibilities.

    d. From these monologues select a story line that integrates the figures.

COMMENT: Appropriate characters from fiction, comic books, video games, and various pop media, then endow, imbue, or alter them with personalized and individuated traits. Explore techniques for rounding or flattening characterization. A rounded character possesses depth, dimension, and complexity. A flat character possesses limited, individuated traits, operating within a functional range.

DOMINANT FIGURES

In general, Jenkin constructs his plays around dominant figures and archetypal stock figures. The dominant figures control the story line, as narrators alongside the action, or as characters in the center of the action. Structured within the framework of travel or journeys, his dominant figures play out that action in search or quest of someone or some object. This restless, wandering aspect of their nature stimulates the movement of the play (his plays are character driven), through an array of bizarre settings and encounters (such as the *mise-en-scène* of the carnival sideshow or wax museum). Jenkin's characters are American adventurers, romantic individuals struggling for a larger share or a better "take" on the whole; or, they are simply trying to escape the present. In some cases, it is a search for an individual, as in the Author's quest for his uncle Sam in *My Uncle Sam*. Sometimes the voyage is mundane and comic, as in the Guest's search for the wedding in *The Country Doctor*. The dominant figure keeps the play moving. In Jenkin's latest play, *Margo Veil*, the eponymous character is in constant movement by either train or car, as she tries to evade capture. The fact that the mover is in crisis, and presented with obstacles or distractions, provides a dramatic grounding or level of interest, however absurd the crises may appear. The traveler figure is by nature an outsider, and being outside of his element creates the tension or energy in the play. Margo's continuing identity shifts in the play create a tension between her character, and the various actors who play her shifting personas. When the movement through place is dramatized, the term *journey play* is accurate and helpful.

Sometimes the traveler can take the more traditional form of an intruder figure: in *American Notes* the traveler figure is grounded at the roadside hotel. The sense of the temporary situation is sound dramaturgically because it creates tension for the character and the audience with built-in mystery, intrigue, or danger: is this the end of the line? In underscoring the stranger in a strange land, Jenkin examines the failed quest of the American dream and the poignant sense of aborted expectations. The notion of the failed American Dream has its legacy in the golden age of the American playwriting, although Jenkin's collection of broken or "stuck" figures (such as in *Like I Say*) seem more redolent of Chekhov than Miller, for example. The *topos* of the stalled journey is present in a number of plays in which the traveler figure is used.

Here are some profiles of Jenkin's travelers:

- The traveler often lives in a hotel or has other temporary arrangements, like the train in *Margo Veil*. (*American Notes, Limbo Tales, My Uncle Sam, Like I Say*).

- The terrain of the traveler maybe real space and time, the product of memory and dreams, or a conflation of both.

- The traveler is usually a male character, although there are exceptions (*Careless Love, Margo Veil*). Often there is more than one traveler (*Pilgrims in the Night*).

- The traveler is a character struggling with a dilemma, looking for solace, a better life or deeper meaning (or to escape) but not really knowing what they want.

- The traveler is in conflict about a certain relationship; the journey works through some of these questions.

- By the end of the play, the traveler arcs to some extent, reaching a deeper level of discovery or wisdom, or poses a deeper premise.

SHALLOW VERSUS DEEP TIME

When the traveler moves forward in a linear way, from point A to point B to point C, the passage of time is shallow. Shallow time is immediate and forward-looking, not self-reflexive or past oriented. When the character is reflective of the past or saturated in consciousness the time progression is temporarily halted, or moves deeper in the temporal sense. Playwrights should be aware of this difference in attempting to manipulate time factors in their plays to the best advantage. The tension between shallow and deep time is particularly evident in Jenkin's monologues (see Chapter 12).

THE STORYTELLER

A second figure that serves a dominant function is the storyteller. Jenkin's theater celebrates the storytelling tradition; his characters like to talk or spin yarns (like the Mayor figure to Chuckles in *American Notes*). Using the techniques of direct address, Jenkin's storytellers "frame" the action and serve as the threshold through which the audience experiences the play. After setting up the frame, the storyteller enters into some dramatized context that elaborates on the givens established in the narrative.

Frequently there are stories within stories, requiring a constant shift of perspective and voice. The multiple storytellers within a Jenkin play can confuse an audience who expect to track its progression through a primary narrator. Jenkin's narrators are never tracked (like Salieri, or the Stage Manager in *Our Town*), but take turns spinning the story. The disturbing loss of context in *Dark Ride*, for example, is suggested in the play's title, but it may not be until the end of the play that the audience accepts the multiple layering and narrative levels. The standard character-related question of "Whose story is this?" is problematic in Jenkin's work because Jenkin categorically works against this dictum. Even *Margo Veil*, which revolves around Margo, has multiple actors playing the part, thus fragmenting any integral character through-line. To critique the body of Jenkin's work against a canonical premise of traditional playwriting would do disservice to his extraordinarily sophisticated level of craft.

THE STORYTELLER AND THE FRAME

Framing is an essential component of Jenkin's figures. Usually, it involves direct address to the audience to set up the givens of a scene that subsequently unfolds in action. (It is a common strategy in current playwriting; Sarah Ruhl's *The Clean House*, Naomi Iizuka's *36 Views*.) This metatheatrical device calls attention to the play's structure, and the matrix of the actor/character. Strategically, it marks the character with the dramatist's function—emplotment. Jenkin's plays are character driven but not in the traditional sense. Multiple characters zigzag us through to the conclusion. There is never a case of a single narrator (like Salieri in Peter Shaffer's *Amadeus*, for example) pitching a particular take across the entire play. *Amadeus* represents the picture-frame model in which the narrator straddles the frame. Salieri brings us in as participant; he steps back out to reflect, to lick his wounds, and only then does he advance the action. His emotional and affective presence mitigates the problem inherent in drama that is episodic, as most biographical plays are. Salieri provides structural unity. In Paula Vogel's *How I Learned to Drive, Lil' Bit* provides a similar function to that of Salieri, although Vogel fractures the chronological framework.

Conversely, Jenkin's plays are more like boxes within boxes, or layers of an onion: the first narrator who opens the frame will lead us to other narrators who open frames. For example, in *Pilgrims of the Night*, Tom begins by telling us a story about a group of people who are telling stories, and then these subsequent characters frame and enact the series of vignettes that follow. *Dark Ride* begins with the Translator having difficulty translating a text, from which characters appear and enact the action discussed. These characters then frame subsequent actions.

The relation between character and space is represented as a manifestation of dream, fantasy, or memory—as in *Margo Veil.* A character may appear as the manifestation of a story in a text, like the Thief in *Dark Ride*, or within travelers telling stories on a trip, as in *Pilgrims of the Night*. As such, characters seem to control the action by creating frames for other characters to appear as manifestations of something they are reading, a dream they once had, or a memory that consumes them.

This character dynamic in Jenkin's plays can be understood in the relationships between dominant and stock figures. The difference may be clarified as a matter of function more than form. Indeed, distinctions are not always clear-cut; the Thief in *Dark Ride* is in the realm of a stock figure, yet is dominant in the progress of the play. *Margo Veil* provides a female dominant figure whose journey provides the core for the play, while those she contacts, the sleazy reverend, marginal magicians, and bogus agent, supply the comic shenanigans.

EXERCISE:
Creating the ten-minute frame play

(Study Jenkin's *Margo Veil* to determine how to handle transitions on stage.)

As is well known, the ten-minute form is now an established contest format. A good model is the character-driven frame format, since some structural density or complexity can be allotted to a relatively brief piece. Moreover, the journey or travel action allows the character a through line to a destination point that marks a successful or unsuccessful outcome. Strong dramaturgical challenges involving the relationship between character and structure are addressed in the format. With the increasing popularity of the ten-minute play, this exercise provides an excellent way to break into the genre. In the workshop, this exercise maximizes the potential number of plays to be read during a typical one-hour period.

1. Start by establishing a dominant figure, either a traveler or storyteller. This figure may or may not be a member of an archetypal group.

   • This character provides the opening frame and must thrust us into some trip, search, or examination. It should be objective, rather than a trip into the psychological realm, for example.

   • This framing character enters into the main action.

2. Determine two to three archetypal figures who enter into the story or provide obstacles for the dominant figure. They should also serve as actors in the story.

   • Allow at least one of these characters to provide an inner frame within the main story.

   • The frame may take the form of monologue (see Chapter 12 for examples).

3. Don't allow the play to go beyond ten or eleven pages. The dominant figure should reach some kind of payoff or payback at the end of the piece.

4. Allow the characters to move through space and time as needed. Keep in mind that you are writing for the stage. Try not to demand large realistic set pieces.

Each character and figure should believe totally in what they are doing, or what they are about. They are working toward a goal, even if it looks hopeless, or they are inept, or others doubt them. Always keep in mind the archetypal relationship between the character and the action. The action should be a manifestation of an archetypal trait. Use strange props or visual elements to provide theatricality.

Be sure to consider the "tenets of theatrical characters" (see page 83) as a guide to creating your characters.

Complete the draft in one sitting, then go over and refine, rewrite, refine. Or, as Eric Overmyer says about the revision process, "hone, chip, sand, rub, and finish." Once you are comfortable with using frames and sequences in this short form, attempt to write a one-act play of between twenty-five to thirty pages.

COMMENT: This format is ideal for the final project in the typical playwriting seminar that runs for ten to fifteen weeks.

JENKIN'S PERFORMATIVE CHARACTERS

A playwright can benefit greatly by studying Jenkin's figures and archetypes. Replete with eccentricities, his stage figures offer the actor an array of performative choices. The performative character emphasizes gesture, movement, and expression over psychological insight or subtext. In practice, Jenkin often develops his characters by including actors in his play development process. In the workshop, the physically trained actor responds quickly and effectively to this external approach of characterization, providing real insight to the playwright in the construction of the play. Remember, in the ten-minute format the playwright can thoroughly workshop the characterizations with actors in a relatively brief amount of time. For optimal results, this developmental strategy should be implemented as soon as an early draft is completed.

7

Mac Wellman:
language-based character

THE EUCLIDEAN CHARACTER

Mac Wellman's consideration of character in traditional theater has become the stuff of legend. He writes:

> One of the most striking features of American dramaturgy is the notion of 'rounded' character. This creature of theatrical artifice with its peculiarly geometric—nay! symmetrical—aspect is so like an object from a math textbook; and one finds it so frequently onstage (and nowhere else) that I have dubbed it the Euclidean Character. Every trait of the Euclidean character must reveal an inner truth of the same kind about the personality in question; each trait must be perfectly consonant with every other trait.
>
> (Wellman 1984, 34)

Wellman is outspoken in his resistance to the traditional approach to characterization. He rejects notions such as character-specific dialogue and subtext, two benchmarks of the Euclidean character. Wellman's Euclidean character is ensconced within his screed on the American theater, "Theatre of Good Intentions," insofar as this formulation of a character intention integrates a relevant sociocultural mission that binds the thematic message of the play. According to Wellman, this "liberal" agenda has privileged the Euclidean character in American dramaturgy since Clifford Odets.

Wellman's distrust of this construct is entrenched in his quintessentially modernist view of the theater artist, a view that he integrates with breakthroughs in chaos theory fractals, and the philosophy of language. As a modernist, Wellman is the master of each inimitable universe that he creates. The actor, rather than "representing" as character, is the "plastic material" that can become whatever Wellman wishes them to be. No one questions the abstract artist for not creating representations of reality, but because the playwright's "material" is the actor, there is the built-in expectation of similitude to characters in real life. Wellman deflates this notion by celebrating language as his primary material and character as a configuration of language, rather than vice versa. An apt corollary might be to the abstract French painter Olivier Debré, who created what he termed *signes-personnages* (figurative or character-like signs) and *signes-paysages* (landscape signs) (Debré 1999). Debré posed these highly evocative *signes-personnages* in oblique relation to each other, suggesting various relationships. The human entities perceived from the shapes were associational simulacrums rather than representational bodies. The landscape signs formed a similar phenomenon, inviting the spectator to form conclusions through association. In his extensively monologic works, like *Cellophane, Jennie Ritchie*, and *Three Americanisms*, Wellman uses language to create transient character-like signs and landscape signs in an aesthetic manner that recalls Debré.

As a playwright, Wellman projects language through the speaking figure, but the language is doing double or triple duty (Wellman 1996). By combining unique syntactical choices with striking sonics, Wellman's language creates a linguistic force field that rivals any current playwright. Moreover, because language is innately culturally bound, and the figure of the actor is necessarily perceived by the audience as a given sociotype or class, Wellman's characters inexorably emerge from the linguistic heat. During these moments his language delineates a certain scale, as well as an architectural, spatial, or iconographic field in which the figure operates. The figure can rage like an Aeschylean hero or squeal like a deposed corporate guru, or bestial Hare, as in *The Invention of Tragedy*. The simulacrum of character is created in a stunningly dialogic manner by the figural presence of the speaking, gesticulating actor conflating with the associations resonating from the linguistic force field.

CHARACTERS WITHOUT NAMES

In several plays, Wellman has abandoned any traditional notion of character. Characters may not even be named, as in *Three Americanisms*, a kind of free-form monologic blast, or more recently, *Jennie Ritchie* and *Bitter Bierce*, these plays provide the conflation or merging of discourses. There are no character titles or additional stage directions. Most individuals shift levels of language to meet the nature or status of the interaction. Mac Wellman provides an interesting twist on this multivocal strategy in his monologue plays. The end result is kind of character by distillation. In Mel Gussow's review of Wellman's *Three Americanisms*, he notes the emergence of three distinct characters confronting aspects of contemporary American culture. When no character names are provided whatsoever, the formation is up to the performer and director, and the perceptions of audience members. Three Americanisms provides us with three distinct characters never mentioned by name, only as Man 1, Man 2, and Woman for the benefit of the script reader. In essence, the audience connects the dots to make the construct.

Bitter Bierce, from Wellman's most recently published collection (2008), is presented by a sole raconteur narrating facets of the life of journalist, Ambrose Bierce. This work conflates Wellman's typical wordplay and whimsy with Bierce's acerbic wit, ensconced within a biographical narrative that tracks the major events of Bierce's life. While Wellman's "voice" is always identifiable and prominent in his plays, it is impossible to pigeonhole him within a particular style or genre. The corollary to modern art would be Picasso from the standpoint of multiple styles, prolific and energetic output, and enormous and persistent impact as playwright and mentor. In his latest collection, *The Difficulty of Crossing a Field*, we get the full array of Wellman's oeuvre from inchoate sketches, to classical forays (*Antigone*), to full-lengths such as the titular play, which derives from an historical event in post-bellum, Selma, Alabama.

EXERCISE:
Creating character from language models

1. Begin by reading *Jennie Ritchie* and *Three Americanisms* and viewing paintings by Yves Tanguy or Olivier Debré.
2. Sense two or three figures as a shadowy presence, not exactly human but as figures are seen in the paintings of Tanguy or Debré. Envision a kind of otherworldly space and locale.
3. Concoct a list of idioms, maxims, or slang belonging to a certain ethnic, cultural, or cultish group.
4. Create a list of architectural terms and forms, as well as terms that might be described as shaping or configuring.
5. Attempt to concoct a different blend for each of the three figures by varying syntax, syllabic structure, and idiomatic choice.
6. Write three or four monologues for each character over about ten pages, allowing the figures to interact at various points. Make no effort to identify characters by traditional names, biographies, or histories—just let language lead the way.

COMMENT: This exercise is much more helpful if you provide the visual sources as indicated above. (Please refer to Chapter 12 for further exploration of Wellman's use of monologue.)

TICKET NAMES

Wellman's range of characterization is broad and complex. As a result, the Wellman concept of character is difficult to pin down. It is experimental in some cases, but Wellman's political series of plays, *Professional Frenchman*, *Bad Infinity*, and *7 Blowjobs*, employs satiric characterizations where characters are named in a somewhat traditional sense. Although considered radical in his innovations, Wellman's "ticket name" approach is traditional, and rings of classicism in the style of Ben Jonson or the melodramas of the nineteenth century. An early play, *Harm's Way*, uses ticket names (Crowfoot described a carnival huckster, for instance) and hip thematic phraseology (By Way of Being Hidden, and Isle of Mercy) to name characters. Beyond these somewhat human figures Wellman delivers alien characters and puppets (in *Albanian Softshoe*), animals (in *Murder of Crows, The Invention of*

Tragedy), and oddities (the fur balls in *Sincerity Forever*). The importance of character naming is often overlooked by writers, or confined in terms of its scope. Wellman's choices remind us that a character's name may offer an interesting sound quality, a relation to a societal question, a way to "point" a script, or establish class or mental state. Ultimately, the sum total of the character list helps to create the overall mood or flavor in a particular piece.

In some cases, Wellman engages character ensembles (the crows in *Murder of Crows*, the cats in *The Invention of Tragedy*) as a throwback to the Greek chorus, thus continually invoking and reworking theatrical conventions in his plays. This aspect of Wellman's writing regarding character should be noted: the reliance and reworking of past traditions long forgotten, or seldom used, in the American theater. This trend is shared with Suzan-Lori Parks: the historicized impact of *Topdog/Underdog* was secured through her use of the ticket names Lincoln and Booth, and the main character Hester who appears in her *Red Letter Plays*, *In the Blood* and *Fucking A* (2001), as homage to Nathaniel Hawthorne's *The Scarlet Letter*.

LANGUAGE AND THE CREATION OF CHARACTER

The philosopher Ludwig Wittgenstein was the first to reassess the relationship between character and language. In traditional dramaturgy the character has a motive that is expressed in language specific to that character: in sum, the notion of character-specific language. Character-specific language is a rubric that posits a causal relationship between an individual's sociocultural class, education, motive, and level of speech. Play developers are enamored of the character-specific rubric, denouncing the character that violates "how that character would really speak." This notion rules television and film writing, wherein the dialogue may be schematic, allowing the actor to bulk subtextual muscle onto the character-specific framework. The problem with the character-specific approach is that it limits both variety and the imagination. Wellman posits the multivocal character, since, as he states, we all change our language styles, and even speech genres, according to the situation. Conflated speech styles may have more impact than the words themselves would indicate: 1960s lingo can jumble with the market-speak of Wall Street to earmark political views and biases, or demonstrate guru-like savvy. Variety in speech is as dependable as the passing of time, and is often contingent upon it. Thus, once slang or speech style falls out of favor it becomes more interesting for the playwright to shape character nuance, historical background, and ideology by elevating dated lingo over dreary exposition.

Wittgenstein noted that instead of language being the result of character, language was the cause of character. In everyday life we assess individuals according to their level of speech, vocabulary syntactical choices, and mastery over jargon, cant, slang, or ability to "text message." Regional background, level of education, literary influence, and age are concluded almost immediately. Wide groups of the population are identified by certain linguistic predilections, whether Cajun, redneck, hipster, sorority sister, surfer dude, rapper, discourse-driven academic, or media-savvy politician. Psychobabble is readily worn on the sleeve and delivered off the cuff as a means to pigeonhole personality types. Texting has superseded everyday conversation in defining the current culture. Language frames character: it establishes the context in which the individual operates. New playwrights need to understand how the presence of language can be weaved through the playful grafting of "real speak" with the imaginative and inventive to create the delightful idiosyncrasies of character.

EXERCISE:
language shaping character (using Wikipedia and Google)

In the following exercise, attempt to establish various figures, phrases, or flourishes that designate various characters. It is important to note how the language serves as a mask or reveals, establishes an emotional place, and so on. It can then be readily manipulated to meet the playwright's ends. For example, the speech genre of a therapist, the jargon of self-awareness, would be about relaxing the consumer toward opening up and revealing certain truths.

1. This exercise can be used in revising a work, or in developing a character in a scene. The use of Wikipedia provides you with some instant research, enough to get you going, and you can use a search engine, like Google, to establish your language lists.

2. "Wikipedia" a particular character type: environmentalist, academic, hip-hop rapper, conservative politician, fundamentalist preacher, anchorwoman, or mortuary owner.

3. "Google" a list of jargon, expressions, and phrases, terms, figures of speech that earmark this character.

4. Determine how each term or expression might be used dramaturgically: to conceal, reveal, to get what the character wants, to create color, to distract, to seduce. In other words, while the language itself is defining an aspect of this character in relationship to the other characters in the play, the language is also functioning in creating a second, strategic level of interest.

5. Write a scene that conflates at least two of these language systems within one character. While not necessarily naming the character, provide a strong passion that governs the character's logorrhea.

6. Create several more or less functional characters utilizing ticket names to describe the characters' main actions.

COMMENT: In the workshop, it's helpful to read excerpts from Wellman's monologue plays to see how this works in practice. Ask members of the workshop at what point they begin to distill a sense of the character from the language. Follow through by identifying moments in the script where readers project actions upon the language or feel an emotional state emerging from the language.

CONCLUSION

Use the various internet tools now available to challenge traditional approaches to forming character. *Chicago Tribune* critic Chris Jones noted that the critically acclaimed Broadway musical, *Bloody, Bloody Andrew Jackson* "is the consummate musical for the Wikipedia age" (October 13, 2010). Young playwrights should explore their potential to create effective characters that draw upon the past or that exist outside their own frame of reference. Perhaps the future of character will bring about the convergence of language-based and psychological models toward some new definition. Particularly interesting is the penetration of the historical or cultural into this model. Recent plays by Suzan-Lori Parks and Sarah Ruhl (*Topdog/ Underdog, The Red Letter Plays*, and *Dead Man's Cell Phone*, and *In the Next Room, or the Vibrator Play*) point in that direction. This conflation of old and new modes of characterization has created a new crossover poetics that is the subject of our next chapter.

8
Crossover poetics:
Sarah Ruhl and Suzan-Lori Parks

Crossover poetics defines the integration or merging of language playwriting strategies in traditional dramaturgical formats. This results in a blurring of distinctions so that it is now difficult to categorize the mainstream and new playwriting as strictly counter-movements. The outcome has shifted the ground of the avant-garde over the past decade, as border crossings have become the rule rather than the exception. Many playwrights now draw upon diverse aesthetics in creating hybrid plays.

Notable for her breakout critical and commercial success is Sarah Ruhl, whose cutting-edge training in playwriting programs at Brown (under Mac Wellman, then Paula Vogel) and Yale universities is evident in her work. She confidently combines the poetics of new writing with traditional dramaturgies. Ruhl is widely produced regionally and in university theaters, has won major awards, and has achieved a body of recognizable published work. She was a Pulitzer-Prize finalist in 2005 and 2010 with *The Clean House* and *In the Next Room, or the Vibrator Play*, respectively. Ruhl's crossover approach provides the optimum study for traditionally oriented playwrights who seek to meld new and old playwriting techniques into their work.

A play representative of her crossover approach, *Dead Man's Cell Phone* (*DMCP*) (Ruhl 2008), juxtaposes characteristics of new playwriting with the framework of a traditional episodic structure. With exceptions, the play is constructed as a series of vignettes triggered by Jean's encounter with the dead man, Gordon, in a café. Described by the playwright as a "nondescript sort of woman," Jean sets the play in motion when she loses patience with a stranger's (Gordon's) incessantly ringing cell phone. At first, she accosts the mute Gordon but to no avail. After several pleadings she picks up his phone to respond. As the morbid jokes and "takes" continue through a series of callers, and she concludes Gordon is dead, Jean develops a bond with the dead man. The first scene concludes in *tableau vivant* as Jean holds Gordon's limp head in her hands, clutching his cell phone as a marker for her loyalty:

… I'll stay with you.
Gordon. For as long as you need me.
I'll stay with you. Gordon.

She holds his hand. She keeps hold of it. The sounds of sirens, rain, and church bells.

(Ruhl 2008, I:1;14)

In his 2009 book *The American Play*, Marc Robinson defines the effect of the nineteenth-century tableau:

Tableaux provided visual codas to the ends of scenes, as actors arrange themselves in ways that indicated their individual importance to the narrative (and to one another) and direct attention to the decisive events in their shared history.

(Robinson 2009, 33)

Through tableau, Ruhl accomplishes all of the above, reinforcing the triangulation that initiates the narrative "bond" between and Gordon, and the cellphone that triggers the play's journey.

In her most recent play, *In the Next Room, or the Vibrator Play*, Ruhl actually sets the play in the late nineteenth century, and uses tableaux in one of their most familiar depictions: to depict the act of eavesdropping. Here, Mrs. Givings strains to listen in on the treatment of her husband's patient, Mrs. Daldry, in the examining room. Mrs. Givings' attempt to discover the cause of the orgasmic cries provides a comic *coup de théâtre*. Later, Ruhl concludes Act 1 with homage to one of the nineteenth century's signature theatricalities: the end of act tableau, underscored by music that crescendos to the falling curtain:

Mrs. Givings puts the vibrator to Mrs. Daldry's private parts.
They look heavenwards. The steady hum of the vibrator. Transcendent music.
A curtain falls. The end of the act.

(Ruhl 2010, 41)

Ruhl "releases" the comic potential in this moment with these theatrics, in essence, defusing the potential for controversy through her salvo to old-school opera-house theatricalism.

EXERCISE:
Creating tableaux

1. Review several scenes that you have already written.
2. Select one or two scenes and rework the ending of the scene into a tableau.
3. The tableau may be a "freeze" that stops a given action and gesture.
4. Set up the tableau so that it foreshadows a future action, relationship, or conflict.
5. The tableau should embody both theme and dynamic as in a still photograph.

CHARACTER AS DEVICE IN *DMCP*

Ruhl's farcical "stiff" presents the strategy of character as device. Dead bodies on stage often educe hilarity, as the playwright sets up a unique set of challenges regarding movement, placement, degree of "deadness," all foisted upon a character (or characters) who must deal with the body. In Mac Wellman's *Harm's Way*, the stiff, Blackmange, is summoned briefly back to life by a Wizard as part of "The con," a kind of carny sideshow. His murderer, Santouche, who seeks and attains vital information from Blackmange, must be kept out of sight. This theatrical setup provides opportunities for humor:

> SANTOUCHE: All right, all right. Shit man! Can't get no peace from a man even by killing him no more.
>
> (Wellman 1984, 29–32)

The more the state of being seems unresolved, the more tension and comic potential in the scene. In *DMCP*, we seem Gordon slumped at his chair in the café but Jean prefers skepticism to certainty: "He doesn't look all that dead. He looks still" (Ruhl 2008, I:1;11). Interest evolves around Jean's spiraling interactions to resolve the issue, while her concomitant conversations on his phone sow the seeds of exposition. Act 1, Scene 1 represents a novel variation of the dialogic monologue as two inert devices simulate live interaction—the dead man and the cell phone. Jean either "converses" with the unresponsive Gordon, or she "responds" to phone calls from offstage characters, portending subsequent scenes. These ringtones each signify "absent others" (Chapter 11), personalities presaged by apposite aural signatures which, when answered, are modulated by the level and tone of Jean's responses.

Beat segments in the opening scene are marked by the intrusions of various ringtones. In effect, Ruhl simulates "French scene" structure (which is traditionally marked by character entrances and exits) as the interruptions change motivation levels for the main character—shifting the dynamics of the scene. These allow for a range of reactions by Jean: from proactive goal-setting, to emotional backsliding, to rhetorical musings. In hinting at traditional well-made play structure, the phone calls do the heavy lifting of expository "introductions," that is, as set-ups for characters we will meet later. (In well-made plays, as popularized by the nineteenth-century French playwrights Scribe and Sardou, the introductory scene was often relegated to the servants who "introduced" us to the major characters and actions of the play.) Ruhl's expanded use of dialogic monologue provides contour by varying speech strategies: conversational (on the phone); speech act (her vow to Gordon); circumstantial commentary, "there seems to be no one working at his café;" gestural, (use of sign language, physical prodding with props), such as '*She checks with a spoon under his nose to see if he is breathing*'; empowered (she takes ownership of the situation). Monologue economizes—as it eliminates functional characters (waiters, other patrons, and so on); but also clarifies—by telescoping the significance of the eponymous cell phone. Ruhl's triangulated monologue positions Jean at the apex between the dead character onstage and the offstage characters linked by cell phones. She innovates upon traditional dramaturgical practices to create novel and effective solutions.

EXERCISE:
Triangulated monologue

(Read Act I, Scene 1 of *Dead Man's Cell Phone* by Sarah Ruhl.)

Just as the addition of a third character multiplies dynamic possibilities on stage, triangulation affects an expanded use of monologue. Before beginning this exercise, review the techniques of the absent other monologue (see exercises in Chapter 11). In addition to the "absent other(s)," your character will address a non-responsive character on stage; or perhaps the audience, if a non-matrixed, presentational dramaturgy is preferred. Remember, triangulation marks the beat segments in the monologue, just as entrances and exits mark the structure of a French scene. It necessitates that the monologist varies ontological levels of presence and absence, moving between task-oriented action beats, and intimacy beats of insight or revelation. Each transition challenges the trained (or in-training) actor with a different threshold of focus, energy, and "givens." These will involve shifts in how the beat is centered in the body. As such, it is ideal if you follow up the written exercise with an actor addressing the challenge of shifting focus and intention; young playwrights are usually surprised at the levels of texture and contour triangulated monologue provides.

1. Establish onstage a "nonresponsive" or unconscious character, who might be sleeping, drugged, ill, or comatose.

2. Write a scene in which the character delivering the monologue confronts or interacts with the nonresponsive "character," with the goal of either affecting a change in character's state of being, or discovering more about the physical state of the character. Task-oriented behavior is ideal.

3. Have the characters interrupted by the "intrusion" of an absent other, represented by a phone call, ringing doorbell, knock on door, text, finding a letter, an email, a picture, or something similar. This interruption should have a determining affect on the action of the scene.

4. The speaking character then returns to the nonresponsive character. (for instance sizing them up, or on task).

5. Optional: have the speaking character address the audience, either directly, or rhetorically.

6. Vary the sequences back and forth toward a resolution of the action of the scene.

COMMENT: In the workshop, you can ask participants to vary their choices between a character who has prior knowledge of the onstage character, and one who lacks prior knowledge (Jean, for example). For students interested in writing one-person plays, this exercise provides a point of entry to viable simulation of interaction on stage. Use actors to fully realize the impact of this exercise.

FAÇADE AND THE PERFORMATIVE CHARACTER

With the setup of *DMCP* accomplished in the first scene, Act 1 proceeds as a Rolodex of scenes in which Jean encounters the major players in Gordon's life, including his wife, lover, mother and brother. Jean concocts various white lies about Gordon's "last words," that, with the exception of Mrs. Gottlieb, engender a positive reaction from each character as they all buy in to the ruse. Buoyed by her power to con others, Jean progresses from a retiring, timid woman to the empowered and successful poseur. Jean's possession of Gordon's cell phone validates her façade as his entrusted confidant. Revered as the person who witnessed Gordon's final moment on earth, she escapes further scrutiny. As this lark gains traction it fuels the comic irony; this diffident messenger turned savior becomes the invaluable healer of their damaged souls. Jean's "moment of truth" with Gordon's lover, Other Woman, typifies this uncanny mystique:

> OTHER WOMAN: So. His last words.
>
> JEAN: Gordon mentioned you before he died. Well, he more than mentioned you. He said: tell her that I love her. And then he turned his face away and died.
>
> OTHER WOMAN: He said that he loved me.
>
> JEAN: Yes.
>
> OTHER WOMAN: I waited for such a long time. And the words—delivered through another woman. What a shit.

Once Jean hooks the character, she elevates her game with unlikely bravura, indicated in heightened language and choreographed cadence. As Other Woman wipes a tear away, Jean's façade becomes transformative—her language is as rhythmic as it is metaphoric.

> JEAN: … He said that other women seemed like clocks compared to you —other women —measured time—broke the day up —but that you — stopped time. He said you —stopped time —just by walking into a room.
> (Ruhl 2008, I:3, 20)

Here, Jean recycles language from earlier in the scene in which Other Women intimidates her by showing her how a "real woman walks into a room." Jean *back channels* this riff, turning the tables to gain control of the scene. Back channel is a term from discourse analysis in which earlier threads in a conversation are woven back later into the dialogue, usually at the conclusion of the interaction. In this case, Jean turns the tables by recapitulating Other Woman's words. This is a counter-intuitive way to construct your lead character, but strategically protects her façade. Utilizing another's language to disarm her foil, Jean must listen more than talk. Ruhl constructs her to "closely observe" what others say and do; she stays "on task" as a means to construct the façade. This speech strategy keeps the audience on the edge of their seats, since her whole construct is built on not saying something that will blow her cover. This necessity creates such a strong intention for this character that it drives the play's action. From scene to scene, Jean patiently sizes up what is said; she holds back for the right moment; then, in quick release, takes her turn with a wallop. The result is a "strong curtain" that concludes scenes. (Another master of the back channel is David Mamet. The device is often an outcome of riffing; see the Riffing exercise in the next chapter.)

EXERCISE:
Integrating back channels in closely observed dialogue

1. This simple exercise involves two characters, one of them is withholding information that the other wants.
2. Write a three-page scene in which one of the characters reiterates what the other character has said, in order to glean or hide crucial information.
3. The other character attempts to evade this through deferring or digression.
4. Culminate the scene with one of the characters winning or losing (that is, gaining the upper hand, or turning the tables). The back channel should be uttered at or near the turning point of the scene.

COMMENT: Closely observed means that the characters are studying each other for clues, are responding to "givens" in the environment, while actively listening to the other character. While it seems obvious, it is essential the playwright play close attention to these interactive and detailed aspects of character. Ultimately, the closely observed character represents a major benchmark of a playwright's craft.

PARKS'S PERFORMATIVE CON MEN

Jean's actions recall those of the skilled hustler, Lincoln, in Scene Five of *Topdog/Underdog*, who touts the importance of watching and being tuned in to the perfect moment to gain maximum advantage over the "mark," or potential dupe:

BOOTH: What you looking at?

LINCOLN: I'm sizing you up.

BOOTH: Oh Yeah?!

(Parks 2002, 1:5:285–90)

That's thuh Dealer's attitude. He acts like he don't wanna play. He holds back.

(Parks 2002, 295–6)

Here, Parks provides the actor with a number of performative clues demonstrating attitudes and behaviors. The fun of this eventually tragic play is in watching Lincoln and Booth play at the various roles: thief, street hustler, and white-faced minstrel sideshow act. In the scene above, after some discussion about the "moves and the grooves," Lincoln provides the *sine qua non* for the con:

LINCOLN: A good-looking walk and a dynamite talk captivates their attention. The Mark focuses with 2 organs primarily: his eyes and his ears. Leave one out you lose yr shirt. Captivate both, yr golden.

(Parks 2002, 319–21)

Parks is urging the actor playing Lincoln to role-play to the hilt.

While Jean's reticence contrasts with Lincoln's swagger, their strategies are remarkably similar. Her unassuming nature captivates skeptical subjects, making her escapes believable. Like the con artist who suspects the "mark" may be ready to blow the whistle, Jean instinctively knows how to "cool down" a situation. The hustler or con man makes for a strong dramatic character because they have a strong "want" and are willing to use deception to achieve their goal. The act of deceiving is where the performative aspect of characterization is realized. This must involve body language, gesture, language manipulation, and the sense of orchestrating the circumstances—all very theatrical and engaging. Thus, it makes for one of the best exercises for playwrights struggling with the notion of "action" in dialogue. While the use of con men is a staple in Len Jenkin's oeuvre, their genus is archetypal—emerging from the hard-boiled genre of pulp fiction and *film noir*.

EXERCISE:
Performative character—the con artist and the mark (dupe)

1. After reading the plays discussed above, or selected excerpts, respond with a short three-page scene of your own.
2. Select two characters: one is the con artist, the other is the mark. Before beginning, determine what the con will be, where it will take place, and what the primary objective is.

3. Sketch out four to five deceptive actions that involve subterfuge, lying, concealing, distracting, hyperbole, and so on.

4. Importantly, the con artist must closely observe the mark, and comment on movements and gestures of the body (or "tells") that give away what the dupe is thinking or feeling.

5. Give some kind of physical shtick to the con: demonstration, sleight of hand, card shark, or similar.

6. Feel the rhythm of the scene building pressure, then come to a quick resolution; what is most important is unleashing the performative aspects of character.

COMMENT: Observing some typical cons on You Tube will help familiarize you with some of the physical aspects of the con. However, in playwriting make sure to have physical gestures reacted to 'in dialogue' by the dupe with a level of specificity that clarifies the action involved. This important element of craft recognizes that the action or reaction is embedded in dialogue versus stage directions.

CROSSOVER CHARACTERIZATION

Jean survives an abortive family dinner in Act I, Scene 5, after which, she falls in romantically with Dwight, Gordon's younger, introverted brother. The infatuated Dwight is no match for clever Jean, as she maintains the façade while winning his heart. Here, the irony is fully apparent because it is a series of lies that brings Jean to the point of true love for Dwight by the end of Act I. Ruhl releases the external façade to provide Jean with an emotional outpouring of passion. This crossover move from the performative construction to provide more character depth is a typical marker in blending disparate dramaturgies.

Suzan-Lori Parks cracks the performative façades of Lincoln's white-faced carny version and Booth's thievery and lying as they reminisce about childhood with their parents. This kind of character revelation and backstory is consistent with the more realistic depictions of a welfare mother and abortion practitioner, Hester, in *The Red Letter Plays* (2001) but a departure from her more radically experimental work. This should serve as wisdom to young playwrights who feel they must adhere to a specific school or genre. Parks constructs her dramaturgy to best suit the material and action of the play. In these crossover plays she embeds various innovations within the strictures of narrative and character arc.

CHARACTER WITHOUT BACKSTORY

In *DMCP*, Jean evolves solely from the action of the play—nothing from her past informs the present action. Her "depth" is created by her emotional passage into love, a throwback to the comedies of Marivaux and his famous *marivaudage*. The *marivaudage* represents the progress of the characters falling in love during the course of the play, an innovation that provided the basis for modern romantic comedy. While Gordon's family history is made transparent to Jean, providing backstory aplenty, her biographical profile is opaque. With the exception of Jean's vague reference to her working in a Holocaust museum (is that made up as well?) we know nothing about her prior life, relationships, or even why she came to the café that day and ordered the "lobster bisque," the iconic link to Gordon's final desire in life before his demise. Jean's alleged connection to Gordon, which Dwight jealously construes as love for his brother, establishes his primary obstacle if he is to win over Jean. For Dwight, mere mention of his brother dredges up a none-too-pleasant history of childhood bullying. In a dialogic manner, Ruhl bundles crossover character formations in this play; ironically, with the lead character providing us the least backstory.

Without backstory, Jean is the quintessential performative character, a chameleon who adapts her colors to fit the circumstances, shifting through genres from *film noir* to martial arts fighter (Act I: 3; Act II: 4 respectively), to stand up comic (Act I: 6); to inhabiting extra-terrestrial "planets" (Act II: 5). Ruhl creates theatrical interest most emphatically with the fight scene between Stranger and Jean that concludes Act II, Scene 4. The fight, which in a realistic play would stretch the limits of plausibility, since there is no evidence to indicate Jean's martial arts background, here seems to suit the character's emphasis on the performative. Placed deep into Act II, the "cat fight" provides a burst of adrenaline for audiences to sustain them through to the end of the show. For playwrights, performative characters offer a wider range of actions than normative characters, since, once the performative expectation is established for an audience, they will accept just about anything the character does.

THE DEVICE AS FETISH (*THE VIBRATOR PLAY*)

The connection of physical object as dramaturgical device to the plays' action provides the fuel for the performative character. For example, Ruhl's latest play, *In the Next Room, or the Vibrator Play* (2010), focuses on the emergence of the vibrator as a tool to relieve female hysteria. This prop has a kind of life-giving, healing force tied to the taboo subject of female orgasm (called "paroxysm" in the 1890s). Like the cell phone it makes sounds, turns on and off, and has talisman-like powers. Its direct application to the women's "private parts" and their subsequent "paroxysm" ensures an in-body catharsis for character and an awkward, ineluctable vicariousness from the audience. Fetishized by the women in the play, the vibrator signifies the transformative basis of Mrs. Daldry's move from misery to bliss. In the larger sense, the vibrator as device cracks the façade of nineteenth-century propriety and manners that defined the Victorian ethos. One could say it resounds on multiple levels.

EXERCISE:

Façade and crafting the performative character

This two-character exercise contrasts a performative character with a normative character, by building a false front that establishes the façade. Note: In this scene, the normative character's need is the driving force of the scene, whereas the performative character goes with the flow, seemingly improvising as they go along. A key to this scene is focusing on the behavioral traits of each character.

1. Develop a normative character who is absorbed in some emotional turmoil or dilemma. Imbue the other character with "special knowledge" or characteristics: they might be a healer, shaman, prophet, lover, psychic, parent, seer, for example.

2. Write a scene in which the performative character adopts a false front or façade through a specific language strategy, special knowledge, or props, costumes, or other objects.

3. Provide some quality or trait in the performative character that is valued by the normative character. In other words, the normative character feeds into and amplifies the façade.

4. The normative character needs to "arrive" at something they want from the performative character, and the latter plays along, relishing the sense of empowerment.

5. Consider each beat segment's "marker" a small discovery or revelation.

6. Create an outcome in which the normative character succeeds in eliminating the turmoil or dilemma, while performative character is transformed.

COMMENT: Performative characters facilitate the action of the play through a variety of strategies. Like Parks, and other contemporary playwrights such as Naomi Iizuka and Martin McDonagh, Ruhl amplifies the realistic context for her characters through theatrical devices such as props, vibrators, makeup, costumes, and heightened language. In *DMCP,* Jean's façade as the confidant and presumed lover of Gordon, validated by her possession of his cell phone, establishes the action. The cell phone ringtones trigger scene transitions, or serve as beat shifters; as a "relic" of Gordon the phone is coveted for its talismanic value by other characters. Jean's "special knowledge" about Gordon's final hours makes her highly valued by others in the play. She facilitates the action, whether in love, business, or marriage.

Table 8.1   Distinguishing performative from normative characters

PERFORMATIVE CHARACTER	NORMATIVE CHARACTER
Plays at roles, facades, fronts	Plays self
None or little backstory or known history	Character biography is integral
Theatrically based	Dramatically based
Non-integral traits	All traits integrated and organic
Behavioral	Psychological
Object or prop as dramaturgic device	Object or prop as extension of character
Theatrical framing of physical scene	Scene as background to action

Table 8.1 offers the playwright a list of distinctions between the DNA of these characters. The conceptual basis for these characters is different and should be understood as such. In exhibiting the performative character, the playwright should be attentive in establishing the staging of the action. For example, the vibrator sequences in *The Vibrator Play* take place in the doctor's office on an examining table, thus simulating the conditions of a medical practice. This creates the platform for the comic incongruity caused by the unexpected orgasmic outcomes. In *Topdog/Underdog*, Parks frames the three-card Monte games as though we were witnessing it on the street, positioning us in the midst of the hustle.

THE *TOUR DE FORCE* MONOLOGUE

From the standpoint of dramatic continuity, what makes *DMCP* anomalous is Gordon's four-page *coup de théâtre* that opens Act II (Ruhl 2008, 39-42). To this point, Ruhl's monologues in Act I are situational or event-driven; as the triangulated monologue discussed above illustrates. Jean's triangulated monologue is in reaction to her happenstance encounter with Gordon and his ringing cell phone. Gordon's *tour de force* monologue at the beginning of Act II recalls Babcock's aria-like monologue in Overmyer's *Dark Rapture* (see Chapter 12). Both characters are in effect viewing their own demise. In *Dark Rapture*, Babcock watches his house (and former life) burn to the ground. In *DMCP*, Gordon observes and comments on the last day of his life.

There is a major dramaturgical difference: Gordon is referencing the events leading up to the first scene of the play, whereas Babcock starts the play with his monologue. If Babcock is elegiac, Gordon's monologue in Act II growls like the comic rants of monologists Lewis Black or the late George Carlin. Ruhl's creature is a cultural cynic, bulking thematic content in grotesque imagery. Gordon lambastes the stage with carnivalesque analogies that juxtapose selling human kidneys with devouring *hamachi* (raw tuna) at a sushi bar. Gordon's inner rage is fueled by the futility of a failed marriage to that "miserable bitch" Hermia. The diatribe expands to extrapolate the dehumanizing effects of train stations, subways, and disconnected souls on cell phones. To execute this heightened bombast, the actor playing Gordon must attack the language with verbal dexterity and physical stamina. The scale and placement of the monologue, fifteen minutes of performance at the top of Act II, demands high-energy virtuosity to realize the desired effect of a collective audience adrenaline rush.

The monologic form resembles the humorous qualities of a *commedia tirata* (tirade), a set speech that twisted through dialects, emotional swings, heightened gestures, and a hodgepodge of seemingly unrelated material—climaxing in a theatrical epiphany, with a classical lament—a rhythmically ecstatic ode to death. Visualize a tenor saxophone solo in the style of John Coltrane or Sonny Rollins, isolating the performer from the ensemble, focusing an extended virtuoso moment, as other players leave the stage.

Structurally, Gordon's monologue mirrors the jazz solo: the major theme of the monologue narrates Gordon's "last day on earth," culminating at the point he orders the lobster bisque; then a counter theme broadens to explore various extrapolations and rants; finally, the reprise of the initial theme crescendos as Gordon, in the throes of a heart attack, recounts his climactic meeting with Jean over the lobster bisque, moments before his death.

The tripartite structure facilitates the staging of the monologue, as it provides coherence combined with mnemonic scaffolding for the actor. Gordon's scale of verbiage rebalances the play in his direction, and through his robust defense of his life's work selling body parts, a thematic emerges that adds a layer of gravitas to the play. The monologue's connection to antecedent forms such as the *tirata* and lament provides a dramaturgical coherence to the structure and a theatrical grandeur.

To distinguish the *tour de force* monologue from monologue's other formats, we establish these primary characteristics:

- It is interpolated into the play, rather than organically or causally motivated.

- It requires an exaggerated presentational style utilizing techniques from related idioms such as stand-up comedy.

- The monologue appears to stand on its own, being complete within itself, insofar as it has a beginning, middle and end.

- There is multivocality, particularly through grotesque or carnivalesque juxtapositions, dialects, political rhetoric, and mimicking. It requires extreme shifts in gesture and movement to underpin or enhance the spoken language.

- There are antecedent corollaries such as the *commedia tirata* and the classical lament.

- There is a rebalancing or calibration in the play toward the character presenting the monologue.

- It requires a performative style with an emphasis on the virtuosic.

The *tour de force* monologue has wide application in a variety of dramaturgies: as a stand-alone monologue, a ten-minute monologue play, a comic routine in the style of Lewis Black, or George Carlin, or a scene within episodic formats. Young Jean Lee's *Church* (2008) opens with Reverend José's parable-like homily, then shifts gears into a personalized fire-and-brimstone diatribe directed at the parishioners (that is, the audience). In essence, *Church* is constructed around a series of heightened monologues delivered by Reverend José and several female reverends. (Lee 2009). In a way similar to Ruhl's Gordon, Lee's monologues juxtapose the grotesque with the more lofty language appropriate to the setting. The *tour de force* monologue can easily be developed independently of the overall scenic structure, which become a dramaturgical strategy of choice across a range of contemporary plays and styles. The following exercise provides a point of entry into developing the technique.

EXERCISE:
Tour de force monologue

Revisit a one-act or full-length play you have written. Select a character from the play. It need not be the major character. In addition to reading through Gordon's monologue, familiarize yourself with both the *tirata* and the lament. You can search Isabella Andreini for examples of the former, and Euripides (Hecuba in *The Trojan Women*) for the latter. Go on You Tube and search John Coltrane and Sonny Rollins, and listen to several of their extended solos. The same site will provide you with examples of comic monologists Lewis Black, George Carlin, and Chris Rock. Young Jean Lee's *Church and Pullman WA* open with *tour de force* monologues. Configure your work accordingly:

1. Like the jazz solo, divide the monologue into theme, counter-theme, and reprise of initial theme (you need to find a theme to get the ball rolling).
2. Establish some relationship to the action or characters of the play in the initial theme.
3. In the middle section, allow the character to comment on various issues, or give points of view, what might be described as thematic content.
4. To close the monologue, reprise the main theme but with some vital difference: a looking forward, a sense of closure, or a call to action. Strive for a crescendo by altering speech patterns. (The classical laments changed the scansion to achieve crescendo effects.)
5. For each section, include specific gestures, takes, and so on to allow for various kinds of role-playing within the monologue. The character, for example, might mock others in the play, perhaps utilizing the accents and the movement patterns of those mimicked.

COMMENT: Playwrights can learn a great deal from observing comic monologists at work, particularly those who use political or cultural material. This trend has increased significantly during the past decade with the success of *The Colbert Report* and *The John Stewart Show*. With the ready availability of You Tube, playwrights can study at close range the comic monologists for uses of invective, political takes, voicings, dialects, and so on.

ORCHESTRATED RESTS

A key music-based strategy utilized by Parks in *Topdog/Underdog, In the Blood,* and other plays, and Ruhl in her prize-winning play *The Clean House,* is the *orchestrated rest.* Their applications in these plays differ from "Pinteresque" pauses and silences, the intent of which was generally ambiguous or indeterminate—obscuring meaning in the free radical of subtext. Parks and Ruhl use rest beats to unlock sibling dynamics represented by the brothers, Booth and Lincoln, and sisters, Lane and Virginia, in their respective plays.

This deft strategy displaces the normative apparatus of textual exposition, by burying it deeply into the body core of the characters, where is then manifest in gesture, facial expression, and movement. By utilizing the rests in this manner, Parks and Ruhl tap into the ingrained body language of filial relationships; the lacunae provide insights into past histories and unresolved tensions deeply embedded in the body. Physically activated "body texts" dialogize with language—unearthing primal or natural behavior that cracks the surface dialogue. As such, the rests provide a paean from the playwright to the actors; moments for the actors to explore unabated their physical self unhinged from the text. The overall effect provides contour to the scene by alternating the rhythm between spoken and unspoken segments. Ruhl's *The Clean House* offers an apt example, as the sisterly argument between Lane and Virginia ceases to verbalize and devolves into something more primitive (and interesting). Ruhl's stage direction reads:

> *For a moment,*
> *Lane and Virginia experience a primal moment*
> *During which they are seven and nine years old,*
> *Inside the mind, respectively.*
> *They are mad. Then they return quite naturally to language*
> *As adults do.*

> (Ruhl 2006, 30)

Herein, Ruhl importunes the actors to physicalize their characters' backstory and shared history. This telescoping of an interactional backstory creates a sudden ontological shift for the audience that could be heightened with lighting and sound effects to expand the comic values. It recalls Richard Foreman's direction of his play *The Cure*, in which he juxtaposed normative dialogue scenes with manic, hyper-kinesthetic interludes to create perceptual shifts for the audience.

Comic values are clearly Ruhl's intent later in the play, when she compresses the act of falling in love into a sequence of three extended rests. Some things happen between the lines, and in *The Clean House* it is love. In Act II, Scene 4 the surgeon Charles (Lane's husband) is telling his patient Ana about her options for dealing with breast cancer, when she insists:

ANA
I'd like to do it tomorrow.

CHARLES
Then we'll do it tomorrow.
> *They look at each other.*
> *They fall in love.*

ANA
Then I'll see you tomorrow, at the surgery.

CHARLES
Goodbye, Ana.

ANA
Goodbye.
> *They look at each other.*
> *They fall in love some more.*
Am I going to die?

CHARLES
No, you're not going to die.
I won't let you die.
> *They fall in love completely.*
> *They kiss wildly*
What's happening?

ANA
I don't know ...

(Ruhl 2006, 53–6)

Here the nonverbal beats provide contour, as the scene zigzags between setting the date for Ana's mastectomy and physicalizing their over-the-top infatuation for each other, indicated through gestures, locked eyes, and physical movement. Like Parks's homage to antique nineteenth-century theater forms such as minstrelsy, Ruhl echoes the *tableau vivant* of melodrama: for instance, those snapshot-like moments when lovers fell into each other's arms. Here, the *gestus* of "love at first sight" counters the impersonal, clinical decorum of patient gowns and lab coats. The grotesque, marked by Ana's imminent loss of her body's symbol of sexuality and fecundity—the breast—is juxtaposed with the heightened euphoria of passionate gazing and sublime caressing. Indeed, if the prognosis for Ana's body is problematic, there is nothing uncertain or gloomy about the romantic bonding. Language, as the marker for illness, disfigurement, and ambiguity, is superseded by the undertow of love, desire, and attraction. This "union of opposites" torques the textual "moment of truth" around comic, gestural relief to propel the scene.

Similarly, Parks's spacer beats in *Topdog/Underdog* are marked by character titles with no dialogue underneath. Parks varies the number of these titles, from the quick back-and-forth exchange of a single pair to multiple pairs of titles that simulate a silent "conversation" between the brothers. These lacunae provide elbow room for Lincoln and Booth to absorb and display the ramifications of their utterances and actions. The actor performs the reaction: is it a con, is it truthful, or simply sizing up the situation? Given the brothers' backgrounds as a "reformed" hustler (Lincoln) and active shoplifter and bullshitter (Booth), these spacer beats often indicate the sizing up of the other. Booth taunts Lincoln for donning a minstrel-like white face and eponymous beard to perform the dead president; while he pushes his brother to the brink, Booth keeps a bead on how far he can go. Through the spacer beats, Parks establishes the physical marker of Lincoln's reserve against the impetuosity of Booth (a ticking bomb that explodes with grave consequences). In the main, Parks's language is the hyperbolic, trash-talking speech genre of the street hustler, contrasted against the unarticulated compassion, caring, and pain physically transmitted in these extended rests. The dialogic tension between the high-octane verbiage and the moments of stasis creates the groove of the play, as these are the moments where the natural rhythm and feel of the characters emerges. For audiences, stasis points allow behavior to be observed unimpeded by narrative, and thus open the play to its broader humanity. (For more on spacer beats, see the next chapter.)

In an age where playwrights are taught to director-proof their plays, Parks steps back to observe her characters *sans* language. Many of the very short plays in her collection *365 Days/365 Plays* include spacer beats. In this detachment from insistent action, Parks seems to be like the jazz composer who gives room for the players to stretch out or improvise on the basic theme. She relaxes the forward pull of the play, takes pause, senses the resurging rhythm, recalibrates, then goes forward. It is risky—the playwright letting go of the play, a kind of anti-dramaturgy that opposes the putative hegemony of total control by the playwright. The double spacer beats in her play *Fucking A* offer a very wide range of interpretations for the actors and director. Scene 15 opens with the character Canary giving Hester a bath:

CANARY: Am I scrubbing too hard?

HESTER:

HESTER:

CANARY: They're reconciled again. Word is she went to her daddy ...

(Parks 2001, 192)

The director's first inclination might be a "double-take," as if to say, "Are you kidding me, back off?" This would most likely invoke a comic reaction. However, Parks leaves it open for any interpretation—what about a sensual take, or ironic, as if she isn't scrubbing at all? In her latest play, *The Book of Grace*, produced at the Public Theater in 2010, Parks "urges audience members to create their own books of grace to evidence good things in the world and complete the work of the play" (Colbert 2010, 666).

A further extreme of this kind of creative democratization is playwright Charles Mee, whose website encourages theater artists to adapt freely from his work. Parks encourages artistic *disponibilité*, that moment of availability to the moment: marked by accepting the contributions of all collaborators in shaping the specific performance. In her strategic use of stasis, Parks invites audiences to share a moment with the performers, to gauge reactions, to sum up. As the respite from language creates a vacuum, it paradoxically propels us to experience more deeply the presence of language in the play, while also acknowledging that pieces of the story may be missing. In essence, Parks is creating a shadow dramaturgy that the audience is invited to construct.

EXERCISE:
Integrating rests and stops

(Read *Topdog/Underdog* and *The Clean House*.)

By interrupting the flow and cadence of language, the playwright can create contour through the tension between interruption and sections of dialogue, providing moments for the audience to "catch up" with the characters and probe the relationships more deeply. Ruhl and Parks maximize the potential for embedded behaviors to emerge during these moments as a natural outcome of their sibling rivalries.

1. This scene is a two-hander that works best if the characters have a shared history. As shown by the above discussion, siblings are ideal and within the shared experiences of most young playwrights.
2. The exercise can work very well as a revision of an earlier scene.
3. Interpolate rests and stops as markers for beat segments, either ending or beginning segments.
4. Rewrite accordingly to integrate the rest or stop.
5. Consider writing in stage directions (as in Ruhl) or in simply providing character titles without dialogue (like Parks).
6. How does the integration of the rest or stop alter the nature of the scene or relationship?

COMMENT: Discuss with the playwrights their intentions for the rests and stops against the feedback from members of the workshop. What can be done to clarify intention, or are these moments up for grabs? Does the playwright consider this loss of control a liability or an asset?

THE DRAMATURGY OF ECOLOGY: TRANSFORMING SPACE IN *THE CLEAN HOUSE*

Many playwrights neglect how the space or setting might serve to not simply enhance but actually drive the action of the play. It is important for the playwright to ask "what if," to probe their creativity more assiduously. If the setting seems realistic or conventional, does the subject matter somehow offer unique opportunities? Sheila Callaghan's *Crumble (Lay Me Down, Justin Timberlake)* transformed the play's setting, The Apartment, into a character in the play with monologue, dialogue, and a full range of character feelings and commentary. She moved the "speaking site" around the apartment from the radiators to the walls, windows, and so on. This defamiliarization device immediately established the darkly comic tone of the play. Defamiliarizing the typical living room set is exactly what happens in Ruhl's *The Clean House*, as the space takes on an organic life inextricably linked to the action of the play. Unlike Callaghan's Apartment, which opens *Crumble* with a monologue, the first third of *The Clean House* proceeds in Lane's nicely appointed suburban living room, with the set seemingly an afterthought.

After Charles leaves his wife Lane, he leaves the marital home and moves in with his beloved patient and *bashert*, or soulmate, Ana. However, the so-called "balcony that overlooks the sea" in Matilde's description of Ana's home is, in the play, overlooking Lane's living room. Architecturally, they are all in the same house. Even Matilde's domestic services are now shared between Charles and Ana, and Lane. The recycled space now both separates and brings together, an example of Ruhl's "union of opposites" aesthetic. Paradoxically, the viewer is forced to "read it" as both an external and internal space. Subsequent actions reinforce this challenging aesthetic. When Charles and Ana toss apple cores into the sea they are actually flung below into Lane's living room. Ruhl plays both sides of the coin, never truly isolating the romantic playfulness from its more gross underpinnings. We see this cut both ways at the end of Act II, Scene 8, when Charles disrobes and throws his dirty laundry into a heap of clothes on Lane's living room. Rather than reject this humiliation, Lane picks up the sweater longingly, while reveling in the scent of her wayward, "absent" husband. Ruhl's ecological "recycling" of food and clothing informs the dramaturgy and reverses expectation—rather than disconnecting the characters through normative "distancing," Ruhl uses every action to bind her characters ever closer.

In a traditional, realistic structure, the extramarital relationship would unfold separately from Lane. She would be dealing with it through conversations with her sister Virginia, Matilde, and in confrontations with Charles. Ruhl theatricalizes the psychological effects of this affair through the set, as the architecture of the lovers' balcony hovers overhead, a looming reminder of her husband (and maid's) betrayal. The conflation of "marital" living room with the lovers' balcony dialogizes the clash between absence and presence. In this sense, the set is now the spatial metaphor of the play's action. Lane ultimately capitulates to the mess in her life, the failed goal of the clean house (and the title's ironic conclusion), as she succumbs to the flotsam and jetsam from above. Ana, whom we find out is refusing chemotherapy and thus succumbing to breast cancer, doesn't end up at a spatial distance from the play's center; quite the opposite, by the play's end she is brought into the heart of it. Indeed, the transformation from clean house to accumulated detritus to tomb comes full circle when Lane's living room becomes Ana's hospice. The transformative scenic arrangement externalizes the play's subtext, as the spatial "arc" becomes a player in the action—its dynamism catalyzes the dramaturgy. Ruhl achieves the paradoxical effect of deep emotional engagement with constant reminders that we are in a theatrical play.

Similarly, the first-half of the title *In the Next Room, or the Vibrator Play* suggests that for Ruhl, the play is as much about the "next room" (that is, the locked, off-limits office of Dr. Givings) as it is about the vibrator. The next room is the site of intimacy and pleasure, as opposed to the sterile, living/ waiting room inhabited mostly by Mrs. Givings. The division in architecture is the spatial metaphor for their estranged marriage. It is only after Mrs. Givings demands that the doctor use the vibrator on her that he begins to recognize his distant coldness toward his wife. Ultimately, the dismantling of spatial boundaries in the play mirrors their emotional and sexual reconciliation that culminates the play.

Parks's *In the Blood* is set under a bridge, a marker for a family that is exposed to the harshest realities, existing "underneath" in a socio-economic substratum, within the most tenuous framework possible, subject to immediate and total disintegration. In setting the play under the bridge, Parks defamiliarizes the normative choice of the family home, however squalid, thereby establishing a powerful spatial metaphor for the play.

EXERCISE:
The "what-if" premise and spatial metaphor

(Review *The Clean House*, *In the Next Room, or the Vibrator Play*, *Crumble*, and *In the Blood*.)

1. The premise is a useful exercise for encapsulating the action of the play in a sentence or phrase. It works better when you divide the workshop into teams of two, either working toward one premise, or each developing their own.
2. Participants in the workshop brainstorm over how conflict between characters can be reinforced spatially, so that the set becomes a player in the action.
3. Stipulate that the set must in some way be transformed—not just a set change.
4. Consider how the scenery serves as a spatial metaphor.
5. Whittle down the "what-if" premise to one or two sentences that embody the above.
6. This is primarily a conceptual exercise at this point. You are trying to awaken possibilities, and the ability to articulate ideas, succinctly.

COMMENT: New playwrights are finding innovation through ecological means, such as recycling objects and space during the course of the play. Do not lose sight of these opportunities to advance your dramaturgy. If characters have arcs, why not space or costumes or other devices that make for powerful theatrical messages? Consider Callaghan's choice to make her setting a character in the play. Certainly risky, but again risk is often where the true voice of the playwright can be found.

CROSSOVER POETICS

Crossover poetics encourages experimentation on the larger canvas and scale of the full-length play. As a matter of credo, Clubbed Thumb requires their produced work to run no more than seventy-five to ninety minutes and without intermission. This predilection for the short form has generally been the case with language playwrights, particularly of the new generation. Historically, this had precedence in the absurdists' preference for the one-act form, since experimental work had other foci than narrative or character development. Just as Edward Albee built upon absurdist-based one-acts like *Zoo Story* and *American Dream* and amplified his oeuvre to great success, new playwrights can be encouraged to tackle larger subjects in expanded forms. The crossover map provided by Ruhl and Parks is to dialogize old and new forms to create a new kind of theatrical experience that reaches a broader audience. For mainstream playwrights interested in how new playwriting might expand their skill sets, these plays provide rich sources of smart dramaturgical innovation upon which to further develop their craft.

PART II

Strategies of structure and form

9

Units and building blocks

THE DIALOGIC BEAT

This chapter explores how dialogism shapes the creation of beats in a play's script. It examines how the component beats in the script interact to create interest. The concepts and techniques feature characteristics common to plays of the new playwriting. In a number of cases, they expand upon traditional approaches and, as such, should stimulate craft development and dramaturgical acumen. Rather than impose a formulaic way of writing, each playwright can assimilate and adapt these strategies toward novel configurations.

CONSIDERATION OF TECHNIQUE: THE DIALOGIC BEAT

PREMISE: The play in itself is a dialogic system. The basic structural component in playwriting is established in beat juxtaposition. The playwright envisions the script as an interactive mechanism in which each beat is in "dialogue" with other beats.

Beats constitute the smallest identifiable units of language, action, or thought in the play. They represent the fundamental building blocks of the playscript. In traditional playwriting, beats should cohere to form an overall unity of intention in the play. The causal linkage of beats provides a consistent progression of action that is considered a benchmark of good dramaturgy. From this perspective, the beat is the fundamental means toward the larger end—the finished play. This relegation subordinates the potential of the beat in the immediate moment to how it services the wholeness and unity of the play.

Conversely, in new playwriting the beat is given its due; the direction of the play exists or is discovered from moment to moment. The beat becomes the site of innovation, shifting the direction of the character or play, and by doing so, contradicting the expected or conventional. Means and ends are no longer hierarchal distinctions since juxtaposition supplants linear progression as the prevailing structural scheme. The dynamic meaning of the play occurs at the interface or junction between beats. This strategy is paramount in new playwriting: Naomi Iizuka's shifting theatrical genres in *36 Views*; Eric Overmyer's use of languages that "osmose the future" in *On the Verge*; Len Jenkin's shifting narrative and dramatic voicings in *Margo Veil*;

Jeffrey Jones's juxtaposed "strips of found language" in *Der Inka von Peru*; Peggy Shaw's split-second gender shifts in *Menopausal Gentleman*; Lane's transformative living room in Sarah Ruhl's *The Clean House*. It helps to visualize this effect as if it were a synapse operating within the larger nervous system of the play. By definition, the synapse is a charged impulse interacting between two or more nerve cells. The dialogic move is synaptic, providing an energizing, nervy impulse between beats. The more striking the dynamic shift between beats the more impulses are awakened in the text.

Beats offer the potential for disruption—for immediate shifts in intent, purpose, and narrative. To write the polyvocal play, the playwright must be open to the beat's capacity to shift the language or action. This move against monologism requires the writer to share the authorial function with this "second voice." This expansion of the beat's function concomitantly allots more indeterminacy in writing the play. The playwright actualizes his dialogic relation to the script, pro-acting synaptically (like a synapse) rather than reacting synoptically (with a view of the whole). This notion of energy is similar to the actor's unleashing psychic and physical associations located in the body through exercises or games. The dialogic playwright responds to associational shifts across the text, crafting them to maximum advantage; or allows more input from actors to create unique voicings. Playwrights like Sarah Ruhl (see the opening scene of her play *The Clean House*) and Suzan-Lori Parks (*365 Days/365 Plays*) encourage the actors to come up with their own actions to affect a sense of spontaneity in the text. The playwright, open to the "second" voice, is empowered to break free from dramaturgical orthodoxy and fully release the potential energy of the script. Table 9.1 distinguishes the beat in new playwriting from its use in traditional dramaturgy.

Table 9.1 The shifting beat	
TRADITIONAL BEAT	NEW PLAYWRITING BEAT
Language (word) as part of system	Language (word) as free radical
Language toward coherence	Language discoheres or innovates
Language as meaning	Language as sign or sound
Conventional syntax	Unconventional syntax
Gesture dependent on language	Autonomous gesture
Synoptic: gives view of the whole	Synaptic: partial, immediate
Playwright's control and intention	Actor may shape performance text

At close range, the play is negotiated in the moment. This primary emphasis of the beat as shifter focuses the playwright's intuition and imagination toward language and character explorations as the primary building blocks of play structure. In effect, the shifting beat simulates real life better than realistic or traditional methods. We constantly change roles and levels of speech to fit the given situation. Our lives move at "cyber-speed": we key in a word and we can instantly access places and information across the globe. New playwriting keys in a virtual, parallel world, where the word is the shifter, where language takes on protean characteristics, providing the material means for transition and transformation.

EXERCISE:

The beat shifter

1. The objective is to create reverberations in the script through rapid shifts in direction. To begin: consider the shifting beat in relation to language; then, explore possibilities with character, or theme. Trigger the shifts with resonant words and reactions to established "givens" in the play. Givens can include physical surroundings, physical props, mood states, time of the day or night, and so on.

2. Shift the vocal level from high-toned to lowbrow; or move from a plaintive state to a wildly exuberant condition (see Santouche in Mac Wellman's *Harm's Way*).

3. Use a mundane topic to trigger a furious interaction. Then shift to a topic of huge import or consequence (see Young Jean Lee's *The Appeal*).

4. A peace-loving character rapidly shifts in a beat of radical violence. Locate a trigger word or phrase to set it off.

5. A seemingly innocuous "given" element in the play triggers a character's impulsive action.

6. A character's "front" of propriety is momentarily suspended with a subversive intent: The supposedly upstanding Reverend D and the Doctor in Parks's *In the Blood* suddenly shift "noble" intentions toward the welfare-mother, Hester, to exploitative sex.

7. The beat as interrupter: give one character the action "to interrupt" the established flow in the scene. Find a word that serves as the interrupter.

COMMENT: An apt analog to the beat shifter is a synapse in the brain that hurls us into another train of thought, fires an emotion, or changes sense perception in some way. You want to create a perceptual shift for both the character and the audience.

Interruption is a fundamental beat-shifting strategy. By interrupting a series or progression of beats, the playwright forces the audience out of its comfort zone to "work" at the play, actually increasing rather than decreasing its involvement. Interruption is akin to the formalist device of "impeded form." In creating his alienation effect, Brecht used the device to redirect audiences from emotional to intellectual involvement. Breaks in continuity compel the audience to "see anew." The beat of interruption energizes the play, as it shifts focus and direction in the script. (Interruption is discussed at length in Chapter 5, particularly as it concerns the equivocal character.)

With our attention on language playwriting, it may be helpful to describe the shifting beat in the terms of linguist Ferdinand de Saussure. Saussure used the term *langue* to describe how current conventions and rules in language and culture give them coherence and understanding. Changes in *langue* are gradual; once competence is achieved the individual operates within the system without giving it a second thought. Traditional playwriting is oriented toward *langue*, since it applies familiar conventions (representational, fictional matrixed characters), which are familiar to the majority of audience members (competence). The primary reason mainstream audiences have not fully embraced the new playwriting has to do with their lack of "competence"; quite simply, as the familiar moorings are unloosed or parodied, the audience is made uncomfortable, or is uncertain about how to react. However, the increased prevalence of innovative dramaturgies has created a more tolerant audience, and thus more audience satisfaction with experimentation. Conversely, the dramaturgy of the traditional play (as a system of *langue*) aims for coherence over formal innovation or disruptive experimentation. In this sense, it does not favor the beat as the site of innovation. A good example of the latter is David Lindsay-Abaire's Pulitzer-Prize-winning play *Rabbit Hole*. The play tracks a careful journey through the parents' grieving process after the accidental death of their young son. Every action or reference in the script ties back to this emotional thematic. While an emotionally satisfying and well-crafted play, *Rabbit Hole* stresses coherence (*langue*) over innovation (*parole*).

Saussure used the term *parole* to describe "how" a word means in actual practice—in its endless variety of contexts, intonations, and syntactic arrangements. As such, *parole* suggests the potential for innovation or deviation from the conventionalized system. Playwrights such as Mee, Parks, and Ruhl who welcome actor-created beats in shaping the performance text are acknowledging the value of *parole* in their work. Over time or a long run, these innovations (in fashion, usage of slang, foreignisms, and so on) become assimilated into *langue* as conventional or mainstream parlance. Eventually, slang dates itself and passes out of general parlance. After a generation passes it becomes historicized, and is then useful to designate a particular feeling or mood about a given period. Playwrights can rebottle historicized slang to establish variations on American character types. The new playwriting favors *parole* in its capacity to innovate; for example, Mac Wellman's unique syntactical choices extravagate how language is configured in current American culture. Ruhl invites the maid character Matilde to improvise a joke in Portuguese at the beginning of *The Clean House*. Mee welcomes interpreters of his adaptations to change or alter the script as needed. In this sense, *parole* can be defined as a gesture of openness and innovation.

The following techniques, examples, and exercises are designed to create more immediacy in the construction of beats. For the most part, these are language-based strategies that open you to your "second voice."

RIFFING

Riffing occurs when one character "picks up on" a phrase or line of dialogue, then embellishes it, rephrases it, or emends it. The concept derives from blues or jazz music, in which a short musical phrase is repeated with continual variation or embellishment. Overmyer's use of the effect in *The Heliotrope Bouquet* is mostly lyrical, although it serves the story function of identifying the brothel the women work in, the House of Blue Light. This beat occurs in the middle of Scene 1, labeled "Joplin's Dream":

SPANISH MARY: There's a lacy breeze.

HANNAH: Lacy breeze fluttering.

SPICE: Lacy breeze.

JOY: Spanish moss lacy in the live oak trees.

FELICITY: Fluttering.

JOY: Morning, morning, morning.

FELICITY: Morning in the House of Blue Light.

(Overmyer 1993, The Heliotrope Bouquet, 231)

This beat riff functions lyrically, poetically interpreting everyday phenomena. The first four characters repeat the word "lacy" in various manifestations and probable intonations; the fifth character's "fluttering" refrains the second character's "lacy breeze fluttering." Riffing links the characters through sound and expressive intent, while maintaining a sense of immediacy. The riffing "ladies of the night" simulate the music of Joplin—the variance in phrasing has its corollary in New Orleans jazz or ragtime.

Riffing divulges lyrically what would otherwise be a labored expository scene. In traditional dramaturgy, the women would "volunteer" information about setting, time, and action that the playwright felt necessary for the play to progress. The scene's placement at the beginning of the play would probably ensure that there would be some discussion about the major characters about to be introduced. This riffing approach transcends the cliché, and in doing so proves that expository information can be handled in an aesthetically satisfying manner.

Anne Marie Healey's *Dearest Eugenia Haggis* opens with a riff that allows the exposition to reveal itself in a rhythmical, interactional, and intimate way. The character Pauline (PK) is taking notes as Mister Blind Johnny Knoll (MBJK) recounts:

MBJK: Well, she was beautiful.

PK: (*She writes it down and adds ...*) And she was rich.

MBJK: She was beautiful and she was rich.

PK: She was ... careless. (*She writes it down*)

MBJK: Yes, she was careless.

PK: But she was only careless because she could be.

MBJK: You mean she could be careless with me?

PK: (*writing*) She could be careless with you because she had so many other men to choose from.

MBJK: ... She did. I forgot she had so many other men to choose from.

PK: (*Looking up to speak*) But that's why you're special Mister Blind Johnny Knoll.

MBJK: Remind me again. Why am I special?

PK: You're special because you have experienced. Love.

MBJK: I have experienced. Love.

(Striar and Detrick 2007, 231)

For Healey, riffing is dramaturgically the best choice because it leads to several character revelations that otherwise would be hidden; for example, if the character read from the notebook to start the play. This opens us as well into the heart of the character and the play by providing an intimate moment upon which to build the narrative. Healey is aware as well that repetition in the beginning of a play eases an audience's transition into the world of the play.

Exposition is generally defined as the information needed for the play to progress: especially, what crucial information audiences must know. To be effective dramaturgically, exposition must appear unforced and earned; it should be sprinkled deftly throughout the playtext, and not simply "front-loaded" in the beginning of the play. Experienced playwrights know that expository material works best when delivered under pressure, as the by-product of conflict and complication. Otherwise, the divulging of information will appear gratuitous or contrived. In new playwriting, the two prevalent forms of handling exposition are riffing variations and the point-of-view monologue. Playwrights such as Susan-Lori Parks, David Mamet, Matthew Maguire, Madelyn Kent, and Anne Marie Healey favor the former, whereas Len Jenkin, Sarah Ruhl, and Tony Kushner favor the latter. The point-of-view character usually has an ironic or politicized take on expository material that includes significant commentary. In *The Clean House*, Ruhl introduces her major characters and actions through a succession of "point-of-view" monologues. For younger or more inexperienced playwrights, riffing offers more immediate results readily apparent in the workshop. The

following exercise will get you through some tedious exposition by explor- 151
ing riffing variations.

CHAPTER 9 UNITS AND BUILDING BLOCKS

EXERCISE:
Riffing and exposition

1. Write a two-person scene in which Character A reacts to a word used by Character B that relates to something expositional (consider this in an associational manner, as in the scene in *The Heliotrope Bouquet* where "lacy" ends up at the place indicated). The expositional beat should relate to an offstage character, an event, or place.
2. Have Character B embellish on Character A, varying the phrase by repeating and reforming or transforming the word. The riff can rhyme, or disclose etymological derivations or foreignisms that provide onomatopoeia, and so forth.
3. How does the riff serve as the shifter in the scene?
4. Find an end or stasis point in the exchange. Note how the riff should be doing double duty, accomplishing both expositional and lyrical functions.

COMMENT: Students love this riffing exercise which has the added benefit of demonstrating dialogue as "turns" rather than separate speeches.

WELLMAN'S SOLO RIFFS

In *Whirligig*, Wellman's character Girl engages in lengthy solo rifts:

> GIRL: [a fragment of her speech] Zero the ozone layer. Zero the Museum of Natural History. Zero the pink tennis shoes. Zero the green hair. Zero the heroes, Ollie, Poindexter, rolling uphill, are dead, blast, brightness nothing.
>
> (Wellman 1995, Whirligig, 149)

Wellman configures shifting phenomenon and places rifting off of the trisyllabic ([Zero the] ozone layer. [Zero the] Museum of Natural History, etc.). The repetitive riff provides coherence, grounding the freewheeling conflation of unrelated phrases and terms. The associations ultimately release into Wellman's point of departure, after "Zero the heroes." The repetitive riff accumulates energy in the text, shifting it in another direction.

Butcher's solo riff in Parks's *Fucking A* becomes a hilarious testimony to his daughter Lulu's many "failings." Here is an example from the early part of this lengthy "nouning" monologue:

> BUTCHER: ... claiming to have multiple parents, claiming to have multiple orgasms, claiming to have injuries she didn't have, claiming to have been places she never was ...
>
> (Parks 2001, 180)

This riffing technique is analogous to a typical musical composition by Philip Glass, which builds through subtle variations and accumulations. Glass's music from his collaboration with Robert Wilson, *Einstein on the Beach*, is a good example. Following these examples, the playwright can repeat a rhythmical phrase or motif and then allow associations to come forth. Moreover, the repetitions produce a mantra-like effect that mitigates the intrusion of the self-censor, freeing the playwright to explore dynamic shifts and juxtapositions.

TURNS AND THE SHADOW RIFF

Turns relate dialogue to pairs of speakers. Turns concern the structure and dynamic of dialogue between speakers and responders. Turns are weighted toward power dynamics: a question from a leader to a subordinate demands an immediate response, whereas a question from a subordinate to a leader might be deferred without protocols being violated. Other rules apply. Speakers are expected to take their turn in everyday discourse. For example, a greeting that is ignored or met with silence might be considered insulting, rude, or indicative of an underlying' antagonism between speakers. On the other hand, turns often reflect a mirror-like patterning whereby one speaker mimics, questions, or reiterates the utterance of the other (as in the excerpt from Healey's play, above). This pattern of repetition is called shadow riffing. The shadow riff is a variable type of turn. It may involve the responder "topping" the speaker, or permuting what is said. The shadow riff foregrounds the surfaces of language as it probes the subtle power plays that underlie conversational exchanges. For playwright David Mamet, the shadow riff is a signature stylistic feature that offers flexibility through shifting intonation, context, and pace. The following example from *Speed The Plow*, recently revived on Broadway, is indicative of what critics like to call Mamet-speak:

> FOX: I just thought, I just thought she falls between two stools.
>
> GOULD: And what would those stools be?
>
> FOX: That she is not, just some, you know, a "floozy."
>
> GOULD: A "floozy" …
>
> FOX: … On the other hand, I think I'd have to say, I don't think she is so ambitious she would have to schtup you just to get ahead.
>
> (*Pause*)
>
> That's all.
>
> (*Pause*)
>
> GOULD: What if she just "liked" me? (*Pause*)
>
> FOX: If she just "liked" you?
>
> GOULD: Yes.

FOX: Ummm. (*pause*)

GOULD: Yes.

FOX: You're saying, if she just … liked you … (*Pause*)

GOULD: You mean nobody loves me for myself?

FOX: No.

GOULD: No?

FOX: Not in this office …

(Mamet 1985, I: 35–6)

Gould shadows Fox's statement regarding "stools" with the question, "And just what would those stools be?" The statement shadowed by the question is a trademark of Mamet's dialogue style. The phoneme intoned (oo) in stools riffs into the alliterative "floozy," an anachronistic descriptor. As an anachronism, the word is foregrounded while both men take pleasure in the sound play. Then, in a turn reversal, Fox shadows Gould's limpid, "What if she just 'liked' me?" with his sarcastic take, "If she just 'liked' you?" Here, intonation provides contextual and rhythmical variety through the shadowed "liked," in quotes, preceded by affirmations and followed by negations. The riff pays off with Fox's punch line, "not in this office"—the follow-up to Gould's setup, "You mean nobody loves me for myself?" Mamet's shadow riffing reflects the gaming nature of language in *Speed the Plow*. Rather than character-specific dialogue, Mamet orchestrates the sequence to suggest subtle moment-to-moment advantage between the characters. The power dynamics disguise the underlying formalism of the shadow riff and the necessity of careful crafting to maximize its effect.

EXERCISE:
The shadow riff

The shadow riff exercise is particularly helpful to young playwrights who generally have difficulty keeping their dialogue "in the moment." The stratagem simulates the "mirror game" that actors play as one speaker provides the language for another actor to copy, mimic, and extrapolate upon. The playwright should maintain the surface level of language, while exploring the subtleties of power relationships. One character must strive to gain some advantage over the other or the riffing will sound mannered and strained.

The shadow riff exercises should be read in the workshop in order to heighten the variables of intonation and rhythm.

1. Characters A and B discuss a third offstage Character C.
2. Establish a key word or phrase uttered by Character A.
3. Character B shadows the phrase of A in the form of a question.
4. Character A answers by restressing the phrase, after several turns of spacers (umm, uhh, ahh) or affirmations; negations reinforce the shadowing.

5. Character B mimics, embellishes, or "reframes" the shadow.

6. A conclusion is arrived at regarding Character C.

VARIATION: Alter the above sequence by riffing on expository material rather than conflict or action material.

COMMENT: The shadow riff will go where it wants to go, and is not predetermined by the playwright. Allow the characters to enjoy and engage the moment without overt interference or "forcing it." An overly controlled shadow riff will sound stilted and calculated, rather than light and quick-witted. Nevertheless, the shadow riff remains an optimum exercise for instilling the practice of dialogue as turns between a pair of speakers. Use this exercise to wean playwrights from the common fault of having characters make speeches rather than listen and respond to each other.

BEAT ROLLOVER

New playwriting offers the director and actor various choices in determining what beats should be pointed or emphasized. At times, it may be warranted to roll over beats rather than playing every beat for its transitional or transformational potential. Playwrights should be particularly attentive in listening to their work to gauge when beats are being overplayed or calculated. Beat rollover occurs when you play through a beat to attain a larger effect or impact. An analogy from music is the soloist who, instead of "marking" the end of the eight or sixteen-bar measure, plays through the transition toward a more impactful end.

DICTIONARY STOP

The introduction of external language sources to redirect the course of the play is characteristic of the new playwriting. In Dictionary Stop, an exercise devised by Mac Wellman, a word is selected at random out of the dictionary and inserted into the text. The character or characters riff on the word as it ineluctably shifts the scene in another direction. Wellman vaunts the effectiveness of the technique in his own plays, particularly as a means to mitigate writer's block. He draws the corollary with physics: the inserted word is the free radical that creates a fission-like reaction within the text, releasing the stored energy in the script. In his one-person play, *Bitter Bierce*, Wellman interpolates "word: definitions" from Ambrose Bierce's sardonic *Devil's Dictionary* to structure the thematic transitions in the play. The group exercise below works very well in the workshop to raise energy levels and camaraderie.

Dictionary Stop

(Read Wellman's *Bitter Bierce*.)

Exercise A: Solo

The purpose of this exercise is to unlock writer's block by freeing the playwright of the responsibility to produce language. This dialogic engagement embraces the "other" and reorients the putative notion of "ownership" in the playscript.

1. You have come to a temporary impasse in writing dialogue. Go the dictionary and randomly select a word (however obscure). Insert the word into the character's dialogue at the point of impasse.

2. The dictionary stop becomes a free radical pivot beat. Have this character and others riff off of the word, allowing it to lead or channel the scene in a different direction.

COMMENT: This exercise always yields unexpected results. As the dropped-in word piques the curiosity of the playwright, the imagination is awakened with new possibilities. The playwright relaxes, allowing this "second voice" to motivate the direction of the script.

VARIATION: The three-word play. Before the workshop, write a bunch of proper names and nouns each on a chit of paper and throw them into a bowl. Have each participant draw three words and write a short play that incorporates the three words.

Exercise B: In the group

Use this exercise in the playwrights' workshop with up to eight to twelve participants. The entire exercise is conducted in the workshop or classroom.

1. Begin writing a two-character scene with a simple premise, such as: one character attempts to get the other character to leave (a room, a house, a car, whatever).

2. Make a list of terms or bring in the dictionary, and at two or three-minute intervals stop, and then drop the word in a line of dialogue.

3. Pass the scripts from left to right. Give from thirty seconds to one minute for the next playwright to read the text, and then continue the process of writing and passing the text, stopping at regular intervals to drop in another word.

4. When you reach your time limit (ten to fourteen minutes), direct the final playwright in the sequence to finish the scene with the instigating character accomplishing or failing the objective.

COMMENT: This exercise builds camaraderie and trust in the workshop. It also takes "ego" out of the mix and involves multiple, often indiscernible voices in the text. Do not overly emphasize the narrative thread; the playwrights should focus on how the inserted word motivates the script.

Many beginning playwrights have difficulty making dialogue sound immediate or in the moment. Typically faulty dialogue is overly expository, has
too many ideas per speech, or expends excessive time describing offstage
events and characters. As a result, scene work lacks presence and verve. The
most effective way to immediately correct this problem is to employ speech
act beats. A *speech act* is a word, phrase, or sentence that suggests immediate
or deferred action. It is dialogic because it requires the "other" to respond;
moreover, the speech act inherently conflates word and circumstance.
Prolific playwright Richard Nelson, whose dinner party cum political party
play, *That Hopey Changey Thing*, recently played at the Public Theater in
November 2010 during election season, considers the speech act the *sine
qua non* of writing for the theater:

> There's this wonderful English philosopher, J. L. Austin, who conceived
> what he called the "speech act." He was asking, "When does speech
> become an action?" For example, if I'm in a marriage ceremony and say,
> "I do," I become married. That involves an action, an action beyond the
> act of speaking. Theater is one giant "speech act." That's its very nature.
>
> (Nelson 2000, 25–6)

The speech act takes a number of forms. Here are some examples:

- **The threat.** When Character A threatens Character B, apprehen-
  sion and suspense are created. The tension is immediate and
  sustainable because the speech act defers to the moment that the
  threat will or will not be realized.

- **The promise.** When a character makes a promise, they set up anticipation. If the promise is not delivered we learn something about
  the makeup of the character. If the promise is delivered we have a
  plot point.

- **The command.** The power move demands an immediate response.
  Those characters receiving the command are compelled to react.
  This reaction determines the relationship of the characters at the
  moment of utterance. What is the power dynamic in the play? How
  will the commanded respond? What is the potential for reversal?

- **The vow.** A vow establishes a bond of trust between characters, or
  between character and audience. It calls to question the credibility
  of the character making the vow.

- **The strategy.** Planning an action keeps the play in the moment.
  Characters must role-play as leaders, followers, instigators, and
  soon. The relationship between the plan and the outcome establishes a dynamic tension. The sequential nature of a strategic plan
  provides ready-made plot points.

- **The dig.** Contains an array of put-downs, character assassinations, or insults from Character A that forces a response from Character B.

Most speech acts are considered truth statements until broken. Unless a playwright establishes the character as untrustworthy, the audience will accept characters at face value. Playwrights can manipulate this "tacit bond" to create interest and surprise. On another level, there is a "force" potential to the speech act—how it is said, and with what intonation, and in what context, are crucial to its effectiveness (Petrey 1990, 15). This makes it a crucial tool in shaping strong dialogue and characterization.

A speech act demands a performative response. It is neither ideation nor idle chat, but must involve behavior. When reactions are conflicted, the speech act beat accelerates the rhythm of a scene. So, if you want to accelerate the audience's heart rate, use the speech act to launch your attack. If Character A says, "Get up!" then we will anxiously await Character B's response, which plays out in the form of an action: to comply, to resist, to defer, to ignore; and in a certain manner: rashly, sluggishly, or distractedly. Speech acts are playable for actors since they externalize intention. Harold Pinter was a master of the speech act, using it to threat, intimidate, accuse, and browbeat, thereby creating a sense of menace in the plot and characters. His early works like *The Homecoming* and *The Birthday Party* are indicative of this usage of language as weapon.

EXERCISE:
Speech acts

To curtail the impulse of young playwrights to describe past events, telegraph internal states, or simply front load expositional material, undertake a scene that utilizes various speech acts. To avoid diluting the force of the speech acts, require that the playwright limit individual speeches to one sentence or phrase.

1. Initiate a brief two-character sequence (made up of three to four beats). Character A utters a speech act that compels Character B to respond. Examples include threats, promises, agreements, vows, denials, commands, directives, and orders.

2. While responses may be immediate (to commands, orders, and so on), other speech acts anticipate later results (promises, wows; or threats). Character B thus has a number of options in responding.

3. At the end of the sequence determine the "truth quality" of the speech act. In other words, was it a bluff, a lie, a subterfuge?

4. How does this "truth quality" inform us about the character?

5. What were the varying degrees of force for each speech act? What was done with the dialogue to create shifts in intonation?

COMMENT: The speech act exercise is a game-changer for young playwrights, and should be brought into the workshop fairly early, since it forces immediacy and the ability to limit dialogue to one idea per line. Playwrights often cite it as one of the most important exercises in their development.

Although we have considered language beats primarily, a beat may also be a gesture. The influential Marxist critic Walter Benjamin said that Bertolt Brecht's plays offered the actor the potential for the quotable gesture, one that could recast an earlier moment in a different light. The quoted gesture interrupts the present context (Benjamin 1977, 7), causing the script to be self-reflexive as it reveals the underlying form of the dramaturgy. The gesture may be repeated or "shadowed" from another character, and thus is related to the beat variations we have referred to above. In productions of Mac Wellman's, Young Jean Lee's, Erik Ehn's and Suzan-Lori Parks's plays, performers can formulate extreme gestures, particularly to clarify or amplify sections of monologue or in spacer beats, during extended pauses and silences. Young Jean Lee's *The Shipment* "quotes" the familiar gestures from a popular video game to "frame" a gangsta moment: "His arms and shoulders resemble the movements the characters in the video game Grand Theft Auto make when they are in their holding pattern" (Lee 2010). For Erik Ehn, gesture provides a frame for the segment of text, as it reinforces the dialogic relation between text and physical action, two autonomous systems that converge and mediate with each other. The following example from *Thistle (Rose of Lima)* in his collection *The Saint Plays*, is indicative as the character Rufina is joined by three performers:

> RUFINA: I was, then lay face down
> (*They stand back up*)
>
> I was in—
> (*Two: they drop as if thrown down, they stand back up.*)
>
> I was—
> (*Three: they lie down slowly, as if shot through the back and falling through water.*)
>
> (Ehn 2000, 48)

This level of gestural specificity creates the primary *mise-en-scène*, or element of spectacle in the play. Where no specific physicalization is indicated by the playwright, gesture can provide intention to beats of nouning or syntactical phrases that would otherwise defy categorization. As gesture marks the text with intention, it provides a performative structure that stands side by side with the text: Actor Stephen Mellor has been the most adept at bringing a gestural intention to the language beats in Mac Wellman's plays. The effect bundles spectacle with language. As Mellor scans the play text, he determines an external gestural form to link passages in the text.

Peggy Shaw uses highly exaggerated gestures to accent transitions in her work. The acting approach conflates the heightened spirit of an Eastern model such as Kabuki with Western *Grand Guignol* or *film noir* stylization. These genres feature exaggerated physical gestures and facial expressions executed with style and formal precision, and recall the style of Andre Serban's early breakthrough adaptations (such as *The Trojan Women*), which was entirely gestural and aural. Ehn's predominant gestus seems derived from Brecht or the 1960s psycho-physical experiments of Grotowski. Mellor uses makeup to exaggerate or shadow features of his natural visage, emphasizing a strange, macabre quality that seems the perfect complement to Wellman's verbal assaults. Young Jean Lee draws upon iconic movements from the Sesame Street character Big Bird in her wildly imaginative adaptation, *Lear* (Lee 2010, 89). Shaw "inhabits" a male suit to clash with her own female menopause. This "masking" promotes a broader, gestural interpretation of the text, just as the male Kabuki performers typified certain female gesticulations to arrive at a performative (not sexual) basis for gender.

A gestured beat can quote itself to create a structural link or unifying device. For example, a gesture that is repeated several times within an act will serve as a linking device across the act.

TAG LINES

In effect a *tag line* is a "quotation"—the character is quoting himself. Since the content of the beat, or in this case tag line, is shifting through the course of the play, the beat is dialogic. In the same way, a "running gag" will provide a *topos* of unity in a comedy, and it will adjust to the given circumstances to build a laugh. Odd syntax, slang, or maxims can serve as interactive links, serving the larger purpose of defining a character. Wellman's recent one-person play *Bitter Bierce* offers an excellent example of the tag as linking device, as the eponymous character makes intermittent 'stop' quotes from his *Devil's Dictionary* across the entire script. Here, two quotes bookend or frame Bierce's marriage to Mary Day:

> "Love, noun.
>
> A temporary insanity curable by marriage."
>
> (Then, after a brief narrative description of the wedding).
>
> "Bride, a noun.
>
> A woman with a fine prospect of happiness behind her."
>
> (Wellman 2008, 192–3)

These rhetorical interpolations serve to cohere the script as structural pivot points, reframing the narrative, and then catapulting us forward to another anecdote in the life of Bierce. Concomitantly, Bierce becomes associated with a rhetorical phrase or style laced with sarcasm and wit. It is really in revision that quotable beats are first discovered or interpolated, then honed and reshaped, to maximize their effect across the text. In revision, examine your script at ultra close range: explore the beats; then exploit their dialogic potential. When revision is perceived as an extension of the creative process, rather than an entirely left-brained, analytical procedure, the playwright opens up to the artistic opportunities their script presents. A seasoned new play dramaturg may be able to help facilitate this process for the inexperienced playwright.

BEAT SHIFTERS AND GROOVE: FROM PAUSES TO PUNCTUATION INDICATORS

SPACER BEATS AND THE ABSENCE OF SPEECH: PAUSES, RESTS, SILENCES AND SPELLS

The function of pauses or ellipses is often misunderstood by beginning writers, who overuse them in an attempt to seem profound or mysterious. Aping the "Pinter pause" will bring detrimental results. In Pinter's dramaturgical scheme, pauses shift power dynamics, submerge truth under the spoken lie, or further a sense of menace and terror. As in real life, the lack of a verbal response may be construed as an insult, or may at least frustrate an antagonist. These reactions are imploded by the pause. Each pause has a definite, calculated, and often subtextual reason for being there. Conversely, beginning playwrights use pauses indiscriminately or gratuitously, and rarely with a sense of strategy or dramaturgic purpose. Pinter's complex dramaturgy involves a system of dialogue breaks of varying duration: the brief ellipsis, the one- or two-beat pause, and the protracted silence. The multiple beats of the silence represent a plunge into the abyss, and theatrically may exact a period of total stasis.

A prevailing trend in Suzan-Lori Parks's plays is to simply use character titles without any dialogue, what she describes as "a spell." (She uses the term "rest" to describe a more normative pause.) These spells can be set up in units to create varying degrees of "actor space" in her script. When the spell involves both characters, their character titles appear sequentially *sans* dialogue. Sometimes, only one character will "spell —the number of dialogue-less character titles indicates the length of the spell. The effect is related to music where the soloists lay out and let the "groove" happen. Parks wants the actors to find their own groove in performing works like *Topdog/Underdog* or *365 Days/365 Plays*. In *Topdog/Underdog* the unspoken exchanges between Lincoln and Booth settle us into the deeper time and history that these brothers have shared.

Playwrights should be wary of the interpretive latitude that pauses and silences afford the director. The pause is a gift to the actor, offering, in the moment, a sense of the improvisational, particularly in terms of gesture, movement, or stage business. For the director, they offer an opportunity to tap into the groove or soul of the play.

The playwright utilizes pauses the way the composer incorporates the rest—for rhythmical syncopation or alteration, to set up a payoff, to explore the characters' gestural histories, or to interrupt and refocus. However, there are differences to be noted as well. For example, a pause in drama often reflects an awkwardness, or inability to verbalize, whereas the same cannot be said of music. Moreover, in the theater it is impossible to be as precise in assessing duration, since composers provide a definite metrical rate that is more or less constant. Nevertheless, both the pause and the rest affect timing and pacing, and are therefore reliant on feel. The pause provides a spacer not only for actor and director, but for audience as well. By interrupting the flow of dialogue the pause draws attention to what has been said. The pause allots the audience a moment to reflect, to anticipate, to discover, to laugh, or to renew interest. Pauses must be paced judiciously or the results will be static, awkward, and overly stylized (not appropriate for a realistic or naturalistic approach, but potential fodder for an anti-naturalistic play). Auteur-director Richard Foreman in the production of his play *The Cure* used stylized pauses and rapid shifts in pace as a means to juxtapose various sequences in the play.

Mac Wellman's pauses frequently indicate a gestural response, a chance for the body to rearrange itself. When used in succession, the pauses allow a director to orchestrate a series of movements, whereby each beat can be specifically focused in rehearsal. Wellman also uses pauses to set up tag lines, buttons, or punch lines in longer speeches. This short segment from *7 Blowjobs* indicates how the pause opens up space for the actor, as it establishes, or refocuses the action:

EILEEN: BAG IT DOT!
Pause.

SENATOR: Cool down, Eileen.
Pause.

      And get him out of here.
BRUCE comes to.

(Wellman 1994, *7 Blowjobs*, 232)

Eileen's command, "BAG IT DOT!" freezes the moment. The pause acknowledges the shift in energy, and the senator's response, "Cool down, Eileen," addresses the momentary vacuum. Because the pause creates a vacuum, it serves as an attractor. Wanting to be filled, a shift in the rhythm or dynamic of the segment now occurs. In the first pause, the senator takes control of the scene. In this sense, the pause can be an important dramaturgic factor in establishing power dynamics in a scene or act. The pause puts matters "up for grabs." The second pause places the senator in charge, as he shifts focus from Eileen to Bruce on the floor. Physical options are made available to the actor during this pause.

Suzan-Lori Parks's use of "spells" lends what she describes as an architectural look to silence. Indeed, its effect is dialogic, as it creates a distinctive marker for a beat transition. The following passage from the twenty-seventh play, *Hole*, in *365 Days/365 Plays* is indicative:

WOMAN: Yr digging.

MAN: Yeah?

WOMAN: Yeah.

MAN: Suit yrself it's a free country.

WOMAN: Is it?

MAN

WOMAN

MAN: Yr one of those agitators, arentcha?

(Parks 2006, 28)

The silent, albeit dialogic, exchange during this spell indicates a summing up, or discovery by Man, and therefore a transition in the action of the scene. It simulates the illuminated lightbulb in old cartoons—Man sees the light. This is a normative usage of the spell: as a transition in thought, the beat of recognition. The spell provides a moment in which we are invited to closely observe her characters, and by so doing, experience their essence.

PUNCTUATION MARKERS: JENKIN AND THE DIALOGIC ELLIPSIS

Jenkin frequently employs ellipses to achieve structural goals such as linking speakers or scenes. At the end of Scene 2 in *Dark Ride*, the Translator, whose translation establishes the action of the play, reads a passage from his work:

> TRANSLATOR: [*At the end of his speech*] I quote. "Margo lies back on the couch in her apartment, and opens a book. She turns the pages slowly until she finds her place. Her lips move slightly with the words she reads, like a child ...."
>
> (Jenkin 1993, *Dark Ride*, 65)

The ellipsis provides the transition into scene 3. Here, Margo takes over, as the scene shifts locale:

> MARGO: Chapter Nine. At the Clinic. [*Her speech continues*]
>
> (Jenkin 1993, *Dark Ride*, 66)

The beat of the ellipsis serves the structural function of shifting the theatrical environment. It is dialogic because it bridges the "present" world of the Translator with some distant past literary world that he has translated. Jenkin's ellipsis is a connector—a dialogic conduit between the two ontological levels. This use of the ellipsis represents a dramaturgic innovation.

THE ELLIPSIS AS INTERRUPTER

While the ellipsis may function as a connector, it may bring about a beat of disruption or interruption. In Part 3 of *Limbo Tales*, "The Hotel," Jenkin sets up two audio speakers, stage right and left. These two sound areas represent the adjoining rooms to the center chamber occupied by the character, named Man. As speakers they simulate typical noises from the adjoining room, thus interrupting the narrative of Man:

> MAN: [*At the end of his speech*] I was sending money home all the time, so Eileen must have liked the other guy a lot, cause the money must have made her feel bad ...
>
> SPEAKER C: [Humming of a little song, coughing, very soft, ...continuing and fading ...]
>
> MAN: ... She should have, too, cause all I thought of on the road was her and the kid.
>
> (Jenkin 1993, Limbo Tales, 42)

Jenkin uses the ellipsis to show the points where Man's train of thought is interrupted—then renewed. The in-and-out-of-focus aspect of the Speaker C intrusion serves several functions: creation of tension and anticipation; reorientation of the audience's attention; rhythmical interpolation; and theatrical use of sound and space. The disruption ultimately draws attention back to Man's reaction.

Wellman's use of the ellipsis is often contingent to the pause, as the opening of Whirligig indicates:

> GIRL: I dreamed I had a wicked sister ...
>
> *Pause*
>
> She was a girl Hun.
>
> (Wellman 1995, Whirligig, 143)

In this example, the opening line, "I dreamed I had a wicked sister," establishes the premise and narrative thrust for the entire play, while the ellipsis is the continuant, open-ended frame for the story. The pause represents the transition into the body of the play.

CONVENTIONAL USES OF THE ELLIPSIS

Playwrights have used ellipses to simulate telephone conversations, the "..." that is the convention for the voice of the other. Another traditional use is to simulate doubt, vacillation, and quick shifts in thought, where the ellipsis defines the transitory mind. The ellipsis is thus a playwright's tool for dealing with a character's inner dialogism. When taken to extremes, the ellipsis presents the opportunity for the multivoiced character to emerge: witness Hungry Mother's levels of language in Overmyer's *Native Speech*.

EXERCISE:
Ellipses

1. With the excerpt in Chapter 12, page 213 from *Dark Ride* as an example, use the ellipsis to segue from a character's closing line of dialogue to a subsequent line of action that is begun by another character. Envision the ellipsis as if it were a relay-race baton: Character A hands off a phrase or sentence to Character B, who channels the play in a different direction.

2. With the above excerpt from *Limbo Tales* as an example, utilize ellipses to frame an intruding character that interrupts Character A. After the interruption, allow Character A to continue his speech.

COMMENT: What are the effects of these two exercises on your sense of playwriting structure? Do they open up certain possibilities? Sequence and points of transition ultimately define structure. Structure is about the interrelationship of parts. Therefore, carefully introduce the use of ellipses in the workshop as a means to integrate monologue and dialogue sections, effectively.

THE ASTERISK AND THE SLASH

Wellman's signature punctuation mark is the asterisk (*). Anyone who reads his plays is initially baffled. Wellman explains, in the notes to *Whirligig*:

> The occasional appearance of an asterisk in the middle of a speech indicates that the next speech begins to overlap at that point. A double asterisk indicates that a later speech (not the one immediately following) begins to overlap at that point. The overlapping speeches are all clearly marked in the text.
>
> (Wellman 1995, *Whirligig*, 142)

This section could be included in the chapter on monologue, although it is clear that the overlapping creates a kind of dialogic dissonance, a more aural than semantic phenomenon. Its use is similar to Caryl Churchill's application in *Serious Money*, in which the forward slash (/) indicates the point in a character's dialogue that is overlapped by the subsequent character's speech. Overlapping or dovetailing dialogue is a regular phenomenon of general discourse. The collision of speeches on stage can be a highly effective means to build pressure in a scene, realizing the payoff as a relief in the pent-up tension.

EXERCISE:
Collision of speech

1. Transcribe a taped conversation between two persons. The persons should not be aware of the taping which should last five or six minutes. Note in the transcription points where voices overlap before the first speech is concluded. Other aspects to consider:

- the use of pauses
- paralinguistic spacers like well, hmmm, and uhh
- how beat shifts and changes in topic correlate.

COMMENT: This transcription exercise demonstrates how speakers interact with no expository material, limit speeches to short phrases, overlap and interrupt each other. It is a very effective exercise if used early in the workshop process, since students at this stage will be constructing dialogue without regard to how people actually converse.

EXERCISE:
The asterisk and the slash

1. Revise some turns (dialogue pairs) in a script by inserting the slash at key or intentional words.
2. Use the asterisk in several long speeches or monologues that are sequential; note the effect of density in the text.

COMMENT: See how these techniques can alter the rhythm and tension of the scene, then establish where the release point is. This will create a marker in the script, and a "moment" for one or more of the actors.

We can now turn our attention to the larger building blocks of the script, the most significant of which is the beat segment.

CREATING THE LARGER STRUCTURE: THE BEAT SEGMENT

The building of several beats around a given action or topic constitutes a *beat segment.* It would be nearly impossible to form a play that was based solely on isolated beats. Perhaps the futurists could be considered, since their plays (really fragmentary sketches) lasted seconds in real time. The sequential quality of the play script mandates certain organizing factors. The beat segment groups beats together, providing a grounding from which the playwright can establish larger units within the play. The beat segment can vary in length from several beats to a dozen or more; thus, it is a significant structural component in the development and later revision of the playscript. Sometimes the beat segment is the same as a French scene, defined by a character's entrance or exit. (While the term *French scene* is useful to pinpoint entrances and exits, under this system of nomenclature, the French scene is more akin to the beat segment.) The following beat segment from Jenkin's *My Uncle Sam* is typical of the latter approach:

[*The MANAGER is gone, The LITTLE PERSON in the dirty yellow vest appears; The PERSON is carrying a box with holes in the top.*]

LITTLE PERSON: Got a butt?

YOUNG SAM: It's you again. Who are you?

LITTLE PERSON: I'm nobody. Who are you?

YOUNG SAM: My Uncle Sam, Hey ...

LITTLE PERSON: Just kidding ... I'm in show business. Show's in here.

[*Holds up box.*]

Rats. I run a rat theater. But the show's not in A-1 shape. Yesterday, we were doing a matinee of Romeo and Juliet when a dog broke into the show tent and ate the cast. These are only the understudies.

YOUNG SAM: You been following me.

LITTLE PERSON: Or vice-versa. I'll put my cards on the table. In fact, I'll put my cards on the floor. You got troubles ahead. Go to the church of St. Christopher. Watch out for Lila.

YOUNG SAM: Lila?

LITTLE PERSON: Then go to the Blowhole Theater. Gotta run there's the travel agent.

YOUNG SAM: Hey—wait ...

[*The TRAVEL AGENT appears with his female ASSISTANT as the LITTLE PERSON runs off.*]

(Jenkin 1993, *My Uncle Sam*, 184–5)

How is the above a typical beat segment? It is marked by the entrance and exit of Little Person, and several internal beats: the introductory "Got a butt?" and the questions of identity, and then the rat theater show, with the preposterous rejoinder that the rats are indeed understudies. The rat theater is foregrounded in the beat segment. After that we return to essentially narrative information—"You've been following me"—to specific directions that take the form of speech acts. These speech acts are most effective tools of dialogue since they not only suggest a present action, but anticipate the future: "Watch out for Lila," which can be construed as a warning, or threat; "go to the Blowhole Theater" is a performative command or direction that anticipates Young Sam's actually going to the theater. Little Person's quick exit ends the beat segment with a build-up of suspense and interest. The structure of this beat segment contains a clearly marked beginning, middle, and end.

The beat segment can also establish a rhythmic or gestural thrust and parry. In *The Bad Infinity* Wellman utilizes labels and pauses that establish an interesting form of dialogism, a kind of call and response. Near the end of the play, as Sam prepares to leave the Chef and the forest, there is the following exchange:

CHEF: What will you find? Will you find
love in the city? Bah!

Love is for children. For idiots.
A beautiful woman is a false
beautiful woman.

SAM: But she is still a beautiful woman.

CHEF: True.

SAM: I'm going now.

CHEF: Clown!

Pause.

Compromisist!

Pause.

Tool of the bourgeoisie!

Pause.

Fascist!

Pause.

Pessimist!

Pause.

Gourmand!

SAM: I've got to get out of this place.

He exits.

(Wellman 1995, *The Bad Infinity*, 100–1)

The Chef's scurrilous labels attempt to demean or villainize Sam. Wellman sets up a gestural parry in each pause, although it can only be inferred that some response from Sam is indicated. Each label and pause represent a beat in this segment that can be isolated from other beats and staged accordingly. Sam's exit concludes the segment, so the beat segment in this case is tantamount to a French scene.

EXERCISE:
Beat segment overview

Examine some of your recent scene work in different plays. If you have not reached the stage where you have a body of work, then review several scenes. Begin by defining the beat segments with adhesive notes or flags in a hard copy, or use track changes in Microsoft Word, or the edit feature if you are working with an online script program. With either approach, you should be able to establish a clear reference point from which to begin. Len Jenkin favors this method of revision by segment.

1. How many beat segments are there per scene? How much variance in the number of beat segments per given scene? For example, does one scene contain twelve segments, another scene one or two?

2. How many beats are there per segment?

3. How does each segment affect the progress of the scene?

   a. Number each segment or give it a letter designation.

   b. Note which segments are keys to the scene and which segments float or bloat.

   c. How are segments juxtaposed? Are transitions smooth or arbitrary?

4. Alter the sequence of segments: cut and paste .

   a. Which segments seem superfluous, no longer serve the play?

   b. What are the "synapses" between segments?

   c. In an early draft, the playwright will often construct transitional segments for her benefit-as a means of getting to beat segment 3 from 1. Once the scene is written, however, 2 may become superfluous, and the jump from 1 to 3 may energize the script.

   d. Consider how the juxtapositions of segments might work after revision.

5. How does each beat affect the progress of the segment?

   a. Which beat gives the segment some punch or pull?

   b. Which beats seem to wobble, wander aimlessly, or feel (to you) awkward or uncomfortable? Why?

   c. Highlight where you really detect a synapse between beats.

COMMENT: Ask members of the workshop to reflect on the typical pattern of their beat segments. Most often they will discover that there is a lack of variety in the length of segments. By addressing this often overlooked component, the playwright will be able to create more rhythmical interest in developing scenes.

As a rule, the more variance from segment to segment, the more interest will be created in the script. Len Jenkin's *Margo Veil* is a recent example of how beat segment variance can be effective. Sarah Ruhl's plays (*The Clean House* and *Dead Man's Cell Phone*) rely upon beat segment interpolations to create the sense of structure. Lisa D'Amour's *16 Spells to Charm the Beast* juxtaposes the somewhat realistic scenes with Lillian and her daughter, with those of the fairy-tale like Beast; as the script progresses the beat segments converge with Lillian and Beast's increased interactions. Emphatically, the proximity and length of the beat segments becomes the corollary to the action of the play.

Because it interacts dialogically with neighboring segments and across the play, the beat segment is a key structural component. Therefore, in early drafts you should "rough in" the optimal sequence of segments, before

polishing the specific segment. It is useful to determine how the segment is
primarily working within a scene, an act, or across the entire play. Never in
isolation, its variable nature allows the segment to be moved, shortened,
lengthened, or deleted entirely. The beat segment must be mastered for the
playwright to effectively write the polyvocal play. Once these chops are developed, the playwright can orchestrate juxtapositions, interpolations, conflations, and transitions with more confidence and facility. Further, an
examination of how you construct beat segments will deepen your understanding of your predilections as a playwright. This self-awareness will prevent
you from falling into familiar traps that now stymie your development. Now
let us turn our attention to some major components of the beat segment.

CONTOUR

Each beat segment suggests a certain definable shape, or contour. While
the beat segment is a structural term, contour is primarily a stylistic
consideration since it describes how or in what manner the material is
handled. Jagged, sinuous, flat, rounded, straight ahead, angular, S-shaped,
or elliptical are metaphoric descriptors that are used to describe contour.
The contour for a given playwright may vary somewhat from play to play,
and contours can vary throughout the play. However, there is usually some
benchmark present in most of the playwright's work. Contour throughout
segments of Anton Chekhov's plays could be described as elliptical or
sinuous. Segments of *Three Sisters* and *The Cherry Orchard* seem to flow into
and out of each other without sharp breaks or delineation. A traditionally
structured play like David Lindsay-Abaire's *Rabbit Hole* (2006) pushes
forward with a pattern of detours that alternate between sharp and rounded
contours, as the playwright strengthens or mitigates the grief effect through
displays of raw emotions alternating with dark humor. Conversely, a play
that dehumanizes through brutality, such as Sarah Kane's *Blasted*, contains
sharp, jagged, or blunted contours that accentuate its underlying message.

The above beat segment from *My Uncle Sam* has a jagged contour: information is given or asked for, but conditions remain mysterious; a gratuitous
story is told, then there is a sudden shift: "You been following me." This
jagged contour of the beat segment reflects in microcosm the action of
Young Sam's search, and suggests the overall contour of the play.

Contour can be varied or manipulated by altering the rhythms and tempi
of speeches, or through collisions in style or genre. The playwright who is
adept at contour will influence the breathing of the actor, since contour is
akin to lyrical phrasing in music. Young Jean Lee's *The Shipment* utilizes significant contour shifts across segments of the play: moving from Chris Rock-
like standup, to sequences of black stereotypes, including rappers and
thugs, concluding with naturalistic "sitcomia." *New York Times* critic Charles
Isherwood, quoted in the introduction to the published play, described the
contour well: "cultural images of black America are tweaked, pulled and
twisted like Silly Putty" (Lee 2010, i).

Contour is paramount in determining the effectiveness of monologues, providing clues for the actor and more engagement for the audience. Wellman's (*Bitter Bierce*) and Peggy Shaw's (*Menopausal Gentleman*) monologues demonstrate zigzag contours that propel us forward with hairpin turns and rapid shifts. So while the character's speeches appear longish on the page, in performance they quickly transpire with vertiginous effect. Words are crafted toward specific "shaping" effects. Contour provides a discernible signature of the master playwright. When contour is fully realized as the shaping corollary to content and theme, the play will achieve its groove.

CONTOUR AND THE DESIGNER

To understand contour in your own work, ask a stage, lighting, or costume designer to read and respond to the contour of your play; the feedback is of a different ilk than you will receive from directors, actors, or dramaturgs. Designers are trained to think and speak in terms of line, shape, form, and mass. For production designers, contour will manifest itself in intuitive terms, a feeling about the shape of the text that emerges over several readings. Follow up by asking the designer how the contour of your work would affect a production design.

EXERCISE:
Contour

1. Write several two-character beat segments, using no more than four words per phrase, sentence, or utterance. How would you describe the contour of shape of the segments?
2. Insert a third character into these segments whose utterances run on without punctuation containing many words in a single breath. **Important:** These insertions should not be monologues, but contain between seven and twenty words that can be spoken fluidly.
3. How does this insertion affect the sense of contour across the segments?
4. How can pauses and ellipses affect contour?

COMMENT: As an addendum to this exercise, have workshop participants draw, on a separate piece of paper, shapes, lines, and forms that indicate the contour of the beat segments.

THE MARKER

Each beat segment finishes with a marker placed at or near the end of the segment. The marker can be an exit, an exit line or button, a pause or stage direction that underlines or defines a transition. Markers are signals for the audience that suggest a change in direction or character; an anticipation of forthcoming events; a key name or identifying characteristic. The marker is a signpost for the reader/audience, and as such is a definable structural unit. When Little Person in Jenkin's *Uncle Sam* says, "Watch out for Lila," the audience not only receives future character information, but an anticipation of suspense, danger, or threat. So the speech act—"Watch out for Lila"—combines a character marker with one that is plot related. A skilled playwright like Jenkin is able to provide markers and fascinating beats that digress (the rat theater story) within the same beat segment. Markers are the playwright's pact with the audience. They allow the playwright greater latitude to experiment because they give the audience some clear indicators to follow.

Markers provide directors and actors with focal points as well. For the actor, the marker represents the crucial moment in the character's arc where an important action or discovery is registered and made, or a change in direction is indicated. For the director, the marker provides the opportunity for directorial choice, and production coherence. Without attention to each marker, the production will appear unfocused, as the director will have neglected making choices in the script.

In traditional playwriting, markers could be as easily notated in a scenario or synopsis as they are in the script. If language is the marker, it resists reduction because the marker is embedded in itself. For example, to produce language-based plays effectively, the director and actor must predetermine markers based on shifts in the intention of the language. These shifts in intention are reflected onstage in dynamic changes of rate and intensity involving voice, gesture, and movement.

The comparison in Table 9.2 demonstrates how markers function in traditional versus new playwriting.

Table 9.2 Markers in traditional versus new playwriting

TRADITIONAL PLAYWRITING	NEW PLAYWRITING
Story markers	*Story markers*
advance the story	advance and/or reiterate the story
create exposition and backstory	create divergent stories and narratives
single narrators	multiple narrators
Plot markers	*Plot markers*
advance the plot	advance the plot
provide progression	create interruption and shifts
exposition	break causal schemes
discoveries and reversals	theatrical vs. dramatic
Character markers	*Character markers*
provide vital information	provide vital information
consistent traits and behaviors	provide breaks and shifts within beats
character-specific language	multivocal speech
"organic" character	equivocal character
Language markers	*Language markers*
are metaphors and figures	create structural links
are a means of drama	levels of discourse
seek historical accuracy	are the material of the play
	are devices
	are historicized and dialogized

In traditional, plot-oriented dramaturgy, dialogue represents the link between markers—the means of getting from A to B. This tracking rationale lends more credence to the scenario approach, as it diminishes the importance of language in the play. The result is to diminish the artistic opportunities in writing the play, as the schematic approach collars creativity, emphasizing analysis to the detriment of the creative process. Countering this tendency, language playwrights rescued language by foregrounding interruption, repetition, intonation, and other devices that stressed the importance of language as a component of dramaturgy. Foregrounding, as discussed earlier, has several connotations. It can be manifested as a word, speech, or object taken from the background and thrust into a closer, more immediate range; or as a device, is given special emphasis to make it stand out from surrounding factors or circumstances. The goal of foregrounding is to alter our perception about a word or object by extricating it from a familiar context. In new playwriting, foregrounding devices are themselves markers, just as the V-effect would be considered a marker in the dramaturgy of Bertolt Brecht. As these devices become more dominant in play making, they shape the dramaturgical aesthetic toward formalism.

In Eric Ehn's saint play, *Thistle (Rose of Lima)*, character utterances are continually shaped or reshaped to echo the opening narrative that describes a horrific massacre in El Salvador (Ehn 2000, 39–62). Repetitions, reiterations, and variations provide a sense of form to the script. Fourteen successive scenes reiterate segments of the narrative almost verbatim, yet performed by different characters. Each scene is titled with a "strip of language" from the opening narrative that is announced or projected in Brechtian fashion. Soon after, the uttering of this "strip" during the scene reinforces it as a marker in the script. Ehn's choice of fourteen scenes is iconic, as the slaughter mirrors the number of Stations of the Cross in Catholic liturgy. In essence, Ehn utilizes the Stations of the Cross and the language strips to structure his play into a powerful, sacrificial statement. In each "station" the ensemble enacts a group gesture that requires a series of specifically defined physical moves. The effect is a dialogic frisson between word and gesture. In the final scene of *Thistle*, Ehn has the ensemble "enact a series of gestures, one per each of the fourteen previous scenes." The structural effect is a kind of gestural "tag line" first enacted by one or two performers and later by the ensemble. This creates a doubling or compounding effect that reinforces Ehn's careful structuring of the play. Ultimately, the language and gestural markers establish a structural thread that combines repetition with difference. Ehn bundles dramatic action narrative, and *gestus*, then the play culminates with a hefty theatrical payoff.

While Ehn's links narrative and gestural "tags" to create the entire structure for *Thistle*, the playwright also has the option of utilizing tags and repetition for more compressed effects, or detailing. The old vaudevillian trick of linking by threes occurs early in the first act of Wellman's *7 Blowjobs*:

DOT: Hello. Senator X's office. Hello, nothing of value inside, please,
Please don't steal our stuff …
  Pause.
Yes. No. Maybe.
  She hangs up. Pause. Phone rings.

DOT: Hello. Senator X's office. Hello, nothing of value inside, please,
Please don't steal our stuff …
  Pause.
Yes. No. Maybe.
  She hangs up. Pause. Phone rings.

DOT: Hello. Senator X's office. Hello, nothing of value inside, please,
Please don't steal our stuff …
  Pause.
Yes. No. Maybe.
  She hangs up. Pause. Phone rings. There is a knock at the door.

DOT: Phone. Door. At the same time, wow.

(Wellman 1995, *7 Blowjobs*, 207)

Wellman uses repetition to establish the satirical/farcical nature of the theatrical world, but also to set up the punch line or payoff: "Phone. Door. At the same time, wow." While providing exactly the same lines in each case, Wellman recognizes that intonation, or actor inflection, will alter the meaning in each delivery of the same utterance. The above beat segment is a marker, since it represents a microcosm of the entire piece: to director and actor, the slant to the writing suggests a farcical, exaggerated mode of performance. For all he is due as an imaginative and innovative playwright, Wellman is also a master craftsman playing old school theatrical tricks for a payoff.

DIALOGUE, THE MARKER, AND THE PRINCIPLE OF INTONATION

When a marker is repeated, particularly when an utterance is repeated verbatim, dialogism is present through intonation. Intonation distinguishes dramatic dialogue from other literary forms including novels, essays, and short stories. How a word or phrase is spoken means a great deal in performance. Intonation allows a semantic shift to take place, even though an utterance or phrase appears the same on the page. Ehn calls for this device quite blatantly in *Thistle*.

RUFFINA, GIRL, BROADCASTER: Upon seeing this river of blood, the women began to cry and scream. (*This sentence* [begun as a whisper] *is repeated, volume increasing to no more than a conversational level, as lights fade.*)

(Ehn 2000, 52)

The shift in intonation intensifies the meaning to a strong "curtain." However, it is a calculated build that is ironic, since Ehn only wants his actors to reach a conversational level, not "to cry and scream," as indicated in the dialogue. The effect is to create a dialogic tension between what language does and how it does it. For Ehn, "how language is breathed or sung is more important than what it says. Language wants to be spectacle" (2000, x).

In performance, these ramifications are calibrated by the director and actors' choices. The playwright should not underestimate the strong dramaturgic effect of varying intonation.

In conclusion, the marker carries with it another signal—the playwright's level of craft. Markers are the playwright's clues or imprints; they focus the audience's perception, guiding the spectator through the play. For this to be effective, markers must be deciphered and interpreted by the director and actors, allowing these collaborators to make sense of the play for an audience.

SOUNDING THE SCRIPT

A truism of playwriting posits that dialogue is meant to be spoken, not simply read. While this fundamental precept seems obvious, it gives function and purpose to the staged reading: if we as playwrights were certain how the script sounded, the process would be more direct from page to stage. In new playwriting, the playwright is creating a secondary linguistic system that offers its own set of rules and challenges to the audience. As Ehn shows us, there is also a "breathed or sung" aspect to language that brings in an aspect of spectacle to language. The test upon hearing experimental work comes in understanding what language is doing in the play, and what you as the orchestrator must do to improve it, whether that means eliminating sections of text, adding new beat segments, rewriting segments, leaving it alone, or beginning anew.

10

Scenes, acts, and revisions

SCENES AND POINTS

A scene is made up of one or more beat segments that come to a point. The point could be described as the super marker, revealing something of crucial significance in the scene. The point is the culminating moment of emphasis or action in the scene. It indicates the purpose or function of the scene in the play. Generally, in new playwriting, it is more accurate to describe the play in terms of scenes and points rather than acts and climaxes. Screenwriters use two or more plot points to describe first the inciting incident at the end of the first act and then the major reversal or change of fortune—the climactic point that ends the second act of the three-act screenplay. In new playwriting, however, the point may define aspects of major emphasis unrelated to plot. Rather than the traditional *peripeteia*, the point may be a device of language or form that functions to provide linkage or coherence. In *On the Verge*, Scene 4, "The mysterious interior," Fanny's machete whacking leads to the discovery of an "old-fashioned egg beater," which had not yet been invented by the starting date of the play's action (1888). The women presume it may be a talisman, totem, amulet, or marsupial's unicycle. The point represents Fanny's discovery, which culminates the marker in the first scene that focuses the forward movement of the play toward the discovery of unknown lands. This point in Scene 4 establishes the gulf between objects and language, which not only underscores a specific action but clarifies the thematic direction of the play.

Good dramaturgy dictates that every scene comes to a point—no matter how brief the scene. For example, scene 22 of Len Jenkin's *Dark Ride* consists of two words of dialogue:

22.

(*The Ballroom. Music. All characters except the THIEF appear. COOK emerges from his cage.*)

DEEP SEA ED: Edna!

DEEP SEA EDNA: Ed! (*A stately dance, during which the THIEF arrives, and places the diamond on a pedestal among the dancers. The dancers stop their movement.*)

(Jenkin 1993, *Dark Ride*, 117)

Here, the dialogue is incidental to the major action of the thief placing the diamond on a pedestal among the dancers. As the penultimate scene in the play, the action represents a culmination and merging of several facets in the play's structure. The unifying device, the dance, theatricalizes the convergence of the ensemble. This scene indicates the relation between the point and what theater practitioners describe as a *moment*. Every play and production should have its moments; this moment in the play is clarified by the transition from movement to stasis, and by the fulcrum-like effect of the pedestal among the dancers. This point is both a dramatic and theatrical moment, and becomes one of the primary images of the play.

For example, in Parks's *In the Blood*, Hester's first lover, Chilli, who is the father of her oldest son, Jabber, returns to propose marriage to Hester (a dramatic moment). However, when her other illegitimate children interrupt this romantic moment, Chilli gets cold feet and backs out of the marriage (dramatic point). A hopeful moment turns horrific as Hester, desperate to win Chilli, denies that these children are hers. The culmination of Hester's revenge at this loss is the tragic point when she kills Jabber (dramatic point), who is played by the same actor playing Chilli. This multiple faceting of points compresses to increase the dramaturgical effect (Parks 2001, 95–6, 106).

Points, then, provide clarity and focus to scenes and can be described as markers with greater dramaturgical significance. Points emerge during the act of writing and should not be overly predetermined in a scenario or synopsis, since optimally, there should be a rhythmical build—like an ascending guitar solo. At first roughed-in to the initial draft, points are further clarified during the shaping and refining of the play.

As the play takes its final form it becomes important for themes or theatrical ideas to pay off in a point. Otherwise, the conceptualization will be unclear. In revision, pointless elements can be reshaped or cut. Falling short, the playwright will be accused of "playing fast and loose" with themes and theatrical ideas. Ultimately, points are a barometer of what the play is about; the playwright thus needs to follow through and be selective.

SCENE SEQUENCE AND STYLE

A scene establishes references to a specific place or time; it focuses on a given topic and demonstrates significant action. The arrangement or sequence of scene units determines the plot of a play. The nature of transitions from scene to scene will define the structural style. For example, when transitions involve leaps in time or space between scenes, the structure is *episodic*. Conversely, a *classical* style favors a more compressed time frame that promotes a logical or causal progression of scenes. The major scenes are linked causally or at least logically, sometimes with interpolated choral commentary. The time factor is compressed, limiting the range of action.

Ideally, the choice of the structural style is contingent on the subject matter, and how the playwright feels it is best served. In general, a playwright gravitates toward a specific structural style, tending to shape content within a given style, rather than vary formats accordingly.

Until recently, new playwrights have favored an episodic style. This format suggests loosely related, noncausal relationships between scenes. What is antecedent may have little or nothing to do with what follows; temporal and spatial conditions can alter with the turn of a phrase. The open-ended episodic approach offers numerous variations:

1 In the *serial episodic approach,* the progression of scenes builds toward a climax or major point of complication. There are frequent shifts in time and place. Scenes are rarely extended beyond several beat segments. Generally, a central character provides a through line for the disparate scenes. Examples include *Venus, In the Blood, Fucking A* (Suzan-Lori Parks), *Interim* (Barbara Cassidy), *Sachiko* (Madelyn Kent), and *Demon Baby* (Erin Courtney).

  • Journey plays as a subgenre are serially episodic. *Margo Veil, Dark Ride,* and *Harm's Way* are examples from Jenkin and Wellman. Usually, the journey structure provides linkage between scenes through transitional devices I explore elsewhere in this book.

2 In the *parallel episodic approach,* succeeding scenes disclose separate story units, but at some point in the story lines converge or characters intertwine. Some hybrids fall into this category; see *16 Spells to Charm the Beast* (Lisa D'Amour), *Dead Man's Cell Phone,* and *The Clean House* (Sarah Ruhl). Earlier examples are *Angels in America* (Tony Kushner) and *American Notes* (Len Jenkin).

  • Here the operating aesthetic is juxtaposition and fragmented sequence. Scenes are compartmentalized and self-contained. There are two or more story lines that may comment or inform each other. Historically, William Shakespeare perfected this multilayered dramaturgy. Lope de Vega used this baroque approach by shifting serious with comic scenes to ensure his various classes of audiences were always entertained. Tony Kushner juggled several story lines effectively in *Angels in America;* his approach exploited the opportunity for the grandest sweep—the truly epic play.

  • This scene aesthetic is most effective when there is a convergence of characters or themes that link or interlace at a given point.

3 In *nonserial juxtaposition,* scenes are juxtaposed and individual scenes are repeated with variation. There is never a real sense of story lines coming together in a cohesive narrative. See *Apparition* (Anne Washburn), *Albanian Softshoe* (Mac Wellman), and *Ajax (Por Nobody)* (Alice Tuan).

  • The structure may be collage-like. The resolution or conclusion exists outside of the play. This style seems to be favored by performance artists such as Guillermo Gomez-Peña, Peggy Shaw, and

Karen Finley. Some contemporary adaptations, like Jesurun's *Philoktetes*, are resolutely thematic and open-ended, rejecting the original Sophoclean narrative and quick fix, *deus ex machina*. A strong thematic thread holds together the disparate scenes.

• Jenkin's *Poor Folk's Pleasure* establishes several basic scenes that are repeated with variations throughout the play. It is described by Jenkin as a play developed in a workshop, constructed as independent vignettes, then assembled as a whole. While Parks's *365 Plays/365 Days* establishes this format in short plays or vignettes, the overall effect is similar, amplified to a larger scale.

Television and film have been pervasive in elevating the episodic approach. Increasingly, playwrights are writing scenes that are more truncated than extended. This proclivity has led to plays that feature frequent shifts in place, but along with it, numerous difficulties in handling transitions. New playwrights have innovated bold solutions to solve problems of transition and sequence. (See Chapter 12 for further discussion of transitions.)

Nevertheless, the episodic format can be difficult to execute effectively because the playwright must constantly reestablish the "givens" for every scene. Moveable settings and wagons, or unit settings, provide several approaches to staging a multiple-scene show. Frequent scene shifts and blackouts will appear awkward unless integrated into the dramaturgy. Blackouts that exist solely to cover scene changes create more problems then they solve. Playwrights can mitigate this problem by using narrative or dialogue bridges that cover the change. Too often playwrights leave the execution of transitions up to the director without fully recognizing how the nature of transitions affects the overall structure.

ADAPTING THE CLASSIC APPROACH

While admiring his colleagues who work in episodic formats, Wellman laments that these difficulties with exposition and shifting scenery are the reason he does not favor this style for his plays. Wellman points out (with a wink) that he is simply writing in the grand tradition of classic American playwriting. Eugene O'Neill, Tennessee Williams, Arthur Miller, and Edward Albee have all written major plays for a single, nonchanging unit setting. Wellman, with notable exceptions, establishes a single environment for his plays: the recent *Bitter Bierce* and *Antigone* are examples, as are some of his seminal works, *Bad Infinity* and *Professional Frenchman*: all progress sequentially from start to finish in one setting. Dissimilar works, such as *Terminal Hip* and *Three Americanisms*, require a theatrical (not representational) environment and utilize only a simple unit set, which is more suitable for the extended one-act format of Wellman's plays. In *Murder of Crows*, the production requirements include a steady rainfall on stage; indeed, any set changes would diminish this striking visual image. Moreover, in *The Murder of Crows* premiere at Primary Stages the execution of rainfall and proper drainage, as well as the insulation of electrical materials, mandated that the set be stable for the production. Unity of place was not the only classical dictum Wellman was following. His use of the crows to simulate a Greek chorus intimated a core tenet of classical dramaturgy. To this extent, Wellman's plays underscore the dialogic tension between innovative approaches to language and character that are grounded in established dramaturgical principles.

There may be a return to the unity of place as found in the recent play by Martin McDonagh, *A Behanding in Spokane*, which takes place entirely in a rundown hotel room. Indeed, Parks's *Topdog/Underdog* could probably use the same set, if converted to a seedy apartment flat. The entire play takes place in the apartment the brothers cohabitate. Sarah Ruhl's *The Clean House* is built primarily around a living-room environment which goes through a physical transformation during the play. Another trend is to create an entire environment, in which selected portions including the auditorium are inhabited during the production. Young Jean Lee's *Church* defines the entire theater as the church and congregation, and the play opens with Reverend José entering in darkness from the back of the house. This unit set, environmental approach indicates changes in place through lighting or actors moving furniture on and off, without changing the playing space. The 2010 musical *Bloody, Bloody Andrew Jackson* was staged entirely on a unit set; meanwhile the entire house and lobby featured early nineteenth-century Americana.

CONCEPTUALIZATION: DIALOGUE AND SCENE

In traditional drama, dialogue is conceived and executed according to a general overall strategy. The following three categories, loosely derived from Jan Mukarovsky's studies on dialogue, are helpful in assessing the playwright's conceptualization of dialogue and scene. These categories are challenged somewhat by the new playwriting.

In the first category, the *conflict-driven scene*, the dialogue between characters A and B clashes, with opposing viewpoints or objectives being expressed. It establishes a clear objective/obstacle situation that drives the scene. Dialogue may be written on the line, when characters say exactly what is on their mind or reveal what they feel, or written indirectly, off the line, whereby characters mitigate, evade, suppress, or willfully ignore the present conflict. Indirect dialogue creates tension between the given circumstances and what is actually spoken. This tension translates into subtext for the actor, and is characteristic of psychological realism.

New playwriting is trending toward more conflict-driven scenes within non-traditional formats. In new playwriting, oblique rather than direct conflict is generally the rule. Conflict, in the traditional sense of the term, does not exist at all in Wellman's *Bitter Bierce* unless it is Bierce's ravings against the world. When you don't have characters with opposing needs, conflict is not the driving force of the play. In plays with a central character–Wren in Erin Courtney's *Demon Baby*, for example—conflict is built into the circumstances (the displaced Wren trying to adapt to her new life in England). The character of the Author may face numerous obstacles in locating Sam in *My Uncle Sam*, but the conflicts are less than central to Jenkin's dramaturgy. There is tension and suspense, yes, but not the classic high-stakes protagonist/antagonist struggle. Where conflict is central, and a protagonist is clearly defined, the conflict is embedded within bizarre antiworlds or the atmospheric picaresque. McDonagh's *A Behanding in Spokane* presents the lead character, Carmichael, in conflict with a con artist, his girl friend, and even his mother, but the circumstances (his search for his lost hand) are bizarre, and the play stands as a kind of ironic joke. In Overmyer's *Dark Rapture*, the lead character Babcock flees pursuers across a shifting tropical landscape that promotes rapid changes in atmosphere (local color) and mood.

In the second category, the *circumstance-driven scene*, a dialogue can emerge from the speaker's reaction to prior events (back story), to circumstances, or better, to events that occur during an actual scene in the play. In other cases, the anticipation of impending circumstance or fate drives a scene. These conditions guide or shift the direction of dialogue. They are most powerful if they are introduced at or around the point in the scene. Because discovery takes place, this type of scene is almost always material to plot. When dialogue responds to given circumstances within the present environment, *deictic* dialogue is favored: a spatialized language that connects characters (you, we, us) and places and objects (here, there, this, that). Gestural indicators such as pointing or referring to objects present in the environment perform this function visually.

Len Jenkin's plays generally explore some longstanding condition facing a character that has in some way come to a crossroads or reckoning point. For example, the Kid in *Kid Twist* reexamines his life through dreams and imaginative flights as he is holed up in a rundown hotel room, interred by federal agents. The Translator in *Dark Ride* has come to a critical point in translating an arcane text, and has difficulty assessing the credibility of his findings. In *American Notes*, Jenkin combines an ensemble of feckless characters who seem to be at the "ends of their ropes." The dialogue in these plays explores the character's search for some meaning, or the hope of a new identity. The marginalized settings, particularly seedy hotel rooms, suggest a longing for roots and a legitimized identity.

Topdog/Underdog spins around the circumstances surrounding the lives of the two brothers. Booth wants Lincoln, who is a master at three-card Monte, to show him the ropes. The card game provides numerous opportunities for exposition and interaction. Conflict emerges when Lincoln refuses to help Booth, a circumstance that drives the play until the penultimate climactic scene in which Lincoln succumbs to the temptation of the game, promptly, hustles Booth with his superior skill at it, and ultimately becomes his victim.

The same could be said of Parks's *The Red Letter Plays*, since Hester, the main character in both contemporized versions of *The Scarlet Letter*, reacts in the first play as a welfare mother (*In The Blood*), then in the second as an abortionist (*Fucking A*). Both places focus on the difficult quotidian pressures Hester faces.

In the third category, the *belief-driven scene*, dialogue may also reflect thematic variables, ideas, or beliefs that form the playwright's or character's personal views. This type of scene might be about satirizing something or someone, or advancing specific ideological ends, or exploring a specific phenomenon. Several of the above conditions are present to stimulate the dialogue in a scene. Christopher Durang uses consecutive scenes in *Betty's Summer Vacation* to satirize the overly talkative roommate, then the over-sexed jock with limited brainpower. Tony Kushner utilizes the backdrop of a funeral and AIDS treatment area to launch into an exploration of current cultural mores. The first part of Young Jean Lee's *The Shipment* is a comic send-up on race relations.

Erik Ehn's *The Saint Plays* are examples of plays that hold belief as the core animus of the action. Generally, plays that deal with strong credo and belief systems are driven by matters such as values and faith. Sarah Ruhl's *Melancholy Play* deals with the state and definition and historicity of melancholy through various vignettes and narratives, beginning with the character Frank's four propositions (that is, belief systems) on the state of melancholy (Ruhl 2006, 221).

THE SCENE AND THE SPACE

A scene bears some relation to a specific spatial/temporal field. Language playwrights have been particularly effective in creating shifting scenes, usually in the form of landscapes altered and formulated by language. The seemingly desultory relationship between scenes is mitigated because language provides a structural linkage.

In part 1 of *Limbo Tales*, Len Jenkin establishes a scene with the anthropology professor, Driver, commuting to his girlfriend's house two hours away. Jenkin's stage directions require a miniature highway and landscape that illustrates the sights and sounds described in Driver's narrative. Phenomenally, we experience a shifting highway environment, although the scene itself situates Driver's relation to the action on the set piece: a miniaturized landscape featuring roads, street signs, lampposts, and the like. Jenkin's novel solution creates a vast changeable space reduced to the scale of an intimate stage. Moreover, the spatial distance between Driver and his destinations affects the character's mental processes; the comic effect is enhanced by the miniature representation of his car in a scale model.

Driver's academic specialty as a professor in Mayan anthropology is exploited during a subsequent scene. An ancient Mayan tomb is constructed on the miniature highway board, suggesting an interesting dialogic relation between cultures and histories. In this sense, we have a meeting or clash between present and past time, immediate and distant space.

Indeed, Naomi Iizuka's *36 Views* provides this same dialogic relation between cultures and histories and past and present time. Her innovative use of ancient Asian iconography and texts is theatricalized through Kabuki movements and costumes, creating a stunning counterpoint to the interactions in the contemporary art gallery, where the play is set. Both ancient art and texts trigger momentary spatial and character transformations to reinforce the themes of the play.

As described earlier, Sarah Ruhl's use of the living room space in *The Clean House* serves as a spatial metaphor for the action of the play. It essentially transforms from a well-appointed suburban living room to a heap of detritus, and finally to a hospice. Each one of these transitions correlates to the transitions in Lane, the major character's life—from professional married woman, to divorced woman dealing with the fallout of her husband's affair, to caregiver for the dying Ana. The title of the play, then, becomes immensely ironic, since the journey of this house has led to anything but tidiness.

The protean qualities of the space may not work for every play, but there are cases, as in the above, where the use of stage space theatricalizes the dramatic aspects of the play. Here are some general guidelines:

- Link spatial transformations to transitions in the script.
- Evaluate "triggers" that will effect transformation.
- Triggers include text, iconic or visual sources, specific actions.
- Consider interstitial (in-between) spaces in transitions (bathrooms, hallways, elevators, stairways).
- Visualize the transformation or transition.

EXERCISE:
Stage space

This exercise is based on the use of stage space in Limbo Tales.

1. Develop several scenes based around the use of a miniature set board that contains a cityscape, an airport, or a train set, for example.
   - Consider characters who regularly commute, and draw given materials from their particular line of work.
2. Have the dialogue in the scene interact with the space: a character might set off on a trip, another is on her daily commute, and so on.
3. Create a sense of wonder, as if a child playing with a train set under a Christmas tree.
   - Introduce other characters on the board that your primary character interacts with.

COMMENT: To demonstrate this in the workshop, a visualization tactic that works well is to upload a virtual chess board with chess pieces and project it on a screen so all participants can view the board. Find some end game variations so your pieces and options are limited. Have members of the workshop move one piece at a time while each workshop participant writes a corresponding line of dialogue. The chess moves serve as an analog to the written dialogue, and progress toward a climax, win/lose (end game). Set a limit on the number of chess moves and time between moves.

CAPTIONING

One device shared by language playwrights is the captioning of scenes with a telling phrase or quote, as is done in Erik Ehn's *Thistle*, or as in the case of Overmyer's *On the Verge*, a journal entry. Sarah Ruhl uses the device in her *Melancholy Play*, and Parks utilizes scene titles like "The Reverend on his soapbox" in her play *In the Blood*. These captions mark the shift from scene to scene. This shift in locale indicates scenic properties or other design changes in lighting or sound. Ehn uses quotes drawn from the opening narrative testimony to make up the headliners for fourteen consecutive scenes. The journal entries in *On the Verge* provide the audience with a kind of play map. When captions establish the scene, they are considered markers. A designer, for example, would factor any shift or cueing signal based on this type of marker; it is a unit of transition.

Ruhl's *Melancholy Play* uses captioning to establish various vignettes and songs in the play. These titles, "Frank and France's account of their labor," "Tilly visits Lorenzo," "The vial of tears," "A song from the company," and so forth, serve to break the play down into scene-like units, underscoring the "points" in the play, while creating a commedia like feel to the action. In *Melancholy Play*, captioning anticipates the "points" of the scene.

Jenkin uses captioning in a number of plays. The transition from Scene 9 to Scene 10 in *Dark Ride* is uncanny as the Thief character, functioning as a narrator, establishes the segue while the chorus provides the caption:

THIEF: But in case you people think I'm only interested in the sensational—there's another article in this magazine that's different. I been thinking about it—reading it over and over. It's by a Mrs. Carl Lammle, who is someone I'd like to talk to sometime. It's called:

ALL: THE WORLD OF COINCIDENCE.

10.

MRS. LAMMLE: All of you are, I'm sure, familiar with what I term the WORLD OF COINCIDENCE. In this world events seem to be more connected . . . than they are in our everyday world, where they most often seem, random, absurd-if not perniciously unrelated to each other. In the world of coincidence, however, the most common expression is:

ALL: What a coincidence!

(Jenkin 1993, *Dark Ride*, 82)

The ensemble serves an essentially narrative function: to establish the forthcoming scene. Captioning is a fundamental unit for implementing transition and sequence between scenes. Therefore, it is always a marker for the audience. The "world of coincidence" indicates or suggests a kind of theatrical "world" while not designating any specific place. The designer and director are prompted by inference rather than direction.

On the other hand, Jenkin might use narrators who stand apart from the action and announce the place of the scene. For example, scene 13 of *My Uncle Sam* begins with the narrator's indicative statement, which reflects the preliminary stage description:

> 13
>
> *The garden. The stage is almost bare. Green. DARLENE and YOUNG SAM. OLD SAM, alone, toward the rear.*
>
> NARRATOR: IN THE GARDEN.
>
> (Jenkin 1993, My Uncle Sam, 199)

Captioning is a theatrical function of language, serving several purposes: indicating, describing, suggesting or differentiating scenes; or dialogizing between levels of language. The use of a narrator, a flashing sign, or a verbal announcement, gives the captioning presence, a theatrical rather than representational construct. In scene 2 of *My Uncle Sam*, two narrators parody the use of captioning:

> NARRATOR 1: Now's Lila's telling Sam she'll marry him if he'll find her brother.
>
> LILA: I'll marry you if you find my brother.
>
> NARRATOR 1: She's listing some people who might have some information about his whereabouts …
>
> LILA: A gentleman with a big book.
>
> YOUNG SAM: A big book
>
> NARRATOR 2: A gentleman with a big book.
>
> LILA: A lady in a golden vest
>
> YOUNG SAM: A lady in a golden vest.
>
> NARRATOR 2: A lady in a golden vest.
>
> LILA: A man with eight flags.
>
> YOUNG SAM: Eight flags.
>
> NARRATOR 2: A man with eight flags.
>
> (Jenkin 1993, My Uncle Sam, 137)

By juxtaposing direct address (the narrators' captions) with the descriptive dialogue between Lila and Young Sam, Jenkin achieves a comic effect. Although this passage is more representative of a beat segment than a scene,

I have included it here as an extreme example of captioning, one which also demonstrates the dialogic relation between narrative and dialogue passages that is at the heart of the new playwriting.

THE NUMERICAL BREAKDOWN OF SCENES

The numbering of scenes may be used to isolate specific blocks of dramatic text from each other. While the traditional approach has been to label in progression (Scene 1, Scene 2, and so on), some recent plays eliminate the word scene. By changing the traditional nomenclature the new playwrights can elevate single beats or beat segments as their structural unit. If the traditional nomenclature suggests some linkage between scenes, the use of numbers alone isolates or telescopes the playwright's focus. Clubbed Thumb member Adam Bock does this effectively in his play *The Typographer's Dream* (Striar and Detrick 2007, 17–51). The length of his numerical "scenes" varies from no dialogue, to several lines, to fully realized scenes with a beginning, middle, and end. This numerical technique indicates a level change even when there seems no topical shift or transition. In other words, Bock is indicating slight beat changes that it would otherwise be impossible to decipher. In production, these "changes" could be augmented by movement, gesture, and directional lighting shifts to create a theatrical dialogism in juxtaposition with the text.

In general, the independent scene, with its beginning, middle, and end (or at times, simply middle and end) remains the building block of all playwrights. In episodic structures, each scene takes on a vitality of its own, as the arranged sequence builds toward a climactic *scene à faire*, the major confrontational or "obligatory" scene. Tony Kushner's *Angels in America* is indicative of this desire to compartmentalize within the limitations of the episodic form. Separate story lines develop and intersect at various points in the play. The separation and distinction between the worlds represented in each scene can create considerable dialogic tension. Kushner does this successfully in alternating Roy Cohn's McCarthy-era tough guy discourse with more contemporary and familiar discourses from gay society (a young Mormon character who is coming out of the closet; a flamboyant "queen" who serves as the nurse). The interweaving of spiritual realms, particularly in Part 2, is in fact more representative of the dialogic principle at work. Sarah Ruhl accomplishes a similar task in *Dead Man's Cell Phone* by alternating scenes with Gordon, Gordon's family, the women in his life, Dwight as Jean's romantic interest, and ultimately the "dead man" Gordon in their *scene à faire* "spiritual awakening"—on Jean's "planet." The result is a series of juxtaposed vignettes, leading to the moment of truth in the play's penultimate scene.

Sarah Ruhl (*The Clean House, Dead Man's Cell Phone, Melancholy Play*), Suzan-Lori Parks (*365 Days/365 Plays, Venus, The Red Letter Plays*), Young Jean Lee (*The Appeal*), and Erin Courtney (*Demon Baby*) utilize the episodic scene as the structural unit. The reason: unlike a sprawling act structure, evident in modernists first, like Eugene O'Neill (*A Long Day's Journey into Night, The Iceman Cometh*), then Lanford Wilson (*Hot L Baltimore*), or Sam Shepard (*Fool for Love, Curse of the Starving Class*), the scene provides the writer with a limited scale, and the ability to compartmentalize the revision process. The playwright can work unit by unit. During revisions, entire units can be abandoned, or restructured to form the wholeness of an act, or play.

In politically committed playwrights (Tony Kushner, for example) there is an underlying thematic intention to dialogue in the scene. These thematic intentions construct the larger presence of the character in the scene. When characters represent an unpopular ideology, like that of Roy Cohn in *Angels in America*, we can expect that somehow these characters will be taught a moral lesson; that they will ultimately receive some psychic or emotional pain to redress their actions. In this sense, the scene bundles its markers toward some payoff later in the play.

SCENES INTO ACTS

To a degree, the process described above for each scene can be expanded to serve as a microcosm for the act. Indeed, in some cases, the act may serve as a microcosm for the structure of the play. But this practice varies considerably; many plays of the new playwriting have radically different approaches to the acts, particularly, as producing trends favor eliminating the once-sacrosanct intermission. It is difficult for the playwright to consider an entire act until later in the evolution of the play. Range and breadth are too large. Nevertheless, the effectiveness of an act can be determined by:

- the quality and flow of the beat segments, particularly how they work together and interact
- the buildup or arrangement of points across the scenes
- the theatrical and dramaturgic effectiveness of the convergence point, or the major moment in the act
- the sense of scale.

Convergence points provide major dramaturgic resonance because they establish points of contact across juxtaposed scenes and seemingly disparate narratives. The role of the act, after all, is to gather the scenes into an aesthetic or formal pattern that is dramaturgically effective. Convergence can happen when characters from disparate scenes share the same space, or even sing the same song, dance together, or are brought into some form of interaction that is dramatically conclusive, which, in traditional terms might be the *scene á faire* or perhaps the climax of the play.

After the first draft of a script is completed, elements need sharpening and clarification. In revision, the play's dialogism is consciously considered. The buildup of dialogic units begins with beats, then proceeds to beat segments and markers, then to scenes and points, then to acts and "moments" of convergence.

Scale determines the crucial relationship between the volume or weight of the subject material and its dramatic treatment. In many cases, there will be too much material, and like the sculptor, the playwright will need to determine what needs to be chiseled off in large blocks versus what needs to be honed and buffed. The proper way to address this revision is by examining the effectiveness of each individual beat segment rather than lopping off a line here and there.

Scale may be a pragmatic consideration. A popular format for the past ten years has been the ten-minute play. In most workshop or classroom settings, it has become the advisable format for beginning student work, where the powers of conceptualization and technique generally are not up to the challenges of the longer formats. While there has been this elevation of the ten-minute play through the many competitions that now celebrate the form, my experience has been that it is often difficult to distinguish a ten-minute play from a focused, extended scene, even when the playwrights are renowned. For example, the first anthology of ten-minute plays, *Take Ten* (Lane, Shengold 1997), contains a monologue as prologue (as ten-minute play) to an evening of plays by Christopher Durang, and pulled scenes from longer formats by other playwrights. However, for many reasons, it is the optimum format for the beginning playwriting workshop.

Since Mac Wellman has conceptualized most of his plays as extended one-acts, the short play has become a most viable trend in new writing, as noted in the anthologies: *Funny, Strange, Provocative: Seven Plays from Clubbed Thumb (Striar and Detrick 2007)* and *New Downtown Now: An Anthology of New Theater from Downtown New York (Wellman and Lee 2006)*. The seventy-five or ninety-minute play without intermission is becoming more standard, and we are seeing this trend even on Broadway, where historically plays and musicals could run well over two-and-a-half hours. A midweek performance that closes before 10 pm rather than after 11 pm will be more attractive to business people and families, especially when commuting time is a factor.

There are various pragmatic reasons dictating the shorter form. In avant-garde theaters where the pay is marginal at best, it is difficult to do extensive work when rehearsal schedules are restricted and actors and directors have other obligations. This is the reality of noncommercial theater in New York. If rehearsal means repetition, then Wellman prefers to have a more concentrated approach to rehearsal. The short play allows the flexibility of either rehearsing the entire play, or exploring segments and scenes in intensive, albeit brief, rehearsal periods. Another practical concern is sustaining audiences' attention through a three-hour show that necessitates one or more intermissions. Producers fear walkouts during the interval, particularly during previews or early in the run, when an emptying house can signal a show's death knell. The preference for the short play may be a by-product of our technological age. In our telecommunication age forms of communication are brief and getting more abbreviated—texting is replacing conversation, and has its own shorthand vocabulary. Facebook means we don't drop in on family or friends, we see them virtually as much as (or more than) desired. If the frequency of our interactions has increased, the scale and scope of these interactions have been vastly reduced. While rarely noted as a factor in dramaturgy, scale is increasingly becoming a determining factor in conceptualizing and executing the play.

In the dialogic play, scale should be a consideration whenever narrative and dramatic elements are interlaced. The attempt is to achieve an understanding of balance and weighting in the script. Examine, in particular, how the monologues are functioning in relation to dialogue sections. Since monologues create a sense of mass in the script, you need to assess whether they are supported by the dramaturgy or balanced by sections of dialogue. This is particularly true when utilizing long sections of direct address, a common feature of many current plays. Monologues that go on for pages not only seem self-indulgent, but tend to weigh down a script like an anchor. Take note of Erik Ehn's work in *The Saint Plays*, or Maria Irene Fornes's *Mud*, which are painstakingly realized in terms of balancing the scale between monologue and dialogue sections. Ultimately, scale affects the size relationship between segments and scenes, and is an important technical indicator in assessing the formal quality of the script.

A general critique of the short play is that the finished work may appear slight, more of a gesture, than a polished, finished work. This sketchiness would imply a lack of depth that plays on surfaces, and masks itself in irony. Where substantial scale has been realized, new work is blending old and new dramaturgies. The time is ripe for new playwrights to realize language-based playwriting at a larger scale and scope—to challenge their work to move beyond irony and cleverness toward a deeper awakening of innovation and insight.

THE REVISION PROCESS, AND DEVELOPING CHOPS

As a founder of Clubbed Thumb and a longtime supporter of new work, Jeffrey Jones has developed somewhat of a guru status among young playwrights. His additions to two recent volumes of new work are not plays, but guideposts for the reader. He provides the introduction (or apologia) to *New Downtown Now* (2006), and an afterword chapter, as benevolent reviewer, to Young Jean Lee's recently published *Songs of the Dragons Flying to Heaven and Other Plays* (2009). These unique entries seem an effort to protect the playwrights from untutored scrutiny by readers not familiar with language playwriting. While his championing of new playwrights is laudatory and necessary, the respective titles of these entries: "Introduction: how to read a curious play"; and, the ironic, "Afterword, what's wrong with these plays," may suggest to some readers that the plays cannot stand on their own merits, without detailed interpretation and guidance.

Jones's process as a playwright is noteworthy. At an ACT playwriting workshop fifteen years ago in San Francisco, Jones stated that the play develops from "stuff"—that is, from the written play material. Jones was alluding to the rough draft, a species with a wide range of definitions, from a first go at the material to a script that needs a mere polish to become performance ready. Jones continues to assert that the real work of the playwright begins after a threshold of written material is reached. While some playwrights such as Sam Shepard seldom revise initial drafts, the opposite is more often the case: the play is "discovered" after numerous rewrites. Jones meticulously labels subsequent drafts during the revision process. His first draft provides the benchmark for the initial impulses behind the script. Later drafts offer significant room for expansion or deletion of characters, scenes, and so on. In this process, Jones's drafts dialogize with each other in the creation of the ultimate script.

The playwright needs a revision process that will maximize chances of success. Many playwrights reach an impasse at this phase; students, in particular, will balk at the forecast of rewrites as tedious and frustrating, and start to "defend" their idea about the work, even if the idea doesn't cotton with the actual text. Many scripts fail to improve at this phase of the process. Part of the resistance and difficulty stems from traditional thinking that defines playwriting as linear and monologic rather than interactive and dialogic. The dialogic method seems more natural than prescribed linear approaches because it seeks to discover the optimum relationship between parts in a playtext. Once this process for conceptualizing the play is established it is a matter of the playwright having the craft, stamina, and willpower to execute the plan.

Stamina may be the most important attribute in a playwright's arsenal. First, it gives the playwright power to cut through lows brought on by frustration, rejection, and bad reviews, or simple laziness, and to continue writing. Second, the play itself must have stamina to "cut it"—in other words, to "hold the boards" for over an hour or more. Balance must be struck between imagination and solid dramaturgical craft. A great deal of stamina is necessary to complete revisions with attention to detail, while not losing the perspective of the overall play. Put another way, lack of stamina probably drives out more would-be playwrights than anything else. While every established playwright has several plays that were never completed, this prospect may discourage the young or emerging playwright. Many promising new play projects never get finished or are half-realized. This matter is compounded in new playwriting, where until the first edition of this work, no effective criteria or methods were available to aid the playwright through the revision process.

With this factor in mind, the craft, or "wrighting," of the play is a foremost concern in the revision process. The playwright needs to find this extra gear of focus and commitment. The demanding nature of playwriting often grinds down to the common denominator of craft. Craft is effective dramaturgy; paradoxically, it is the conscious application of form in the script, yet at the same time it is intuitively felt. A play is well crafted when the playwright has solved its challenges and problems; to be a masterpiece the crafting must be exquisite. Learning the craft is not the most difficult step for young playwrights, but it is certainly the most humbling. Some genres rely more heavily than others on craft. Whatever the case, there is no way around the mastery of technique as a means to achieving potential.

The synergies of conceptualization, stamina, and craft equal *chops*. In music, chops have to do with the player's musical concept, sound presence, and, of course, confidence and facility of technique. In playwriting, chops separate the lesser playwrights from the truly great: the master playwright demonstrates a level of virtuosity that is signatory. The most difficult aspect of chops for most playwrights is realizing the conceptualization, and for beginners this can be the most elusive to identify. When the basic idea of the play is flawed, no amount of revision will improve it. This is why it is important to stay true to your initial impulses, and write the first drafts as quickly as possible. Effective conceptualization means that the play achieves what it sets out to do. It works on its own terms. This blending of craft, stamina, and conceptualization can be most impressive. Literary managers, dramaturgs, and directors recognize chops as technical execution and dramaturgical savvy, with something more—a distinctive voice. The building of chops is the byproduct of effective revision.

THE REVISION PROCESS

PREMISE: The beat segment is the primary site of revision. Effective beat segments and the optimum placement of markers provide the building blocks of form.

In revising the playscript through the early drafts, the playwright must consider how each beat segment establishes markers, and what the relation between segments is, particularly for those segments that immediately precede and follow. What is dialogic here? Beat segments interact with each other in the formation of scene. How effectively they interact determines the quality of the dramaturgy. Most playwrights, beginners in particular, make changes line by line without first determining or identifying the entire beat segment. The first step should be to define the marker of the beat segment. Once you understand how the beat segment functions you can proceed. At this point, you can choose to work to this marker from the preceding marker, or revise backward from this marker to the previous marker. You can also assess whether the entire beat segment should be moved, deleted, or stored for potential later use. The revision process, rather than a sloppy and difficult procedure, can now be accomplished more efficiently. Developers and dramaturgs who understand the workings of the beat segment can be more specific (and helpful) in discussing revisions with the playwright.

Revision

You probably have several fragments of plays that you have shelved, with the hope of returning to them at some future point. The following exercise encourages you to bring out one of your rougher works and give it a dialogic makeover. If there is a level of trust and camaraderie in the workshop, you can divide the group into duets, with the each playwright responding to the other's work. Often the beginning playwright will be too blocked to enter into a productive dialogue about their own work.

1. Read through the entire draft (without wincing).

2. Since Step 1 is generally not possible, read through the draft indicating in the left margin each beat segment, numbering and bracketing them as you go along. If the segment has no marker, this indicates a certain revision area.

3. Locate the marker in each beat segment. Identify what happens there. If the script is full-length, get a separate sheet of paper and number and identify as above. This is your *aide-memoire,* so you don't forget what you have already written.

4. Assess each marker and its relation to the other markers that precede and follow. Are there shifts in direction? Can the marker be clarified? Should the contour of the beat segment be altered?

   - Examine the potential of opposite outcomes in the marker. Is the opposite outcome better? What are the possibilities?

   - Refer to your list. Can a beat segment be taken and shaped from another part of the text? To determine this, start back from the marker using only the material that you need. Slough off the rest and place it in a file. Another option is to cut and storyboard the numbered beat segments, exploring possible configurations.

   - Does the new arrangement release the energy potential of your script? Altering the contour across the various segments can release stored energy from the texts. Now move on to the next ten pages.

5. At some point in this process, you will sense, or feel in your gut, a direction for the play that may have previously escaped you. Something in the dialogic relationship between markers, or the shifting contours of segments, will trigger a solution to the project. It may be the entry of a character, or a strategy of monologue, the introduction of song or music. Keep yourself open to these possibilities. You might see in the markers the key to subsequent scenes, and excise whole sections of the script. Often, you will need to bridge old passages of script with newly written material.

6. Program your subconscious to trigger the ending of the play. Attempt to visualize an image at the final curtain. Think theatrically: Who is on stage? What has just happened? Does it conclude the script satisfactorily? Once you have determined the landing point you can rework the high points or the most important markers in the play. Endings shape the thematic matter conclusively. After the ending is determined, proceed with revisions. You will have less trouble with the ending (a major stumbling block of young playwrights) if you are tuned in dialogically to the markers in your script. Priming the

subconscious is good because the answer may come from something that comes across your everyday life: a phrase, an image, or a dream. The best revision will come when the imagination tunes in to the dialogic process.

7. Before you begin polishing the revisions clarify the following, in order of importance: the curtain scene; the major markers that precede the curtain; the end of the first act (if there is an intermission); the beginning of the second act; the beginning of the play to the first marker. Most playwrights spend a great deal of time reworking the beginning of the play, and categorically less on the second act than the first.

COMMENT: Either revise what you set out to do in one session, or establish daily parameters for the revision in time units over several days or a week. The rationale is that if you allow time to lapse, your perspective will change or you will lose the intention of the revision. Intention is the operative word in revision.

The mid-revision phase is where the *wright* in *playwright* demonstrates craft and finesse. It can be the most invigorating and satisfying part of the process. If you view the first part of writing the script as creating the raw material, like Jeffrey Jones, then you won't make premature judgments, because you commit to further engagement before true form emerges. A number of texts on playwriting blame the failure to complete a script on lack of planning, but it may be the inability to discover what is inherently valid and worth pursuing in the given raw materials. In this sense, the playwright is in a dialogic relation to the material; the evolving script is in a very real sense in dialogue with them. It is important to subsume the self-censor at this point, so that you are in a state of flow with the material. This dialogism between playwright and the evolving text goes on consciously and unconsciously until the text is finished, or scrapped. Be open to the muse, to the call of imagination. Indeed, an old script often "calls" the writer back—the process is visceral and living. This is the mysterious and seductive dialogue between text and writer that signals a readiness to complete the text.

Too many playwrights send their work out before this phase is concluded adequately, in a sense, hoping that someone "out in development land" will save their play. It rarely happens. You need to establish the craft in the play. Like the "eye music" that attracts the reader, an advanced level of craft provides the pleasure of form.

EXERCISE:
Dramaturgy

Read the following plays for craft purposes only: *The Clean House* (Ruhl), *Margo Veil* (Jenkin), and *Bitter Bierce* (Wellman).

1. Pick ten pages of text at random from each play.
2. Repeat several steps from the above revision exercise: include beat segments, markers, points, contour, and the dialogic relation between beat segments.

3. Play close heed to the transitions. What's happening to create shifts, movement; and so on?

4. Analyze the ending of each play. What is the relationship between the ending and the ten pages you selected? Is a sense of dialogism apparent? How were certain markers drawn to conclusion?

COMMENT: Dramaturgy tends to take in the big picture, but it only becomes a tool for the playwright when operating at close range. The fundamental approach of this book is to analyze these techniques without judgment and then demonstrate the move and how it might work for you.

REVISING DIALOGUE

Most playwrights would envy Sam Shepard's approach to writing dialogue, which is to let the first draft stand as it hits the page. In actual practice, dialogue undergoes a metamorphic process during the vetting of the script.

Metamorphosis is an apt term because it describes how the early drafts molt away, leaving a more evolved form. The script, as the more experienced playwright knows, becomes an active player in the changing process. The writer's total engagement with the material activates it toward its optimum form. Throughout the process, the writer will undertake both revision and polish; the differences between the two are shown in Table 10.1.

Table 10.1 Revision versus polish

1. The revision shapes the material into form: the play takes on life.

2. The revision should remove the awkwardness from the play.

3. The revision deals with beat segments and establishes the markers and points.

4. The revision opens up the potential of the play. The theme or project becomes clear enough that subsequent work can be targeted.

5. The revision reveals the inherent dialogism at work.

1. The polish hones, buffs, and waxes the material into a refined state. Sharpness and clarity of attack are made apparent.

2. The polish reveals the elegance and expertise of the craft and craftsperson, respectively.

3. The polish deals with each beat and the point of attack of each line of dialogue (see below).

4. The polish realizes the potential of the play. The material of the play is worked toward its greatest fruition.

5. The polish reveals the sharpness of the dialogue.

Point of attack traditionally refers to the moment in the story where the playwright begins the play. Early point of attack means that most of the story unfolds before our eyes, and mandates a longer passage of time and greater space. This favors the episodic scenic structure. A late point of attack occurs within a compressed time and space, and often is a response to events that occurred prior to the beginning of the play. The late point of attack suggests a more classical style. There are some exceptions to this: for example, David Lindsay-Abaire's *Rabbit Hole* begins after the death of the protagonists' son, and is a response to an earlier event (late point of attack). Nevertheless, the play's arc covers a long aftermath in which the parents come to grips with their grief. In essence, we begin at an early stage in the grieving process, and the progress is set up episodically. Similarly, Lynn Nottage's *Ruined* picks up on the lives of refugee women who have been savaged by multiple rapes, and the subsequent rejection of their families and tribes. Both of these Pulitzer-Prize-winning plays are dealing with the aftermath of a devastating event. Yet the playwrights' intention is clearly focused on the survivors, and their struggles to deal and make sense of their present circumstances.

In referring to dialogue, *late point of attack* refers to the latest possible point at which to begin a line of dialogue. Note the following example: "I think I will come to see you soon" versus "I'll see you soon" versus "See you. Soon." Clearly the last version sharpens intention. Crafting dialogue to one idea per line is a great exercise for young playwrights. In polishing the point of attack, cut back compound verbs and conditional verbs (would, could, should) as well as most adjectives and adverbs. If the "I" or "you" is implied, it can be eliminated. Generally, avoid the subjunctive or the conditional tenses since the indicative tense creates stronger intentions. Favor the language of presence over the language of ambiguity and absence, unless a particular effect is desired. A skilled actor can play on the line or against the line. The actor can manufacture subjunctive qualities (hesitancy, uncertainty, speculation, and so on) through intonation or behavior. The intention of the line should make this clear.

Polish dialogue from beat to beat. The polish helps to determine the contour of the beat segment and the dialogic relationship between markers. Contour emerges more clearly as dialogue is sharpened and honed. Indeed, contour can provide the *modus operandi* for the polish insofar as the shaping of lines affects pace. The contour should generally reinforce the action of the beat segment. In other words, in a romantic seduction scene the playwright might strive for a sinuous sense to the contour, rather than a staccato angularity (though the latter approach might be appropriate in creating a stylized or comic handling of the same material).

Usually, a polish will decrease the distance between markers in a scene. The rate of the play will appear to quicken, as extraneous material is vetted. This compression will affect the contour across the beat segments, and may change the quality of the scene. At this stage, you should arrange a reading of the script to monitor how the revisions have affected it. A brisker pace is usually preferred, although you may want to alternate a more languidly paced scene that includes longer speeches and pauses with segments made up of truncated dialogue. If the pace is too fast, consider inserting character-oriented beats, or even digressionary material related to the givens. Rather than slow the script, these inserts can add impact and immediacy as the character notices some object, or has a revelation that is prompted by the givens of the scene. These beats can include pauses as well as spoken dialogue. Pay close attention to what your characters are wearing: jewelry, charms, or more mundane items can be worn, transferred, lost, or provide comic relief. Wellman is a master at this technique. A broken watch spring in *Harm's Way* provides a major impetus for Santouche's action.

In a polish, you are detailing your script—honing it to its optimum degree. Because the new playwriting is reliant on language to a greater degree than traditional dramaturgy, it is essential for the playwright to execute the polish with precision and care.

11

Foundations of contemporary monologue

"Show us, don't tell us" is the most widely used caveat directed at playwrights. It demands that good dramatic writing be present tense, immediate, and interactive. While it remains an operative strategy for playwrights, a casual glance at any play anthology suggests that the adage is untrue. Often guised as the single monologic voice, narrative elements in play texts have been present since Thespis. Take your pick from the historical canon of plays: the reportage of the Sophoclean messenger; the soliloquies of the Shakespearean hero; the caustic commentators of John Webster; the rhetorical moralisms of John Dryden; the lamentations of Anton Chekhov's characters; the self-absorbed ruminations of Tennessee Williams's women; the backstories of Peter Shaffer's narrators; or the ideological tomes of Tony Kushner's tormented characters, to mention only a few. These playwrights, and most contemporary dramatists, employ monologue as a significant factor in their dramaturgy.

Moreover, the use of monologue in the theater has increased significantly, spurred by the growth in popularity of the one-person show. This type of monologue in performance ranges from monodramas in which the actor transforms into the biographical personage of a historical character (for instance, Mark Twain, Emily Dickinson, Ambrose Bierce) to one-person shows built extensively from autobiographical materials, such as Doug Wright's Pulitzer-Prize-winning play *I am My Own Wife*, and John Leguziamo's Drama Desk Award winning *Freak* (1997) and Tony-nominated *Sexaholix ... a Love Story* (2002). Drawing on a format successfully developed by the late Spalding Gray, theater performers and others are branching out to create their own, self-contained studies of contemporary life and culture.

Because of the cost-saving features of the one-person show, the format has been effective in bringing marginalized groups to a wider audience. Leguziamo's breakthrough performances were the first to feature the contemporary Latino lifestyle on Broadway. Peggy Shaw, founder of the lesbian theater company Split Britches, won an OBIE award in 2000 for her cross-dressed performance of *Menopausal Gentleman*. Shaw was exploring the ravages of her own menopause—ironically, as she pointed out—dressed as a man who looked twenty years younger—a dead ringer for Sean Penn.

Similar to most one-person shows, Shaw conflated numerous elements in a pastiche that contained references to Frank Sinatra, her own childhood, stories about her father, lip-synched music of the 1960s, and 1940s zoot suits. As part of this format, narrative, visual, and gestural elements are drawn from the respective subcultures. For example, Shaw utilizes lip-synching techniques drawn from her work with drag shows.

The most popular current trend derives from the world of standup and politically satirical performers, such as Colbert, Lewis Black, and John Stewart. While seemingly novel to contemporary viewers, some of the elements of their work, such as the comic rant or tirade, date back to the early *commedia dell'arte tirata*. The former SNL comedian and monologist Colin Quinn recently opened on Broadway (2010–1) with his *Long Short Story*, an abbreviated history of the world, developed with (and directed by) Jerry Seinfeld. This highly successful show will soon be made into an HBO special. If these one-person formats contain a variety of theatrical elements, their textual bases are in monologue; the principles explored in this and the next chapters will apply in most cases.

Most playwriting texts do not consider the practice and strategy of writing monologues. There is a need to cover some basic principles that govern the use of monologue, both as a linguistic strategy and on the stage. So while this text considers the monologue's use in new playwriting, it is first necessary to briefly explore some traditional uses and applications of the monologue. Therefore, this chapter examines the underpinnings of the monologue, and considers several contemporary functions of monologues in plays. The next chapter discloses how the monologue in the new playwriting represents a progress from its monologic aspect toward various forms of dialogism.

THE FUNCTION OF MONOLOGUE IN EVERYDAY LIFE

In daily life, the monologue serves a transactional rather than interactional function. In transactional speech no conversational response is anticipated, as monologue pretends to be the last word. As a result, the monologue casts an air of authority, in spiritual realms and pulpits (from the voice of God to the sermon by the priest) or in more mundane offerings (a presentation by an expert, a lecture by a professor, or the scolding of a parent). The authority of monologue is related to its inherent resistance to interruption or disruption. As practical, everyday language, monologue possesses qualities that are static and planned; it knows where it is going, either in intent or ideology.

Narratology exists as a branch of linguistics that deals with transactional speech. This is to differentiate it from discourse analysis—the study of conversational patterns and strategies. Narratology considers contexts and outcomes where the speaker is largely uninterrupted. Some examples include taking personal histories (for example, from medicine or journalism); using legal narratives such as briefs, affidavits, confessions, and testimonies; and using personal narratives entered into journals and diaries. There is a continued interest among playwrights in creating plays based on these formats. Eric Ehn's *Thistle (Rose of Lima)* (2000) opens with a testimony from a survivor of the massacre in El Salvador. This "testimony" then provides the subsequent plot for the play. Lynn Nottage's Pulitzer-Prize-winning play *Ruined* (2009) was based upon personal histories of the women who were raped by Ugandan rebel and government soldiers, and then abandoned by their families and tribes.

HOW MONOLOGUE TRADITIONALLY FUNCTIONS IN A PLAY

Monologue's contrived aspect is featured on stage. Real-life, intense emotions actually trigger a lack of clearly articulated speech, but that is not usually the case in drama. The convention in which intense character emotions trigger the articulation of carefully composed language is at the heart of the contrivance. Most monologues use selective repetition and figures of speech, as well as negative space—clarified through pauses, silences, or ellipses. The monologue is composed, orchestrated for effect, and marked by a heightened, often formal level of language. Often used to establish the "reality of the character," monologue may theatricalize what Dorrit Cohn has described as the transparent mind, allowing audiences entry into the characters' consciousness: their motivations, history, or point of view. As Cohn posits:

> If the real world becomes fiction only by revealing the hidden side of human beings, the reverse is equally true: the most real, the 'roundest' characters of fiction are those we know most intimately, precisely in ways we could never know people in real life.
>
> (Cohn 1978, 5)

This psychological "rounding" provided by monologue serves to texture the dramatized action. The Aristotelian action expands to include the articulation of thought processes, emotional states, visual metaphors, and so on. Who can think of William Shakespeare's greatest play, *Hamlet*, bereft of the soliloquies?

Before a live audience, heightened by lighting and staging effects supporting the force of the actor, the monologue's impact can be powerful. The theatricalized baring of the one before the many rivets an audience's attention to this character's inner struggles, moment of epiphany or intimate revelation. This convention of monologue remains one of the most tried and true elements of dramaturgy, and its effectiveness is reserved for the stage. Because of their essentially visual, image-oriented basis, neither film nor television suffer long speeches gladly. In film, monologue is invariably formatted as a voice-over: a vocal narrative track that underscores a series of visual images. If direct address to the audience from the stage can represent a powerful dramaturgy, it is not without its critics. The *New York* back: stop talking to me," lamented the proliferation of direct address in contemporary plays: "Direct address has become the kudzu of new playwriting, running wild across the contemporary landscape and threatening to strangle any and all other dramaturgical devices."

He has a point. There has been an increasing trend for playwrights to start the play with one or a series of monologues. Ruhl's *The Clean House*, Kreitzer's *Freakshow*, and Sheila Callaghan's *Crumble (Lay Me Down, Justin Timberlake)* are representative of this pervasive practice. Parks's *In the Blood* kicks off with a choral monologue. Of the above, the most innovative use is in Callaghan's *Crumble*, which opens with the "character" called Apartment addressing the audience, immediately establishing the bizarre world of the play.

The opening monologue(s) should immediately "open" up the play and establish its tone to the audience. *The Clean House* begins with the maid, Mathilde, telling a joke in Portuguese, followed by introductory monologues from the principal characters. Amalia, the legless/armless torso in *Freakshow*, confronts us with her sexuality: "You are wondering if I have ever had sexual intercourse." (Striar and Detrick 2007, 273) Immediately, Kreitzer explodes the character's subtext as a manifestation of the audience's curiosities.

Isherwood does not totally negate the value of monologue, rather laments that it precludes other dramaturgical solutions, and may just be a quick and easy fix. Indeed, strict adherence to the "show us, don't tell us" dictum (the purely dialogue-oriented play text) may render subtextual meaning opaque or hidden. Tennessee Williams's Blanche's transparency is achieved through her monologic rhapsodizing. Novelist Thomas Mann lambasted the limitations of dialogue alone: "I confess that in everything regarding knowledge of men as individual beings, I regard drama as an art of the silhouette, and only narrated man as round, whole, real, and fully shaped" (quoted in Cohn 1978, 7). Mann's cavil targets the silhouetted "agent of the action" that marks the Aristotelian character. Monologue allows telescopic glimpses of characters' motivations beyond the capacity of conversational discourse, thus ensuring a greater possibility of "knowing the character" beyond the plot-inscribed "agent of the action."

In contemporary drama, monologue services the requirements of both actor and audience for explication and clarification of subtext. Since Anton Chekhov, Tennessee Williams may be the most important playwright to examine the psychological world of the character through monologue. Chekhov's ongoing appeal may be partially linked to his characters' solo ruminations. Nevertheless, most experienced playwrights are keenly aware that unless their monologues are functioning to better serve the play, the results will lead to a very static dramaturgy.

In the traditional dialogue-oriented script, monologue expands upon the core of the play script, giving the audience more satisfaction, a sense of coloration, and clarity. As a by-product, its impact defines to an extent the writing ability of the playwright. Moreover, monologue's acceptance as a dramaturgical convention establishes playwriting as the most literary of dramatic media. To prove this point, attend several stage readings of new works and observe audiences' responses. Invariably, they will single out monologues as examples of the playwright's ability to capture an essence or feeling, and as a measurement of their awe regarding the talent of the writing. The skilled theater person will combine this perception with an evaluation of its stage-worthiness.

In traditional dramaturgy, outer motivations are realized through dialogue and dramatic action; thus, it remains for the monologue to clarify inner objectives, especially if those hidden forces run contrary to the more apparent external motives. The unbolting of strong emotions can reveal a sudden shift in intention. The release of hidden forces is a clear marker of definition for the character, representing a level of discovery or reversal. In backstage parlance, this point is where the character gauges the overall arc, or trajectory of the character's journey during the course of the play. Thus, the proper build to this point in the arc can be clearly orchestrated, giving the character structure and definition. Based on these observations we can arrive at the general premise that monologue serves a variety of expansionary functions, and its placement in the playscript generally indicates its purpose. The various functions can be:

- character introduction, exposition or genre setting in the early scenes
- metaphoric or thematic analogue used to emphasize or clarify points of conflict in the rising action
- character discovery, epiphany, or reversals located near the major crisis of the play.

Providing examples of the first two of those functions are the contemporary plays *The Clean House*, by Sarah Ruhl, and *16 Spells to Charm the Beast*, by Lisa D'Amour. Barbara Cassidy's *Interim* is an example of the third function. Characters in these plays, with the exception of the "Beast" in D'Amour's play, are generally imitative of, or based in, real life. Thus, realism defines content rather than formal or structural elements of the plays. For example, we already discussed how space is used in a most non-realistic manner in *The Clean House*, despite the fact that all the characters are grounded in a realistic context.

Ruhl and D'Amour interweave dramatized scenes with monologue sections. In *The Clean House*, the character Matilde uses her monologic "moments" to provide exposition that details her relationship with her deceased Brazilian parents and her rationale for now living in America and working as a maid. These are interpolated between normative dialogue scenes in Lane's living room. However, the theatricalized convention of monologue allows Ruhl to actualize Matilde's parents dancing, and for us to observe Matilde's sense of loss.

In *Crumble*, Callaghan moves the Apartment's monologues (and voice) around the entire space: the floor, walls, ceiling, steam radiator, and window. The Apartment, in essence, mirrors and reinforces the anxieties of its inhabitants. Here, Callaghan's characters expose their innermost thoughts, while the space itself offers a comic counterpoint. In these plays, the monologues have an interpolated structural quality, serving as a bridge between scenes of dialogue. While not advancing the action, they function to establish the tone and world of the play.

MONOLOGUE INTERPOLATION IN NEW PLAY DEVELOPMENT

In play development, monologue interpolation between sections of dialogue can provide an effective strategy for discovering a character's functions and thematic values without massive internal redrafting of scenes. As director of the New Playwrights' Program at the University of Alabama, I had the opportunity to develop *Southern Girls*, a play by Dura Temple and Sheri Bailey. The playwrights nearly doubled fifty minutes of dialogue to about 100 minutes as each of the six characters (three black and three white) were given monologues that flashed from the present back to the 1950s, 1960s, and 1970s. These monologues segued through the historical periods presented in the play. Audiences relished these character moments, but more importantly, the monologues covered the structural breaks of time, and gave unity to the form. Subsequently, *Southern Girls* was chosen as best new play from the southern region of the American College Theater Festival, and has gone on to a number of national productions.

EXERCISE:
Monologue interpolation

A very effective exercise for any level of playwright, the following involves two playwrights working together.

1. Write a short, five-scene play that will be about ten minutes in length.
2. The group should use free association to profile the main character (who should fall within the realm of a persecutor or savior type). A saturated biography can also be manufactured for the main character; this provides a complete history of the character up to the point of attack (the beginning of the play).
3. Playwright A drafts three dialogue-oriented scenes.
4. Playwright B interpolates two monologues at key points interrupting the dialogue. Each monologue serves a distinct function.
5. Playwright B redrafts the dialogue-oriented scenes.
6. Playwright A revises and tweaks the monologues.

COMMENT: Interpolation can be considered late into the rehearsal process as a means of revising a scene or play without wholesale restructuring. Song interpolation in musicals is relatively common, especially recently, with the proliferation of rock composers (Bono, Elton John, and so on) writing for the stage. Remember, monologue in drama accomplishes what the song does in a musical, a corollary that is often overlooked.

EXERCISE:
How monologues function: creating the ten-minute play

1. Write three scenes in dialogue involving a love triangle.

2. Target five scenes, either alternating two monologue scenes with three dialogue scenes, or two dialogue scenes with three monologues. In the latter format, start with a monologue from your major character; the second monologue comes from another character; the third involves the major character in a discovery, or moment of *peripeteia*.

3. One monologue should use an image, inanimate object, song, or prop to describe the character analogically or metaphorically.

4. Play with the structure by interpolating the monologues between scenes of dialogue. What happens to the sense of sequence and transition? You will have to revise a bit to accommodate the monologues into the dialogue.

5. How and what do the monologues tell us about the character speaking, and the other characters?

COMMENT: This exercise is most successful with beginning playwrights because it teaches a fundamental model for structuring a play that is readily accessible. Since the outcome of the exercise will be about ten pages, it is an excellent method to structure a ten-minute play. The alternation of monologue and dialogue scenes affects stage time, seemingly expanding a sense of duration while being read within the ten-minute framework. The concept of monologue as independent scene is made clear.

Note: Try both combinations of structure:

dialogue/monologue/dialogue/monologue/dialogue;

monologue/dialogue/monologue/dialogue/monologue.

Note the differences in the results.

EXERCISE:
The relationship of the monologue to space

1. Select a common household space and integrate it completely into a scheme of character and structure.

2. Consider private or transitional spaces and write several character monologues. Use closets, attics, foyers, and corridors, weight or exercise rooms, laundry rooms, and so on.

3. How does space inform the monologue? What feels safe to the character?

4. Attempt to build a brief one-act play around one of these transitional spaces. For example, think of the dramatic possibilities in a laundry room: its powerful image of clean and dirty and forgotten or ruined clothes. How can this visual reinforce the past, the present? The action of ironing or pressing clothes may trigger emotional responses. Corridors or stairways (transitional spaces) are seldom used by playwrights but impose interesting contextual frames. Playwright Kent Brown and others have written successful one-acts around garage sales. Obviously, items put up for sale have histories that inform us about the characters in a natural way. The space-event-related action provides context for the play. Rummaging in an attic might border on the cliché or banal unless objects and memories become imbued with wonder.

COMMENT: This is an excellent exercise for young playwrights to move beyond living rooms or scenes in bars and coffee shops. For example, bathrooms are often used as a refuge, a place for bathing and relaxing, and thus retreat from daily life. They provide an excellent setting for the reflective or revelatory monologue.

EXERCISE:
Portrait monologue

The portrait monologue can be used as a study of character; providing external stimulation and closely observed detailing for the young playwright. The following exercise has become a mainstay in my playwriting workshops. The more you can get young playwrights "out of their head" and into observation of the other, the more quickly they will progress as playwrights.

1. Download photographic portraits of distinctive characters. These may be comic or serious, but should trigger the imagination of the viewer. Seek out portraits with props or other objects that define circumstances.

2. Set the pile down in the workshop and have the participants choose which one they would like to explore further.

3. As they closely observe the portrait, the participant jots down key features and aspects, then constructs an imaginary "life bio" giving the figure a name, context, and action.

4. Proceed with the writing a one-page monologue that details a particular desire or need of the figure.

COMMENT: This exercise can be combined with the saturated bio to create a full profile based on the portrait.

INTEGRATED MONOLOGUE

Monologue seems most organic when it is completely integrated within the dramatic scheme. In Barbara Cassidy's *Interim* the character Jim comes to his moment of self-perception and self-discovery very close to the end of the play. This crucial placement heightens the impact of the character's epiphany and reversal through the dramaturgical shift to the monologic form:

JIM: (*Addressing Audience*) I used to think that at some time in my existence, I would do something that was important. (*Pause*) Or maybe it was I thought I'd do something that other people thought was important. (*Pause.*) That might be more like it. (*Pause.*) I now realize that I'm not going to do either. My daughter, Alma, is now the only thing I care about. It's true. She's eight years old. (*calling downstage*) Alma. Alma. Could you come out here please?

(Wellman and Lee 2006, 43)

Cassidy's carefully constructed dramatic monologue concentrates traditional elements of play structure: beginning (exposition: sense of context, sense of past), middle (discovery, climax: realization that his measurement of success has now changed); and end (reversal, choice, resolution): He not only realizes that his daughter is the most important thing to him, but reinforces it by asking her to join him onstage.

In his book *The Word and Verbal Art*, Jan Mukarovsky posits that a character's move to monologism occurs "by virtue of the fact that one of the speakers forgets his partners and speaks 'to himself by indulging in recollection or by becoming absorbed in himself'" (1997, 115). Of course, onstage this is accomplished with a subtle lighting special that illuminates the monologic moment in contrast to dimmed background characters and setting. The skilled director, and the actor playing Jim, will find distinct beats in this monologue—emphasizing the transitions from beginning to middle to end—fully working the range of contrast and contour. In its entirety the monologue represents a beat segment with clear dramaturgical markers.

David Lindsay-Abaire's *Rabbit Hole* uses a variety of monologue techniques, including the integrated model. In this play, tense dialogue between the grieving parents builds to pressure points that release in monologue. Here, an altercation ensues after Howie finds out Becca inadvertently taped over a video of their son. Note how intention is clarified with italics, and punctuations and capital letters are used to indicate intonation shifts:

HOWIE: I left the gate unlatched.

BECCA: Well, *I* didn't check it! (*retreats a bit*) I'm not playing this game again, Howie. It was no one's fault.

HOWIE: Not even the dog's.

BECCA: I *know* that.

HOWIE: Dogs chase squirrels. Boys chase dogs.

BECCA: Are you telling me or yourself?

HOWIE: He loved that dog!

BECCA: Of course he did.

HOWIE: And you got rid of him!

BECCA: Right, like I got rid of the tape. I get it.

HOWIE: (*Losing it*) It's not just the tape! I'm not talking about the tape, Becca! It's Taz, and the paintings, and the clothes, and it's *everything*! You have to stop erasing him! You have to stop it! You HAVE TO STOP! (*Howie has been reduced to tears. He moves away from her. She takes him in, more confused than affronted*).

BECCA: Do you really not know me, Howie? Do you really not know how utterly impossible that would be? To erase him? No matter how many things I give to charity, or how many art projects I box up, do you really think I don't see him every second of every day? And OK, I'm trying to make things a little easier on myself by hiding some photos, and giving away the clothes, but that does not mean I'm trying to erase him. That tape was an accident. And believe me, I will beat myself up about it forever, I'm sure. Like everything else I could've prevented but didn't.

(Lindsay-Abaire 2006, 86)

Becca's monologue is an epiphany for her, and a moment of deeper understanding for Howie. Becca is confronting the realities of getting on with life, with actions that cannot be neatly articulated or clearly defined. The erased videotape, is, of course, a metaphor for this process, and Abaire uses it to trigger the monologue exchange. Becca opens the monologue with a series of question, as much for the audience as for herself and Howie. It is an excellent example of the "transparent mind" as we see her doubt, her struggle, and her actions in a complex, messy bundle, that she (and we) are trying to sort through. Howie's invective monologue which precedes her "moment of truth" is crafted expertly. Particularly note the end of the monologue—here, a series of three lines are truncated in sequence, climaxing in the all-caps crescendo. Abaire's building and baring of emotions in these two monologues seems operatic. For example, the pause between the monologues and the separation of characters allows Becca to move the focal point of her monologue outward, rather than inward to Howie, much the way an opera singer would begin an aria.

EXERCISE:
Utilizing the integrated model

1. Write a two-character scene in which the characters are bound in some type of relationship: a couple, business partners, siblings, parent and child.
2. One character should reveal some deep or hidden truth that will change or reverse the course of their relationship.
3. This revelation is accomplished through a monologue that has clear beat transitions for beginning, middle, and end.
4. Create a strong level of self-absorption in the character during the monologue.

5. The character should feel a strong change of horizon as a result of the mono-logue (like a weight has been lifted). Clarify this marker with something visual, a rhythmic shift in speech, a pause, and so on.

COMMENT: One of the contrived aspects of the monologue and one of the problems in rehearsal has to do with other persons who are listeners, but not participants. In fact, part of the effect is achieved by making these listener characters remote. It is easy for the silent character to inadvertently steal focus, for example. In production, the focus on the actor can be emphasized easily with a lighting special while lowering light levels on the other characters. This ensures primary focus and is a convention in the theater. Conversely, if there are multiple monologues in a play, a director will most likely seek variety in staging. In some cases, this will involve total engagement of "the other" so there is less theatrical distinction between monologue and dialogue scenes. As we explore the various monologic formats, the playwright will discover how the function of monologue is tied to an expansive array of choices.

Structuring the monologue with specific beats that indicate beginning, middle, and end is often quite difficult for beginning playwrights. The tendency is to get pulled off track in the middle of the monologue—usually with digressionary material or tangential subject matter. A successful counter-strategy has the playwright construct the end first, and then begin the monologue keeping the target in mind. Just like the special ellipsoidal light beam that captures the monologue's delivery, the monologue must remain focused throughout, with a sharpness of attack and purpose.

Focus can also be achieved by relating the content of the monologue to sensual experiences. The keen awareness of sense experiences will open the playwright to a novel way of triggering theatrical language.

EXERCISE:
Sense recall—the accident monologue

This exercise was given in a workshop by Matthew Maguire, author of the award-winning *Throwin' Bones* and *Phaedra*. Maguire is chair of the theatre department at Fordham University. The key to this monologue is keeping it in the moment. If the writer can visualize the event in slow motion detail this will help create the desired effect.

1. In a monologue, describe a true, nonfictional accident that happened to you.

2. Select the most intense moment of the accident, focus on the phenomenon: what you perceived, what was happening around you, capturing as closely as possible each of your five senses in that moment.

3. Create the impression of time standing still until the abrupt moment of resolution.

COMMENT: The accident represents a moment of hyperreality when time seemingly stands still, and life hangs in the balance. This sense of danger is the very stuff of theater. Keep audiences on the nervy precipice, off balance and engaged. Attempt to write rhythmically, withholding and restraining the monologue until the heightened moment of no return. At this point increase rapidity, by using truncated phrases, accelerated rate, and heightened pitch. Indicate with exclamation points and capital letters. Consider the breathing of the actor—from slow and sustained to ending in a pant.

EXPLORATORY MONOLOGUE

The exploratory monologue is a means to flesh out a character or integrate backstory into the character's actions. Sometimes it can be used to recall sense experience in a particular episode of a character or author's life. It can also be used as a means to arrive at the above exercise, providing the raw materials that can be shaped accordingly into the requisite beginning, middle, and end. To achieve this, have participants construct a saturated bio first, choose specific qualities to include or not, then integrate those elements into your monologue or play. (See Table 11.1.) The saturated bio simply is a fictional and exploratory history of the character concocted by the playwright. Actors-in-training will often construct the saturated bio as a means to explore subtext.

This saturated bio table provides you with a wide range of qualities and characteristics for developing closely observed characters. Once you specify choices you can gauge how important they are for a character in a particular play or monologue. Simply select a handful of the most important as your areas of focus. The saturated bio can be combined with other exercises, such as the portrait monologue. This chart is particularly useful with developing monologues that might otherwise become rhetorical, abstract or disconnected; the "sat bio" can ground a character by emphasizing specific characteristics or qualities across a broad continuum. It can be used to create a range of characters from traditional to experimental depending upon what you emphasize.

MONOLOGUE AND THE ABSENT "OTHER"

A fundamental skill of playwriting is the ability to effectively score monologues to offstage characters. Often, this convention of monologue involves the semiotization of the absent "other." When a character prays to an onstage statue, for instance, the statue is the visual stand-in for the actual saint, for Christ, or for an ancestor. *Semiotization* means that one object stands in for something else, becoming a sign of that object. Perhaps the most prosaic example is the telephone, the use of which indicates and simulates that someone "absent" is on the other end. An empty chair can be just that, but when it is semiotized it could signify the person who just left, or even a deceased parent (as in dad's favorite chair). Tape recorders and phone answering devices have long been used to introduce characters before their entrance. The use of visual or iconic signs can be particularly effective, as when a character addresses a photographic image of a loved one, a painted portrait or bust, or even a tattoo of a lover etched into the flesh. Various symbols may portray the absent other: a piece of jewelry such as a locket, or a flower.

Table 11.1 The saturated bio chart

CHARACTER NAME:	SATURATED BIO CHART/KNOWLEDGE BASE	SPECIFICS ABOUT CHARACTER	RATE IMPORTANCE OF EACH TO THE CHARACTER ON 1–10 SCALE (HOW IMPORTANT IS EACH TO YOUR MONOLOGUE?)
QUALITY	MAJOR DEFINING CHARACTERISTIC		DELETE LOW RANKS FROM MONOLOGUE
Age			
Height	Range		
Weight	Descriptive vs. quantity		
Religion	Devout, atheist, et		
Political	Liberal, fanatic, etc.		
Race			
Gene	Proclivities based on inherited traits		
Handicap			
Attractive	Relative scale		
Emotions	Dominant emotion: anger, envy, etc.		
Communication modality	Primary mode is visual, tactile, or auditory		
Intelligent to incompetent			
Musical?	Instrument, type (specific)		
Art			

CHARACTER NAME:	SATURATED BIO CHART/KNOWLEDGE BASE	SPECIFICS ABOUT CHARACTER	RATE IMPORTANCE OF EACH TO THE CHARACTER ON 1–10 SCALE (HOW IMPORTANT IS EACH TO YOUR MONOLOGUE?)
QUALITY	MAJOR DEFINING CHARACTERISTIC		DELETE LOW RANKS FROM MONOLOGUE
Hobby/sport			
Parents			
Relationships			
Drugs, booze	Dependent, etc.		
Siblings			
Accent or regionalism			
Major action or intention			
What do other characters say about you			
Favorite phrase			
Biggest success			
Biggest failure			
Wants to be	Liked, understood, respected, etc.		
Sexuality	Libido charge		
PROP			

By using these devices the playwright can construct the monologue with confidence that the audience will suspend its disbelief regarding the non-present "other." For instance, in the familiar phone monologue, the playwright deftly disguises the monologue within conditions that are essentially dialogic, or interactional, by presenting disagreements, misunderstandings, and disruptions, rather than a chain of uninterrupted continuity or agreement. In writing the phone monologue the playwright must provide leading questions, followed by credible responses. This device has become increasingly popular with the ubiquity of the cellular phone, which can simply be pulled from the actor's pocket at the appropriate moment. As discussed earlier, the first scene of Sarah Ruhl's *Dead Man's Cell Phone* is really a dialogic monologue with frequent phone breaks, mixing with direct address and "conversation" with the dead man. Of course, the risk for the playwright is in overusing a technique that can grow predictable and stale; it can become as corny as the written letter that is gratuitously recited or dictated to a third party. By altering ringtones in *Dead Man's Cell Phone* a director can semiotize the various "callers" with sounds that reflect their personalities. This not only defines and distinguishes the "other" but also provides comic payoffs to the frequent interruptions.

EXERCISES:
Monologue and the absent "other"

Exercise A
1. Brainstorm over typical professions that use the phone often.
2. Write an opening scene that utilizes a phone device but creates a vivid sense of offstage characters. In other words, use the monologue to focus on the offstage character.
3. Give the offstage character insight into the behavior of the character that is speaking, thus creating a kind of self-commentary, which is ironic and effective onstage.

Exercise B
1. Have a character find the photo of another character at an earlier phase in their life.
2. Have a monologue develop the differences between the past and the present in terms of the character perceiving the photograph (the marker is the moment of discovery).
3. Some change of outlook or emotional horizon is indicated (shift the mood).

COMMENT: While reading a letter on stage seems stodgy from a theatrical point of view, Lindsay-Abaire in *Rabbit Hole* solved the problem by having Jason, the teenaged driver who killed their son, present the letter in monologue, while the mother, Becca, reads it in the background. The semiotized lighting effect translated an old convention into a powerfully theatricalized realization that gave an added dimension to the play.

In sum, the key factor in writing effective monologues is to capture the char- acter's transition in mental and emotional states. You need to provide markers for the actor to affect this end result. If you wish to improve characterization in your monologues, a good tool is to study portrait paintings, paying close attention to visual details in particular. In period portraits, you will notice iconographic elements that show what an individual is about— profession, passions, and private concerns. A most effective exercise that takes this visual aspect to the extreme involves a *fetish object* and the character. By showing the abnormal attachment of the character to a particular object, you unlock a level of visual interest for the audience while drawing a dialogic relationship between the fetish object and the character's emotional states. Used in the workshop, this pushes students or participants beyond their comfort zone and inhibited range of characterization.

12

Dialogic monologue:
from structure to antistructure

DEFINING THE DOMINANT: VARIOUS APPLICATIONS

The dominant may be defined as the focusing component of a work of art: it rules, determines, and transforms the remaining components. It is the dominant that guarantees the integrity of the structure (see Matejka and Poworoska 1978, 82). In this case, the impetus for a change in scene is provided by a literary or theatrical device rather than by a character's psychological motivation or need. It could be considered an arbitrary shifter in the structure of the play. Its function is both literary and theatrical, and in Matejka's terms, it "transforms the remaining components" in the play. Monologue as the dominant has other manifestations that are most valuable for the playwright interested in expanding their dramaturgical skills. A signature component of Len Jenkin's work is his use of the *call*.

The call is the focusing structural component of *Dark Ride*, which remains one of the most important breakthrough plays in the new dramaturgy. The call is at work in other Jenkin plays, like *Kid Twist*, in which the titular character is confined to a hotel room awaiting trial as a federally protected witness.

The calls here are framed as the Kid's dreams; they transport the action to various worlds outside the motel room. Another example of the call is the monologue that begins Jenkin's *American Notes*. The Mayor's opening monologue is delivered to the mentally challenged Chuckles. After telling Chuckles he might be able "to place a man of his talents," the Mayor tells him to look around, at which point he makes reference to the desk clerk of the motel. Lights go up on her area, segueing us into the next scene of dialogue. In the journey play, monologue invariably contains a marker that leads us forward, thus giving the play direction, focus, and progression.

Jenkin's use of multiple, rather than single, narrators creates a structural tension as they continually vie for "authorship" of the story. This dialogism across narrator/characters provides one level of interest. The call provides structural links to the disparate voices. Otherwise, the play would be haphazard and incoherent. For playwrights, the call can have applications along a broad continuum or spectrum: from single narrators and shifting scenes to multiple narrators and shifting worlds. The best example of this phenomenon in action is Jenkin's *Dark Ride*. In a February 23, 2010 interview with Culturebot, Adam Greenfield, current literary manager at Playwright's Horizon in New York, described *Dark Ride* as the most important play he had ever read: it "rocked my world" for reasons that we discuss below (Horwitz 2010).

THE CALL AND THE JOURNEY PLAY: MONOLOGUE AS STRUCTURE IN *DARK RIDE*

In Scene 3 of Len Jenkin's *Dark Ride*, the character Margo picks up a postcard referring us to her lover, a character Jenkin has simply named the Thief. While the postcard suggests the casual regard of the Thief for Margo, it establishes structural links to the next scene. The postcard device exploits one way of dealing with the absent "other," although Jenkin takes the dramaturgical move one step further. The last three phrases read by Margo: "outskirts of some city, for miles alongside highways, feeding out into suburban streets," become the opening lines of the Thief's monologue. More importantly, Jenkin's dramaturgical move is indicative of how structure is created in a journey play. Jenkin's repetition posits a dialogism that is temporal, A to A in terms of the repetitive sequence whereby A reflects itself, but also spatial, A to B, as the shift in character and stage space initiates a new scene:

> THIEF: Outskirts of some city, for miles alongside highways, feeding out into suburban streets, and I'm walking, and I keep looking back over my shoulder to see if anyone's behind me. I have the damn thing in a leather bag around my neck and I'm heading south and I figured I better … after three days on the road I figured I better … I figured I better get inside somewhere, I figured I better eat something. I'm in America, coming into town. There's these long stretches of seedy apartment houses. Some people on the steps of them with a baby, and they're drinking beer, and they say hello in the dark, and they don't even know who they're talkin' to, you know but I say hello back anyway, and that seems to be it cause I just keep walkin' and they don't say anything else. O.K. Now I'm really hungry but it's a long way between neon, and then I see one coming, a red blur in the distance, and I squint at it, wanting it to say Cafe or Eat Here or something but it ends up saying Tri-City Furniture or Red Robin Autos—Used but not Abused—and finally I see another one, and it's a revolve, turning and turning, and it says THE EMBERS. We Never Close, so I go in. I'm here. Jukebox.
>
> (Jenkin 1993, *Dark Ride*, 69–70)

At this point, a waitress appears, seats the Thief, and a dramatized scene follows in a restaurant.

Spatially, Jenkin's on-the-road drifter is set against the shifting ground of a highway landscape. The monologue is evocative in unraveling a closely observed pastiche of roadside Americana. This down-on-his-luck drifter with a point of view is a staple of American lore. This character is drenched in fear, but driven by the desire to satisfy his appetite. The syntax is present tense, yet thrusts us into future events. The transitory narrative casts the Thief in unfolding interactions with his environment. A destination is found, but not in the linear or unified sense. Note the tortuous passage through the seedy apartment buildings, and the inner dialogue between hoped for "Eat here" and actual "Tri-City Furniture." Strong visual images, such as "Red Robin Autos," the revolving neon sign, "Embers," and "jukebox" delineate name associations for the spectators' imagination, and a path for the spectator to follow in the journey through language space. The monologic spatial field becomes interactive as each utterance shifts both the spectator and the actor to a defined "other." Words serve a spatial and temporal function, as language imbues the stage with protean characteristics. Chameleon-like, the stage changes colors and location with fluidity and ease. Jenkin's syntactical techniques in the monologue underscore the scene's action. The length of the Thief's phrases corresponds to his distance from his eventual destination. As he approaches the restaurant, his utterances truncate. Phrasing choices reflect the actual space.

Jenkin's proper-name labeling celebrates the Americana landscape in a panoramic word-field. Within monologue, proper names create vivid images, suggest a mood, or provide concrete detail. Jenkin eliminates past-tense explorations of character psychology as necessary links to present behavior. By doing so, he voids the creation of subtext. Mood states replace subtext in the subjective realm of the new playwriting. Mood emerges as an external condition in which the character operates, rather than as a manifestation of inner psychology. The symbolic nature of the language, and the reliance on transitory mood states, recall certain tenets of symbolist theater, although the new playwriting is rarely static or minimalist.

FASCINATION WITH FORM

Form devices like the call motivate the narrative shifts and concomitant divulgence of content. Form is foregrounded in *Dark Ride* as the audience is readily aware of the device. Jenkin notes to the director in the Dramatists Play Service edition:

> The director and performers should be aware that *Dark Ride* is a weave of tales, of scenes within scenes, like the facets of the diamond. That a scene is within a book, or a picture, or in someone's mind makes it no less 'real' in terms of staging. The 'real' point of view is a shifting one.
>
> (Jenkin 1982, 47–8)

In departing from the unity provided by a central character, Jenkin's statement echoes one of his literary heroes, Franz Kafka (Jenkin is now developing a play called *Time in Kafka*). Jenkin opposes causal linearity, favoring the restlessness of a shifting form featuring an array of characters. Although

steeped in the lore of American types and literary conventions, he rejects
the notion of a dominant narrative or story line. His polyvocal narratives
pull the audience away from empathic identification by creating a field of
diverse plots, multiple ironies, and shifts of mood. These dramaturgical
techniques link him to Brechtian alienation, but without didactic ends.

SUMMARIZING THE CALL

Jenkin provides multiple narrators whose dramaturgical functions are to
call scenes forth into being or intervene within active dramatic sections in
order to disrupt the action and transit the sequence elsewhere. After characters finish role-playing as narrators, they return to the action, move to
another area, or disappear altogether. Thus, each sequence of the action is
literally wrapped within a given narrative, formal device. This may appear
complex and intricate, yet in practice it is really quite straightforward. The
exercise below explores the most prevalent of Jenkin's narrative techniques—the call, or invocation—essential to understanding the concept of
sequence in his playwriting. In the call the narrator's function is twofold; he
must first, establish the basic story or subject matter of the play (usually
from memory, dreams, or fantasy), and second, call forth the dramatized
scene. The call occurs near the end of the narrated story or passage, and is
generally positioned in the penultimate sentence or phrase of the speech.
This placement allows the other characters to enter and assume actions as
the narrator finishes the speech. At that point, the narrator enters into the
dramatic action, assumes another area of the stage, or exits the scene.

The call is a fundamental technique to effect sequence and transition
without cumbersome blackouts. By using the narrator(s), the playwright
can finesse an otherwise awkward stage shift. A narrator can mediate
between simultaneous scenes, bridge gaps in time, or move time forward or
backward. I usually assign this next exercise as a ten-minute play, whereby
the playwrights are required to limit blackouts to one—at the end.

EXERCISE:
The call

1. Have one character pick up a letter, a postcard, a photograph, or painting of
someone they are in a relationship with, or have been in close emotional
involvement with.
2. At the point where reference is made to the other character, the other should
appear at another place on the stage.
3. The character from step 1 reads a direct quote from the other character, the
last lines of which this other repeats, and the transition is made to the next
sequence.
4. The first character disappears as the other enters a building, the house of a
lover, a church or any other place depicted in the monologue. This narration
represents the call for a new dramatized scene to begin.

COMMENT: This fundamental technique must be mastered for the playwright to write fluidly within an episodic structure. It is quite stageworthy as it allows designers to shift scenery and lighting without a break in continuity. The blackout should never be used simply as a matter of convenience for the playwright but should embody some dramaturgical purpose that helps rather than hinders the reception of the play. The call combines resolution with anticipation, two powerful components of dramaturgy.

FORM AND CONTENT REVISITED

Traditional pedagogies in playwriting (and more so, screenwriting) emphasize formal principles that once learned, can be adapted to fit various contexts. In screenwriting, the three-act form is ingrained to the degree that plot points must occur at the 17th minute, halfway through the screenplay, and at the final climax. Student playwrights define their progress by improvements in developing conflict, rising action, and increasing complications within these parameters; craft is defined as executing the content within these strictures. Conversely, new playwriting derives form from content, extricating theatrical rather than rhetorical means to deliver the message. Several of these examples follow.

EROTICISM AND MONOLOGUE

As we have noted, Iizuka's application (in *36 Views*) of Kabuki acting and medieval Japanese iconography and musicality ensures sensate experiences for the audience; the dialogic clash between past and present catalyzes the frisson that releases the stored energy in the material. This risky dramaturgy allows Iizuka to explore the sexual relationship between the art dealer Wheeler and Setzuko's equivocal character without its appearing gratuitous.

Through her displays of *shunga*, antique erotic woodblock prints that were commissioned for a patron's private viewing, Iizuka seeds the brewing sexual tension in the play. Most *shunga* are graphically sexual images created to arouse desire in the viewer, (Some *shunga* add written or poetic messages that are descriptive or personal.) Woven into the progression of scenes, these displays run concomitantly to the growing attraction between Setsuko and Wheeler, reaching their "climactic" moment in Scene 26. Here, the *shunga* transforms from a static image into the *tableau vivant* of Setsuko and Wheeler as naked lovers. Then, Iizuka "captions" the tableau with Setsuko's poetic monologue:

> SETSUKO HEARN:
> No rain tonight, no moon, the air is perfectly still …
> Their bellies slick and wet-
> The tickle of waterweed
> The soft wet moss
> The curve of your neck, your fingertips

The rustle of silk undone—
Your mouth, your tongue
Your lips, the taste of your lips, salt, wet
The warmth of your breath against my skin—

(Iizuka 2003, scene 26: 69–70)

Iizuka artfully wraps the erotic, first in graphic imagery, then tableau, then poetry, before returning to the realism of Scene 28, when we find Setsuko and Wheeler dressing while discussing the image of the Heian-era woman in the portrait. Their passionate interaction is seemingly motivated from the *shunga* iconography in the print as if it came from its DNA.

The Asian historicized content of *36 Views* fits the polyvocal format that defines the play's structure, just as *Topdog/Underdog*'s sampling of minstrelsy delivers a broader statement than a realistic *tranche de vie* (slice of life) between two brothers. Len Jenkin's *Margo Veil* draws upon the visual tricks of the nineteenth-century illusionist to transform the lead character, Margo, into multiple "others." In weaning oneself from the strictures of realism, the playwright acknowledges and incorporates the broader palette of theatrical language. The playwright who crosses borders, or transgresses sexual boundaries, engages risk, but this is not to be feared—risk innately creates interest! Nowhere is this more evident than in Alice Tuan's sexually explicit adaptation of Sophocles' *Ajax,* which Tuan has retitled *Ajax (Por Nobody).* Her artful use of monologue here slightly veils the action of a *ménage à trois* among Alma, Jesse, and Alexander:

> ALMA: To bring man together in one entity. You'd meet somewhere right ... here (points right between her bosom) ... the two of you, right here ... head to head ... head touching head ...think you'll both reach— (They both start fondling her). The brotherhood of man ... filling in all gaps, leave nothing empty ... oh there, an empty continent ... . fill it, yes, right there ... fill it, with your know-how ... your numerals... your roads, I feel roads being paved ... palaces being entered ... .courts being visited ... heads being praised... one's in ... I guess the other waits for my silence, as I bid the sleeping maiden adieu and bend, bend for the brotherhood ... that they may meet, and love, in one.

(Wellman and Lee 2006, 301)

The euphemistic hyperbole of a double entendre maximizes the humorous aspect of this sexual encounter, and distances the audience appropriately. Tuan sets Alma behind a bench so that the physical act may be feigned, while her paralinguistic "Uhn's" mark her progress toward sexual satisfaction. However, subsequent actions of fellatio in the play would be more difficult to feign, and Tuan makes no effort to do so. The production ran for four months at the Flea Theater in New York (in 2001) but as a modified staged reading. Tuan's classical references in the play, as described earlier, provided the theatrical point of departure for the playwright's Dionysian reveries and diverted some of the critical attention from the sexuality. Nevertheless, its bold exposé of unleashed female sexuality represented a breakthrough, and launched Tuan's career.

In the latest and most successful play on liberating female sexuality, Sarah Ruhl's 2009 Pulitzer Prize finalist, *The Next Room or the Vibrator Play*, the subject matter is late nineteenth-century hysteria and the use of the latest technology to cure it. Ruhl's play, which prompted *New York Magazine* reviewer Scott Brown's lead, "Sarah Ruhl should write more porn" (November 16, 2009), delves into the therapeutic benefits of "paroxysm," the term used in 1880 to describe orgasm. (Ruhl also tosses moments of female ejaculation and male prostate orgasm into the mix.) The scientific Dr. Givings's explanatory monologue sets the comic tone:

> DR. GIVINGS: Are you warm enough (Mrs. Daltry nods.) Mrs. Daltry, we are going to produce in you what is called a paroxysm. The congestion in your womb is causing your hysterical symptoms and if we can release some of that congestion and invite the juices downward your health will be restored. Thanks to the dawn of electricity – yes thank you Mr. Edison – a great American – I have a new instrument, which I will use. It used to be that it would take me or it would take Annie – oh – hours to produce a paroxysm in our patients and it demanded a lot of skill and patience. It was much like a child's game – trying to pat the head and rub the stomach at the same time – but thanks to this new electrical instrument we shall be done in a matter of minutes.
>
> (Ruhl 2010, 16)

By setting the play in the late nineteenth century, Ruhl is able to mitigate the reactions of her audience through its relatively quaint qualities. The women's Victorian clothing, for example, presents all kinds of challenges to remove, with endless buttoning and layers. The vibrator itself is first viewed by Mrs. Givings as a "farm tool," and the monologue's references to Thomas Edison, and comparisons with children's games and manual masturbation, provide witty juxtapositions. Dr. Givings's stiff upper lip reserve lends propriety to his work; while he keeps his wife at some distance from "the next room," she comically eavesdrops, ultimately wanting her husband to give her the vibrator treatment. The neglected wife finally wins her husband's attention as the play concludes, and this warms the play from its clinical, albeit hilarious, approach to female sexuality. In its periodization, behavioral protocols, and theme of female liberation, the play echoes Ibsen's *A Doll's House*.

As these playwrights demonstrate, nineteenth-century realism, classical tragedy, Kabuki, *tableau vivant* and minstrelsy which defined historical eras in the past can be resuscitated anew, and, not only "hold the boards," but create magic and wonder for new audiences. Utilizing erotic iconography (or devices) as a point of departure has the solid underpinnings of transferring gestures, costumes, and movements from erstwhile periods. These codes become experienced as living phenomena when transferred to the actor on stage. Dealing with highly charged erotic material in today's theater seems more challenging than it was in the freewheeling 1960s and early 1970s. Ironically, new playwrights can be at their most innovative (and derive the most latitude) when recycling the theatricality of the past into their plays.

EXERCISE:
Theatrical style and transgressive material

Define a theatrical style that you want to conflate within your contemporary scene. Select from historical performance styles, some of which may include historical realism, Kabuki, Noh, puppetry, *commedia dell'arte*, carnival or circus, mime, pantomime, music hall, *tableau vivant*, Ancient Greek, 60s avant-garde (Open Theater, Performance Group, Grotowski), etc.

1. Select an action that involves two or three characters whereby the past or memory is an important component.

2. Select a potentially transgressive subject, either erotic, or some type of taboo.

3. Begin with a monologue in which a historicized action from another character juxtaposes with the narrator.

4. Consider something iconic as a trigger device.

5. Incorporate the theatrical form to mitigate the transgressive subject matter or theme.

6. Vary the theatrical form or style with a contemporary take on the subject matter.

7. Explore the script's potential for juxtaposed theatricality in the workshop, considering how it might be structured into a ten-minute play.

8. Write the ten-minute play structuring key theatrical transitions through the integration of historicized form.

COMMENT: Search Wikipedia then move on to the Theater History website if unfamiliar with a particular historical era or style. Playwrights should investigate four or five aspects of a given performance style before beginning. The exercise will deliver better results if the playwright makes references in monologue rather than stage directions. There should be a link (as in the Iizuka model above) between the language and action.

MONOLOGUE AS ARIA

If monologue traditionally focuses a character's credo or belief system at a pivotal point in the play, then its heightened rendering may simulate the aria of opera. In one of his last major stage plays, *Dark Rapture*, Eric Overmyer, utilizes the backdrop of an inferno to stimulate some virtuosic wordplay. His monologues are often designed toward showstopping qualities tantamount to the operatic aria. He envisions monologue as an opportunity for the playwright to demonstrate virtuosity, for language to be fully explored. This technical crafting is apparent in *Dark Rapture*, in Babcock's first speech. The character is entranced as he watches his California home burn in the near distance:

> BABCOCK: Fuckin A. Nothin' spookier 'n a night fire, man. Makes you feel so all alone. I remember. One time. Big Island. Lava flow. Big orange tongues a molten magma whatever creepin down the hillside like some kinda hellacious glacier. Like some kinda red-hot tectonic taffy. Eerie fuckin' thing to be comin' at ya outa the fuckin' dark, I'm tellin' ya. Fry an egg on that air. That' how hot it was. Softboil one on the palm a your hand. Melt cars. Asphalt like butter, Houses'd just pop. Bang. Like paper bags. Like that. (*He cups his hands and slaps them together, making a popping sound.*) Kablooee. Spontaneous combust. From the sheer fuckin' heat. Kablam. What can you do but grab the cat, count the kids, and say a prayer to St. Jude the lava runs outa geothermal juice 'fore it desiccates you `n yours like so much delicatessen jerky. Just sit back 'n watch it comin' toward you. Like sheer fuckin' inevitability, Lurchin' outa the dark rapture... .

> (Overmyer 1993, *Dark Rapture*, 261)

Opening the play, the monologue points entry into a *film noir*-styled play of intrigue and romantic adventure. The *noir* speech genre, conflated with cartoonese ("Kablam" and "Kablooee"), provides the formal foundation for the character's dialogic flights. The laconic *film noir* style is juxtaposed with the playwright's baroque elocutions with its volcanic force and towering eloquence. The rapturous rhythm of language simulates the swells and high notes of the operatic aria. The character gets caught up in what he's saying—enjoying the phrasing, relishing the articulation. The force of language energizes a vibrant tension between audience and actor. Babcock's soliloquy is fueled from moment to moment by the raging inferno in the background. This landscape of language oscillates between figure and ground. It transgresses the boundaries of more normative, fixed-figure monologues, in which the figure steps forward into the isolating beam of the spotlight.

EXERCISE:
Monologue aria; on rapture

1. Revise or write a monologue in which a character is describing an event. Put it in the present tense—in the moment the event is occurring. Strive for "upmanship" whereby the linguistic force attempts to top the event.

2. The moment should be an epiphany for the character. Explore range from the ecstatic to the catastrophic: the moment one falls in love or loses everything; a near-death experience; an unexpected victory; or a self-discovery.

4. Riff with the language and its suggested rhythms——the character takes joy and energy from what is said or described. Notice how Overmyer riffs with word choices and rhythms ("desiccates/delicatessen"; "grab the cat, count the kids, and say a prayer to St. Jude," and so on).

5. Focus "in the moment" as opposed to the results.

COMMENT: For many young playwrights, theater seems too tame or safe. The desire to pummel the audience with sound, energy, and musical force can be unleashed through the force in language. This exercise gives you a chance to get extreme, as you try to "top" yourself, giving as much energy to the speech as possible. Rapture can be associated with whipping up frenzy—a move toward the ecstatic.

MONOLOGUE AS STRUCTURAL DETERMINANT

As we have seen, new playwriting tends to maximize the structural component of dialogic monologue. If you consider yourself a traditionalist, these strategies will allow you more range in making transitions between scenes without resorting to blackouts or abrupt episodic shifts. Blackouts that exist only for the playwright's convenience will harm rather than aid the dramaturgy. Scene changes that occur during blackouts are usually cumbersome and distracting. The playwright must master the dramaturgy of sequence and transition, and thereby, offer the director solutions to staging the play.

Many playwrights now alternate monologue and dialogue sections to provide the overall structural scheme. Monologue sections supply the scene material for subsequent dialogues among those characters referred to or introduced in the monologue. As we have seen, meta-devices like songs, poetry, or voice-overs may be used. These effects can be sublime and hardly noticed by the theatergoer, yet provide the substance of structure. Lynn Nottage's 2009 Pulitzer-Prize-winning *Ruined* integrates song, poetry, and a narrative to segue transitions in mood and time. These elements dialogize sinuously within the dramaturgical design.

SPINNING

Nottage often relies on spinning dialogue scenes into monologues to create stunning revelations of character. As the pace of a dialogue between two characters quickens, there is a spinning effect to the language that creates an oblique, vertiginous effect in the dramaturgy. At some point in the dialogue a character spins into a monologue that culminates the topic of the dialogue. When the transforming monologue concludes, the characters are at a different horizon level and a new dialogue or new scene ensues. These monologues are forceful dramaturgic components and keys to the exploring the thematic underpinnings of action. Drama Desk award-winning playwright Matthew Maguire utilizes spinning to explore character-related material that would otherwise remain underexplored in the script. Spinning has various applications that afford the playwright an effective mode of linking dialogue with monologue. The fundamental principle at work is that the dialogue has run its course, or emotional peak, and its natural extension is through monologue. It is similar to the practice in musicals where the emotional build finds its release in song.

PIVOT MONOLOGUE AND THE SCALE OF CHARACTER

As the use of monologue evolves in playwriting usage toward increased dialogism, new forms are emerging that are radicalizing dramaturgy while offering virtuosic moments for the actor. The pivot monologue provides the playwright with a structural bridge between larger beat segments as it catapults the play forward in unexpected directions. In dialogic fashion, the pivot monologue introduces or accelerates the development of a secondary character in a manner that is as unabashed as it is unexpected. The pivot monologue momentarily suspends the narrative track, seemingly digressionary in function; however, the true effect is a rebalancing of the play's objectives. Traditionally, when secondary characters are given monologues in plays, they address the main character, or have a coming of age moment within the context of the fourth wall. The pivot monologue, however, elevates the secondary character to primary status, calling into question "whose play is it?" In this sense, the pivot monologue serves as the "dominant." The term *pivot* indicates a dramaturgical 180-degree turn, it can be identified by some or all of the following properties:

- placement at or around the center of the play
- stand alone, presentational, direct address without fourth-wall contrivance
- character is not the central character in the play
- the scale is large enough to warrant its stand-alone status
- it introduces new thematic material and information
- it shifts the monologic (one-view) orientation of the play
- use of a performative character.

In Sarah Ruhl's *Dead Man's Cell Phone*, Act II opens with a four-page monologue by Gordon (the "dead man"). Prior to this monologue, we see (but do not hear) him at two points: the first scene when Jean finds him dead in the café, and as an observer, at the end of Act I when he witnesses his brother Dwight kissing Jean. In a twist on traditional expository introductions, Ruhl uses the phone device in Act 1 to "introduce" us to the dead man's business contacts, lover, and mother. The following sequence of scenes in Act I proceeds episodically and realistically. As Act II begins with Gordon alone on stage, we recognize that the framework of "reality" has been broken. This represents a sharp turn in the Ruhl's dramaturgy from fourth-wall representational to direct address presentational; the structural cohesion of back-to-back interactive scenes is now interrupted.

Until Gordon's monologue, this is unequivocally Jean's play; with the pivot monologue, Ruhl redeems Gordon from comic device (as stiff) to a fully realized character. By setting it in the play's center, it becomes a structural swing point that oscillates between Jean and Gordon's point of view. From this point on, the grotesque and grisly business of body parts is juxtaposed with the "real time" romance of Jean and Dwight (Gordon's brother). Gordon's extroverted, confident manner contrasts sharply with his brother's and Jean's; although "dead," his presence is exuberant and indomitable. Ruhl now examines Jean's dilemma—is she really in love with Dwight, or drawn to him because of her attraction to Gordon? Amplifying the scale of Gordon's character immediately increases dramatic interest, ultimately oscillating the play's perspective from monologic (Jean's view) to dialogic, as Gordon is given full voice.

Similarly, Ruhl opens Act II *In the Next Room,* or the *Vibrator Play* with a long narration by Leo, a character we meet for the first time in the play (Ruhl 2010, 43–4). While the monologue is broken by brief utterances from Dr. Givings, the effect is to insert a new voice and affect some rebalancing in the play. Leo, in addition to undergoing Dr. Givings's sexual therapy, eventually becomes the romantic foil that Givings's wife utilizes to gain her husband's attention. By introducing significant characters to begin her second acts, Ruhl has developed a novel dramaturgy that reorients audiences' attention while reducing dramatic predictability.

Martin McDonagh's recent play, *A Behanding in Spokane,* uses the pivot monologue to perform a similar feat. In the 2010 Broadway production the lead character of Carmichael was played by Christopher Walken, whose towering performance received a Tony nomination for best actor. However, McDonagh balances the dominance of this character by interpolating a long monologue in front of the curtain delivered by Mervyn, the hotel receptionist. A peripheral or "functional character" inflates into a resounding screed of unresolved issues and personality foibles. Yet Mervyn's direct address, presentational format in front of the curtain, seems abeyant from the play—in a sense—a star turn *tour de force* that equals any of Carmichael's rants. Through this pivot monologue, Mervyn's scale now counterweights the enormity of Walken's eponymous one-handed anti-hero. The monologue's placement slightly before the halfway point echoes Ruhl's structural shifter. The result is a double-tracked narrative that oscillates until the conclusion of the play. We are absorbed in Carmichael/Walken's struggles to regain his hand, while at the same time, we have a second stakeholder who as the proprietor of the hotel also has much to win or lose by the violent antics evolving in Carmichael's hotel room.

The pivot monologue offers the playwright the convenience of increased character scale in a play without wholesale reworking of scenes or dialogue. The monologue may be interpolated late in the revision process as the playwright responds to the evolution of the script. The pivot monologue builds scale dramatically, but also, theatrically, as its performative construction creates a virtuosic opportunity for the skilled actor.

Monologue can assume dialogic qualities through *dematrixing techniques*. The actor/character can be dematrixed when, or if, they:

- fracture the mold of a specific character
- directly acknowledge or address the presence of the audience
- foreground the presence of the actor over character.

Direct address forces the audience to experience matrixing—what Erving Goffman, in *Frame Analysis* (1974), has described as the distinction between onlookers and theatergoers. To break the matrix through direct address, an actor might chide the incoming audience as theatergoers (cajoling latecomers, for example); then, "in character" address the audience as onlookers during his participation in the dramatic action. The first instance represents an actor/theatergoer exchange; the second demonstrates the character/onlooker exchange.

In the 2005 Soho Rep production of his *Careless Love* (a stage version of the radio play *Angel Baby*), Len Jenkin theatricalizes the move between actor and character by requiring microphone-aided speech for Bobby's monologues. The voiceover of the miked Bobby dematrixes Marie's "interior monologue." Bobby's presence on stage heightens the moment's theatricality.

> (*In her mind*) You don't need to write poems about us, babe, cause one drop of your sweat when you're on top of me is a coded message that flies out by night, to other worlds. The drop gets translated by intergalactic linguificators into seven thousand hexameters of immortal, feminine, earth verse … [*gentle laughing that fades*]
>
> (Jenkin 1993, *Careless Love*, 28)

With the microphone, Bobby foregrounds the actor as performer, since the microphone marks the moment as a performance. Later, he resumes the matrix of unamplified speech and dramatized event as the character. This semantic/sonic variable dialogizes between alternating levels of amplified and unamplified speech. Rather than Marie recollecting through a past-tense, third-person monologue that summons the idea of the "absent" lover, Bobby's speech focuses us upon the palpable presence of their erotic interaction. Linguistically, the sound or look of words assumes more importance than their meanings as language seemingly floats—apart from character. In both cases, there is a heightened awareness of artifice or device.

The playwright who is interested in combining voice-overs with "natural" speech can create some marvelous dialogic effects. Karen's multivocal monologue in Jenkin's oft-produced *American Notes* gives the impression of "inner dialogue." Singing dimensionalizes it further.

KAREN: (*V.O.* [voice-over]) Where was I? (*LIVE*) Who the hell knows. (*Karen notices the candy bar, picks it up. She looks back toward the door.* (*V.O.*) Oh my God ... am I that pitiful? (*LIVE*) Snickers. Looks like it's been in his pocket in a heat wave. (*She tosses the crushed candy bar into a corner. V.O.*) Three days in this hole. Waiting's just like being dead, except you still have to pass the time. (*LIVE. Sings.*) "I will sing you a song of the New Jerusalem, that far away home of the soul ..." (*V.O.*) That's all I remember. (*LIVE*) Facts. He's late, (*V.O.*) he's very late, (*LIVE*) but he's on his way, knowing I'd wait forever, that I'd be here ... (*V.O.*) ... staring out the window for him till my eyes become two tiny swamps where the moss floats, till my lips are food for crows, till deep in the grass grown up through this crumbling floor, my white bones rot. (*LIVE*) Fuck that. Hell, he'll probably show up any minute, with a hard-on and a mouth full of sorry [a moment's silence].

(Jenkin 1993, *American Notes,* 245–6)

The bifurcation of the character into taped and live presences theatricalizes the inner dialogue. Voice-overs provide Karen with an interactional "other," whereby taped dialogue confronts, contradicts, or focuses her live, "quoted" responses (see Cohn 1978, 58–99). Theatrically, the interactional mode culminates as a dialogue between the matrixed live character and her nonmatrixed (nonlive) recording, where the means or function of expression become as significant to the dialogism as what is being said. A rule of thumb to be gleaned from language playwrights: emphasize various language functions in your plays.

EXERCISE:
Dialogic monologue; the taped or miked voice-over

1. Have a character pantomime an action (dressing, for example) while her concurrent thoughts are played on tape. She answers each thought back in her character's voice, interacting with the taped speech—the theatrical corollary of talking to herself.

2. Have one character impersonate the voices of other characters. For instance, a character is setting a table for dinner, "conversing" with each guest as she sets up their place setting. The running dialogue between herself and the "guest" can vary from the humorous to poignant—an introduction that builds audiences' expectations. (The introduction is a well-made play device: one, two, or several characters describe a character or characters about to enter.)

3. Interpolate the taped voice of another character within the speaker's monologue. The quoted monologue is used frequently in novels indicated by "he said," or "she thought to herself," or "she exclaimed," and so on. This application conflates the dialogic "other" within the matrix of the monologue.

COMMENT: You can create this effect in (3) in the workshop by having another reader assigned to the quoted sections.

Miked speech can create a disembodied eeriness by foregrounding sound quality in the utterance. The actor doesn't have to push vocally, so this opens up certain resonances in the voice that would not otherwise be heard. In *Fnu Lnu,* published in his anthology *Cellophane* (2001, 237), Wellman mikes performers to create a choral effect or startle the audience with "demon voices," a practice used in several productions of his *Murder of Crows.* With current advances in sound technologies, playwrights can now conceptualize monologue to include multiple voices, dialects, languages, and an array of sound-effect options.

Phone devices demonstrate how the distinction between monologic and dialogic discourses can be blurred in the theater. As in everyday speech, transactional and interactional modes of discourse are simultaneously present in a state of continual flux. Generally, monologue and dialogue should not be conceived as two mutually exclusive forms of dramatic language, but as two approaches that struggle for predominance, even within a specific speech (see Mukarovsky 1977, 102). In drama, this struggle is evident when the addressed "other" is the audience.

As we have seen, direct address is now a staple of contemporary dramaturgy as audiences have grown inured to it as an innovation. In fact, it is more rarely the case that the construct of the fourth wall is consistent throughout the play. While its usual placement is at the beginning of the script, a number of recent plays have utilized direct address in the middle of the play, where it serves as a kind of pivot point. The diverse dramaturgies of *Behanding in Spokane, Rabbit Hole,* and *Dead Man's Cell Phone* all have long character monologues near the center of the script. In most cases, these monologues introduce a new character, and as such, are not delivered by the protagonist or anchor character(s). By drawing focus from the protagonist, the pivot monologue shifts the balance of the play at its fulcrum point. Regardless of its placement or function, direct address calculates a certain distancing from the audience that belies its so-called immediacy. This stratagem can become cloying when the playwright poses questions to, or confronts, the audience with responses neither expected nor desired. This contradictory effect combines a dialogic intention with monologic impenetrability.

Part 2 of Len Jenkin's *Limbo Tales* and the opening of Young Jean Lee's *Church* make this point: Whether the actor/character directly addresses the incoming spectators as the emcee, in the former, or as Reverend José, in the latter, the conditions are fixed and monologic: the ad-libs are scripted and will stand without reply. Nevertheless, the potential for dialogic exchange is present whenever the speaker "penetrates" the fourth wall and directly engages the audience. When the emcee and Reverend José introduce us to the cast of characters in *Limbo Tales* and *Church* respectively, they become matrixed as a character in the play. Margaret Edson's 1999 Pulitzer-Prize-winning play *Wit* makes a similar move; in the opening monologue, the actor playing Vivian introduces herself first as the actor in the play:

today? Great. That's just great.

(Edson 1999, 7)

Then she sets herself into the character of Vivian:

(*In her own professorial tone.*) This is not my standard greeting, I assure you. I tend to something a little more formal, a little less inquisitive, such as, say, "Hello."

The monologue then continues to disclose the character's profession, current patient status and obviously dire condition until the end of the speech, when the actor brings us back to the theatricality of the event: "I've got less than two hours. Then: curtain" (Edson 1999, 7–8).

These level shifts in language, intention, and matrix represent a form of internal dialogism. In *Limbo Tales*, *Church*, and *Wit*, the narrators' voices shift between presentational and representational modes, giving the plays a dialogic structure. This dialogic shift is characteristic of current playwriting practices, and it offers the playwright a variety of dramaturgic options.

Sometimes, as in Jenkin's *My Uncle Sam* and *Kid Twist*, the events narrated are different from those staged, with the speaker positioned at the interface between the audience and the dramatic event. Monologue's authority and innate credibility are undermined in its relation to the event onstage. Regarding contextual relativity in *The Dialogic Imagination*, Mikhail Bakhtin posited that:

there is a constant interaction between meanings, all of which have the potential of conditioning others. What will affect the other, how it will do so, and in what degree is what is actually settled at the moment of utterance. This dialogic imperative ... insures that there can be no true monologue.

(Bakhtin 1981, 246–7)

This indeterminate quality of monologue is evident in plays that feature memory or the recall of past events. Harold Pinter's monologues in *Betrayal*, *Old Times*, and *Landscape* proffer the impossibility of memory to capture truths underlying shared events. Sam Shepard uses monologue similarly to Pinter: in the film version of *Fool For Love*, monologue voice-overs describe a different action than that suggested in the narrative. In this case, the dialogic clash is determined contextually rather than textually. This cinematic technique has been adapted by playwrights, who innovate its use as a clash between the narrator's description and the actual image of the mise-en-scène.

The blurring of monologic and dialogic qualities has become increasingly predominant in contemporary playwriting. In Jenkin's plays dialogue may serve a narrative function, while monologue, upon which his storytelling techniques are established, functions in an interactional, dialogic manner. Wellman monologues invariably subvert traditional syntactical and linguistic constructions. This focus on the syntactic and phonetic, an approach common to the early plays of Suzan-Lori Parks, targets language rather than plot, character, or a traditional sense of discernible meaning as the focal point. As discussed in Chapter 2, Parks's phonetic approach to writing dramatic language contains immanent links to African-American dialect and history without overtly stating or reiterating traditional black themes. The street hustler language in *Topdog/Underdog* maintains this strategy, albeit with a greater nod to the "black history" thematic than her earlier, and more radically linguistic, *An American Play*, for example. Parks codifies grotesque descriptors in *Fucking A*, thereby linguistically mitigating the starkness of the content. The cryptic voicings of Hester, the abortionist, utilize the concocted faux language Parks describes as TALK. For example, "die Abah-nazip" translates as "the abortion;" many of the other descriptors such as, "seh tum ... woah ya," refer to vulgar descriptions of women's genitalia (Parks 2001, 117; 119).

SHADOW DRAMATURGY

In the late 1980s, Wellman conflated slang from different eras into neologisms or new combinations, as in his play *Whirligig*. His Obie-award-winning monologue play *Terminal Hip* ineluctably triggers sociocultural contexts within the purview of the spectator. Meaning is not directly apparent, but negotiated in the collision of specific speech genres or discourses: African American, Wall Street market talk, ethnic expressions, street jive, and so on. Through the collision of language the shadow of narrative emerges. This "shadow dramaturgy" is contingent on each performance, representing a countervailing anti-structure to the text itself, and released in the colliding fields of language. Its effect is palpable yet ineffable, and can only be realized in performance. An apt analogy might be that for Wellman language is the mask, and underneath lies the creature that seeks to be released—what Roberto Tessari described as the mask (*la maschera*) and its shadow (*l'ombra*). (Tessari 1989).

Wellman's shadow dramaturgy is triggered by monologues featuring a bombardment of language, still evident in his recent plays, *The Invention of Tragedy* (2006) and *The Difficulty of Crossing a Field* (2002), contained in his recently published anthology bearing the title of the latter play (Wellman 2008). He creates the verbal onslaught through several craft-conscious methods, such as his use of asterisks to indicate that monologues are overlapping and simultaneous. In other words, the subsequent speech begins while the first monologue is delivered. The asterisk is the marker for the second (or third) monologue to begin, an effect similar to overlapping musical rounds. In *The Difficulty of Crossing a Field*, the doubling phenomenon initiated by the asterisk is heightened by phrases that are repeated over and over again to effect a kind of stacking. In *The Invention of Tragedy*, he locks into the alliterative phrase "And chop the chails of all cats." This tag line becomes the marker that provides a sense of cohesion to the text. Here, the simulacrum of structure is through iteration and tag lines, with variance established through intonation. The latter is set up through the articulation stressors on the alliterative "ch" sound, culminating in the hard "c" plosive sound of "cat." In language playwriting, the actor is urged to attack words with muscularity and declaration, trusting that the language itself will release the inherent power and communicative force. This sure-footed approach is akin to a heroic or psycho-physical style of acting such as Suzuki, which strives to connect language to the actor's essential core.

At the end of Act I in *The Invention of Tragedy*, the figure of the Enforcer appears and culminates the tag line with this stage direction: "The axe is raised; the axe is swung; the chail is topped off" (Wellman 2008, 275). As the late *New York Times* critic Mel Gussow noted, Wellman's plays often "work better than they read." The repetitions and tags resound in the text, a phenomenon like waves crashing to the shore, then regrouping and repeating. As in the above, the verbiage culminates in a physical action—much more powerful on stage than in the text. The crescendos are marked with asterisks, difficult to "hear" from the page but profoundly impactful in performance. Between the waves lie the verbal tricks, the whimsy and humor, word play, bizarre bits, and special effects like nouning.

Indeed, his most signature technique, the use of nouning, defined below, can be recognized in many of his plays. Wellman's language is not progressing the plot or character, as in a traditional script—rather, the effect is accretion versus progression. Wellman's linguistic enterprise differs radically from the quotidian, or what is generally considered best practice in formulating stage monologue: beginning, middle, end, point of view, and so on. Wellman's inimitable language is in tension with, or independent of, the current parlance. The "grey look," mass, or density, of his writing appears as monologue on the page, yet its effect and purpose is to dialogize both linguistically (on a cultural level) and theatrically (on an aesthetic level). This expansion of monologue's capacity into the linguistic arena redefines the traditional concept of what constitutes a play.

An analogy might be to the experiments of Jerzy Grotowski and Richard Schechner's The Performance Group in the 1960s and 1970s which focused on redefining the physical functions and spiritual essences of the actor in performance. Wellman reassesses how language can function in a play, as Grotowski sought to reevaluate prevailing assumptions regarding the actors' potential. Grotowski's paratheatrical experiments eventually isolated the actor in an intensive exploration of the acting process. At times, Wellman's inscrutable experiments isolate linguistic foregrounding to the extent that language momentarily eclipses or suspends the need for dramaturgy. Wellman's force of language substitutes for immediate moment-to-moment interest as an antistructural device. If not for the underpinnings of repetition and tag lines, the plays would lose any sense of gravity or architecture, as images and sounds appear, transfigure, disappear, and reemerge. Wellman has staked out his own territory for the playwright, one filled with risk, adventure, and a sense of the unknown. Curiously, while Wellman has mentored a number of successful young playwrights, he still remains the most radical in his use of language; for the past twenty-five years his prolific output and signature style have come to define the eponymous Mac Wellman play.

"FORMING" ANTISTRUCTURE: FROM NOUNING TO *SKAZ*

Nouning is used by a number of contemporary playwrights, including Suzan-Lori Parks (see below), but it was Wellman who first innovated the technique. Nouning exercises are favorites of students, and can be integrated into more conventional monologues with a wide array of applications.

A signature example is from Wellman's groundbreaking *Whirligig* (1988): here, the Girl Hun's last speech provides the effect of hurling us through space:

> Plinth ... Mitake Mura, Dikan'ka, Elmer, Hektor, Doctor Spock, Roswitha, Pia, Wofiana, Erda, Helio, 1935X, McCuskey, Wild, Whipple, Zulu, CrAO, Toro, Hamburga...
>
> (Wellman 1995, *Whirligig*, 173–4)

The linear stacking of word signifiers—Wellman coined the term *nouning*—creates a fission-like reaction, what he describes as the *radioactive effect of language*. This term, *radioactive language*, locates the site of "fission" in the observer: meaning is absorbed contextually in the gaps between words, then through continual deferring until the destination is reached. Fission is the simulacrum of conflict, here displaced to the spectator rather than between actors. The playwright's monologic bombardment triggers an interactive dialogic response from the spectator. Rather than denying the existence of the "other" or pretending to be the "final word," it is now the "other" as audience who becomes the author of meaning (Holquist 1990, 21). In essence, Wellman defers the creation of structure to the audience. This Dada-like move means the audience has to be an active component in establishing meaning to language.

Wellman's interstellar travels through a fictional universe are made strange by juxtaposing "proper" names such as Doctor Spock, Zulu, Hamburga, and others with "space names" such as 1935X and CrAO. Obviously, this "radioactive effect" interrupts any emotional involvement of

guistically theatrical experience. Nouning defers intention to favor sense
experience. To an extent nouning also invites a rational response to the
ironic juxtaposition of the familiar and the strange. An excellent example
of this is Butcher's lengthy monologue description of his daughter in Suzan-
Lori Parks's *Fucking A*, which moves from nouning to juxtaposed phrases of
varied lengths (the following is excerpted):

> BUTCHER: ... Prostitution, racketeering, moneylaundering, cyber
> fraud, intellectual embezzlement, highway robbery, dialing for dollars,
> doing a buffalo after midnight, printing her own money, cheating at
> cheating, jaywalking, selling herself without a license, selling her chil-
> dren without a permit, unlawful reproduction, having more than one
> spouse, claiming to have multiple parents, claiming to have multiple
> orgasms, claiming to have injuries she didn't have...skipping school,
> skipping her monthly, smoking in the girls room, drugging of all stripes
> and varieties, smiling in the off season.... [etc.]
>
> (Parks 2001, 160–1)

Here, sonic and semantic relations combine to create moment-to-moment
interest and humor. Unlike the work of the traditional playwright/craft-
sperson who attempts to control meaning and structure, these monologic
word barrages obscure not only the character's voice but also overall dramaturgical coherence. By negating coherence and dramatic underpinnings,
nouning creates an antistructure that simulates walking a tightrope with no
net. The safe underpinnings of narrative pull and psychologically rounded
characters are offset by the second-to-second unfolding of surprise and the
unexpected. The intensity of the moment supplants the traditional build
toward climax and resolution. The actor supplies interest through the
pointing of specific words, and varying the phraseology by shifting vocal
centers in the body.

Wellman's recent work utilizes increasingly complex "nouning" phras-
ings and stacked neologisms to create bizarre and often droll effects that
would challenge the most nimbly tongued actor. The following example
from *The Invention of Tragedy* is indicative. (Note the bundled polysyllabic
neologisms, along with the intermix of proper names and onomatopeia.)

> FOURTH CHORUS: Three full stops beyond Seti Osiris we mean o o his
> saurian Ahura Maxda domino somononatonatomorpho morpho pie hat
> pie tree forest of whisperz and whimperz on the trellis of Egypt her hat
> who found his bed out out past the o blushbluishngreenbedslipperpark
> where no one had no one had to look at what is not worth the trouble
> and ho they go hoho hoot and hoo like a what it is what does that mean
> damn meant you mean no no yes yes. And chop the chail off all cats.
>
> (Wellman 2008, 263)

Wellman concludes with the structuring tag line ("chop the chail off all cats") that is embedded repeatedly throughout the play. We have traces of the myth of Osiris, a paean to the origins of Egyptian theatrical traditions that may be traced to the origins of tragedy. Wellman peels back the obscure to offer glimpses of deeper meaning. These "clues" continue through a series of choruses, numbered by Wellman, until later in the play, the figure of Hare appears as an oblique referent to the classical *hamartia*, or "error in judgment." Hare's "error" as narrated, was to inadvertently carry a switchblade in his carry-on luggage, which led to his detention at an airport security checkpoint. The ultimate effect was the unraveling of his erstwhile life as a sandwich maker. Hare ultimately provides a salvo of meaning to the play, when he suggests that it is the need for individualism that leads to tragedy: that it happens to the person who steps out of the chorus. This double entendre marker refers back to Thespis, who of course as the first actor stepped out of the dithyramb chorus and created the opportunity of the tragic hero. Thus, if we work hard enough, and are patient, and understand the arcane and oblique references, Wellman ultimately answers the riddle of his title, *The Invention of Tragedy*—a trail from the myth of Osiris through Thespis and the birth of Greek tragedy.

The following exercises offer a point of entry into what may be unfamiliar dramaturgical territory. Since the impact of nouning is most noticeable in its sonic aspect, this interactive exercise should prove helpful.

EXERCISE:
Nouning

(Read *Whirligig* and *Fucking A*.)

1. In Wellman's *Whirligig* and Parks's *Fucking A*, refer to the Girl Hun's nouning monologue, in the former, and Butcher's speech (as quoted above) in the latter.

2. How does nouning create the sense of travel or movement in *Whirligig*? What does the litany of nouning and phrases tell us about Butcher's daughter? About Butcher? About the world of the play?

3. How are these playwrights "making strange" by juxtaposing the normative to the absurd, or the serious to the comic? How are words and phrases affected by their proximity to other words and phrases?

4. Why is nouning an effective dramaturgic device at this point within the play?

COMMENT: The nouning exercises are attempts to free playwrights from normative syntactical choices. Daily life is consumed with lists, and nouning activates this impulse. Most rote learning is achieved through the memorization of facts on lists. Beyond that, an associational barrage can release powerful energies in a text or character. Even within traditional playwriting formats the nouning monologue can be a potent tool in your arsenal.

EXERCISE:
Freewriting

Read the Tenth through the Fourteenth Choruses from Wellman's *The Invention of Tragedy*.

1. Freely associate names that are associated with given rooms, spaces, or businesses; time periods; or cultural phenomena.
2. Use slogans as well as nouns.
3. Set a timer to four minutes and do not lift pen from paper during this word barrage.
4. Attempt to free the "self-censor"—any tendency to censor your writing.

COMMENT: Language playwrights strive to "do things with words." These exercises demonstrate how words can operate in an exciting, vital way. The playwright should not neglect the spatial effect that nouning and proper names have on the sensory imagination of the spectator. Monologue can supply mass in a text, the same way that a large area painted in one color can focus or stabilize a painting. As in the previous exercise on spinning, monologues can become pivot points around which scenes converge—one coming to closure in the monologue as another is born.

TERMINAL HIP AND RADIOACTIVE LANGUAGE

While Wellman's 1989 OBIE-Award winning play *Terminal Hip*, subtitled *The Spiritual History of America through the Medium of Bad Language*, is older than some readers of this book, it remains seminally representative of his most radical dramaturgy. There is no vestige of either plot or character. A characterless monologue, *Terminal Hip* required a heightened theatricalized performance to define it as a work of theater. Actor Stephen Mellor came to the conclusion that the only way to play it was at close range—phrase by phrase and in a hyper-realistic manner. Mellor established a strong intention for each moment to construct a convincing performance. Mel Gussow described it as "postJoycean Jabberwocky," replete with "unidentified flying verbiage" (Gussow 1990, 5). The beginning scene zigzags us into Wellman's idiosyncratic universe:

Strange the Y all bent up and Dented
Blew the who to tragic eightball.
Eightball trumpet earwax and so forth.
Pure chew, loud thump and release pin.
Crabity gotta nail him too sure.
You don't not have no super shoes when as how
you don't need not to never.
Ask for the labernath it's all over sure.
They got music there so bad.
They got music there as do the shame-ball
double up and fall over

three times running while it drills
corrosive z's on that there river bottom.
Technology comes here too am. (1:1)

(Wellman 2001, *Terminal Hip*, 257)

Terminal Hip's words and grammatical aberrations (the same can be said about its companion piece, *Cellophane* (Wellman 2001, 151–84)) become the property of the senses rather than vehicles to convey a character's psychology or the play's exposition. They embody Antonin Artaud's theory that "language cannot be defined except by its possibilities for dynamic expression in space as opposed to the expressive possibilities of spoken dialogue ... [and] for dissociative and vibratory action upon the sensibility" (Artaud, quoted in Bentley 1968, 55–6).

Wellman's stacked sequential nouning, such as "eightball, trumpet, earwax," demonstrates what Artaud described in *The Theater and Its Double* as "this solidified, materialized language" (Bentley 1968, 55). *Terminal Hip* presents "a language in which an overwhelming stage experience seems to be communicated, in comparison with which our productions depending exclusively upon dialogue seem like so much stuttering" (Bentley 1968, 56). Artaud's "stutterer," a metaphor for the theater's inability to assert a breakthrough language, may be contrasted with Wellman's master utterer. Wellman's defiant take on diction is the linguistic corollary to Artaud's overwhelming stage experience. *Terminal Hip* explores the theatrical potential of the monologic format to redeem the "stutterer," by syntactically transcending imitative reality and discourse. Stripped of familiar moorings, we are hurled into a dream of consciousness, constructed by what Gussow's NYT's review called a "crazy quilt of slang and convolutions" (1990, 5).

Terminal Hip ultimately affects a cathartic response brought on by neither pity and fear nor emotional identification, but the intense force (in the sense of Artaud's "theater of cruelty") of the language on the sense organs. It works as theater when the actor brings the strongest intention, or "in tension" from the various centers of the body. The gestural nature of the language then elicits a force field between actor and audience from which a shadow narrative emerges. While radical in its execution, Wellman's dramaturgy is reliant on two basic dramatic principles. First, it is the nature of conflict to create narrative, and while this is not a trackable narrative in the conventional sense, it inexorably springs forth from the conflict between normative discourse and Wellman's field of language. Second, audiences are conditioned by the "willing suspension of disbelief" to engage their imagination in determining the meaning of a script. In this sense, audiences construct an imaginary, anti-world through Wellman's language, just as a Shakespeare's audiences were transported to "a battlefield" in France (through simple declaration), while watching a performance at the Globe.

EXERCISE:
Bad English

A signature of Wellman's dramaturgy is his reliance on "Bad English." Bad English is made up of incorrect syntax, misplaced words, slang, profanity, much of which Wellman gleaned from his study of H. L. Mencken's *The American Language* (Wellman 2001, 151). The playwright rejects acceptable speech norms and conventions of writing dialogue or monologue. Bad English provides an option for multivocal texturing since the playwright can juxtapose it with more normative syntactical choices. It is a formalistic device because the playwright is drawing attention to language function versus meaning. Nouns and verbs are juxtaposed to create strange or unusual effects.

1. Gather in a journal examples of improper but colorful syntax. Tune your ears to peculiarities of syntax, sentence structure and word choices.

2. Refer to Chapter 2 for examples from speech genres. Seek out examples from differing speech genres on available internet sources.

3. Write a five-minute monologue with a multivocal character who is extremely upset about some social wrong such as toxic waste or global warming. Vary normative speech patterns with bad English syntactical choices.

COMMENT: YouTube can be probed for some blatant examples of bad English.

EXERCISE:
Free association

This automatic writing exercise is based on the free association of terms and phrases. It uses the obsessive idea as a focus point. André Breton, the French father of surrealism, promoted automatic writing as a means to unlock and discover unconscious desires. Breton suggested the writer should obsess on an object, person, or idea as a means to focus the intention.

1. Allow a character in a scene to freely associate on a sexual obsession (for example, a woman or man whom the character observes from a window at given times during the day). The regularity and predictability become habitual, then obsessional.

2. Seek closure. Does the love interest vanish? How does this mark the free association? Or does the character act on the obsession? How does this choice mark the free association?

3. In what ways does this practice inform your writing?

4. Does it release the character's voice in any way?

COMMENT: This exercise can be effective in the workshop, although you must implement some meditative or ethereal electronic music so as to create a trance-like state in the playwright. For the exercise to be effective a certain concentrated mental state must be achieved that is free of distraction or interruption. It is a terrific exercise for releasing the subconscious of the playwright, and for many, it will be their first experience with this type of formative playwriting.

One outcome of the free association exercise may be the digressionary monologue. The digressionary monologue is often formatted as a direct address to the audience. Since it does little or nothing to further the plot, the digressionary monologue works as a kind of verbal *lazzi*. *Lazzi* were physical and rhetorical "shticks" utilized by the *commedia dell'arte*. These moments were interpolated in the performance text, providing comic relief. The digressionary monologue may provide diversion, humor, or amplification of theme. There is this caveat for the playwright: dramaturgs or play developers may assert that since the material serves no crucial dramatic function it should be cut. On the other hand, what would the work of Anton Chekhov be without the occasional digression? Indeed, the digressions seem woven into the fabric of his dramaturgy. In the new playwriting, Jenkin is a master of the digressionary monologue. An example from the Young Man's speech in *My Uncle Sam* is typical:

> Tell you what I'm gonna do. Special price for you and the missus on any of the selection of exciting book I have to offer. Here's one called *Confessions of a Nun* ... this one's written in the kind of plain language anyone can understand. I can see you're a man of the world. Here's a copy of *From Ballroom to Hell* by an ex-dance teacher ... awful dangers to young girls in the dancing academy. How about *HIRAM BIRDSEED AT THE WORLD'S FAIR?*
>
> [Aside to audience] This *Hiram Birdseed at the World's Fair* is my biggest seller published by the same company in Philadelphia. For men only. You know the kind—*Sam Savage in the South Seas* ... "the naked maidens surrounded him ..." and so on. It's like the same guy wrote them all, though they got different names on 'em. But *Hiram Birdseed* is different. It's like this writer of all of them was hit by fantasy exhaustion one day and he hadda stay in bed, so for one time he hired another guy ... a little guy with a dirty green cardigan sweater and glasses, and he was given this title, *Hiram Birdseed at the World's Fair*, and the farm boy gets involved in international sex in New York City and this little guy goes back to his furnished room, and he writes. He stays up all night, his mind at white heat, and as the dawn filters through the Venetian blinds he finishes the first half. He falls into a fitful doze. The pages on the desk flutter in an early morning breeze ...
>
> (Jenkin 1993, *My Uncle Sam*, 159–60)

Jenkin's Young Sam continues to discuss the contents of the book, including in detail a chapter called "Hiram Birdseed's Dream." The monologue is framed at the beginning and end to characters in the play; yet in the middle, it is framed to the audience. Thus, the story is a diversion for the audience, but one in which there is a shared intimacy with the performer, and by extension, the playwright. *Hiram Birdseed* is Jenkin's world in a nutshell:

playful, strange, funny, intelligent, marginalized, and wildly imaginative. For playwrights, the key to the success of the digressionary monologue is best described by the French term *disponibilité*, which describes an openness or "availability" to the moment at hand. The great artist must remain open to the moment of *disponibilité*, and audience and dramaturgs must understand its value—not being so ready to cut the digressionary thread that somehow informs, and most definitely, delights.

Young Jean Lee offers some current examples of the digressionary monologue in her adaptation of Shakespeare's *King Lear*, truncated to *Lear*. For example, Regan's monologue, which begins "I wake up in the morning and I am alive...." is set off from the rest of the play, framed by a single spotlight and between two scenes of dialogue. It resonates with some of the themes in the play, such as the image of the old man (Lear) talking to himself, but relates to nothing specifically in the action of the play (Lee 2010, 71). While the digressionary monologue will seem tangential to the progress of narrative, it adds dramaturgical value when it opens a character or thematic element in the play that might otherwise be dormant. In Regan's monologue, Lee offers us a detailed slice of the character's life and a deeper reflection on the old man's (Lear's) desperate loneliness.

SKAZ MONOLOGUE

Skaz as a literary term was first described by the Russian Formalists in the late 1910s. In brief, the Russian Formalists attempted to separate language from meaning, focusing instead on language's articulatory aspects, rhythmic qualities, and its use as a device. *Skaz* foregrounds what is seemingly an improvisational moment within the text, where the speaker or narrator deviates from, or ignores, the narrative. Bakhtin recognized *skaz* as dialogic in that it brought a competing authorial level in the creation of the text. *Skaz* gives the sense of unmediated or impromptu speech. It is the spoken corollary to the spacer beats and rests discussed earlier.

For example, Ruhl opens *The Clean House* with the Brazilian maid, Matilde, telling a joke in Portuguese. This speech is marked only by the stage directions. (As Russian Formalism is a staple of Paula Vogel's pedagogical credo, Ruhl would have been introduced to it while studying with Vogel at Brown University.)

> *Matilde tells a long joke in Portuguese to the audience*
> *We can tell she is telling a joke even though we might not understand the language.*
> *She finishes the joke.*
> *She exits.*

> (Ruhl 2006, 9)

Ruhl clearly is aware that American audiences won't understand Portuguese, so she is foregrounding the articulatory aspect of the language over the meaning. It is similar to having an actor deliver a passage in gibberish, whereby any grasping of intent or meaning is communicated through sound qualities, movement, gesture and facial expression.

In her appendix to the play, Ruhl offers three possible versions of the joke, while urging producers of the work to come up with their own. Here, the jokes are offered in translations by several native speakers. As *skaz*, the joke stands alone from the text, and can be taken on its own terms. It differentiates the character, Matilde, from the author, in that these jokes are outside of the world of the play. The articulatory sound of the Brazilian dialect creates a sense of "otherness" that dialogizes with the hegemonic English language. As Matilde is the maid in this play, her native speech sets up the clash of class structure in the play. As it is a joke she is telling, *skaz* is emphasizing the performative aspect of delivery over the content.

Skaz is a dialogic strategy that features the performance of the narrator or actor over the author, and may or may not be linked to anything in the narrative. In *The Clean House*, Matilde has been in search of the perfect joke since the death of her parents; her mother died laughing, while her father took his own life, unable to cope after his beloved joke partner died. In this case, polyvocality is created by the use of a second language, although, in other cases dialects or slang would be appropriate. The corollary of *skaz* in music is "free jazz" in the style of for instance Ornette Coleman or Sun Ra, where improvisation and sound qualities (for example, overblowing effects) triumph over traditional jazz structures like song forms (such as AABA) and set meters.

EXERCISE:
Skaz monologue

1. A *skaz* monologue can be constructed independently of the play, although its true impact derives from its frisson with the rest of the play.

2. There needs to be a specific strategy of language: foreign (as in the example above), slang (see below), dialect or regionalisms, speech genres, or similar. This should be consistent in the monologue.

3. You can use a portrait as the starting point, a saturated bio, or a secondary or undeveloped character from a scene or play project.

4. For material, have the character either tell a joke, or produce some shtick. This comic business is like a *commedia lazzi* except with emphasis on language and delivery.

5. The insertion of a character from an underclass and foreign country (like Matilde) allots *skaz* an empowering aspect; plus, it provides a theatrical means to embed political or cultural themes.

COMMENT: *Skaz* offers the writer the opportunity to let the character's voice go, in essence releasing control of the play, since it is freewheeling, irreverent, and need not be tied to the narrative thread. As such, it is a freeing exercise for playwrights who are suffering from writer's block.

Underdog contain the slang and dialect of the black street hustler, and embody *skaz* in their improvisatory aspect. While these monologues are clearly written by Parks, they emphasize the performative aspect of the character, and to be effective require a virtuosic display of command. An apposite way to envision *skaz* is as a verbal *lazzi* that calls attention to the performer's "natural ownership" of the material. To develop your "ear" for *skaz*, study ethnic-based comic monologues on You Tube, where the performer's "take" on the material often supersedes the impact of the material itself.

PROPERTIES OF MONOLOGUE

The "knows where it's going" aspect of monologue results from careful composition and editing. Unlike shared dialogue, the monologue is "owned" by the performer. Because it is a "moment" for the actor, they are encouraged to maximize the theatrical potential of the speech. As the primary audition tool, casting agents and directors seek originality, passion, and impressive virtuoso turns by the actor. Critics respond to the transparency of monologue. They receive an unimpeded glimpse of character while qualifying the level of writing talent and dramaturgical skill. The savvy critic knows that monologue deciphers theme. Reviewers allot more language flexibility to monologue than dialogue, where heightened language may be considered stilted or forced. Playwrights satisfy these expectations by embedding their message in a solo speech, even when the risk is of telegraphing. If telegraphing is a fault, playwrights defend it as authentic "writing on the line"—allowing the character to bare true thoughts, feelings, and intentions. Nevertheless, it primarily serves as a playwright's convenience. Playwrights can transcend this problem by pushing the limits of language. The result is a *tour de force* monologue that exalts the virtuosic in performance.

MONOLOGUE EXTREMUS

In the 2010 Broadway revival of David Hirson's *La Bête*, audiences witnessed the extremes of monologue: the voluble Valere's 20-minute rant in rhymed couplets—a star turn by actor Mark Rylance—that brought down the house (as reviewers remarked, and I witnessed the night I attended). As the prolix Valere goes on and on and on, the other characters on stage attempt to shut him down, but to no avail. The feat is pulling off this monologue that is entirely written in Alexandrine couplets. As the repetitive rhyming begins to numb us, Rylance's droll muggings, pleadings to audience, and outrageous performance sustain our astonishment. From the standpoint of dramaturgy, Hirson's attention to this extended beat segment dwarfs the action of the play, and turns our focus of attention toward Rylance's performance. Curiously, the major "star" in the play, David Hyde Pierce, is relegated to a secondary role as spectator to Rylance's rant. In viewing the performance, I felt the monologue could have been trimmed by 25 percent and still accomplished its comic intent. However, from the standpoint of illustrating Valere's garrulous and obnoxious character, it served that purpose well. The dramaturgical issue for the playwright is to consider the monologue's overall impact on the play's structure in relation to a particular moment, effect, or character turn.

Monologue, theatricality, and structure are dialogically linked in new playwriting. Their effective interaction assures a dynamic dramaturgy that goes beyond direct address. While language provides the springboard for most of these explorations, the playwright should be responsive to the theatrical material inherent in the subject matter. Understanding how the dominant works in creating form can provide a map for coherence and artistic unity in your plays, regardless of the subject matter. This heightened awareness is necessary to maximize the potential of your script to deliver a powerful *mise-en-scène.*

THE CLASSICAL MODEL

The theatricality of monologue has its basis in the drama of classical Greece. Like new playwriting, the classical tragedians made frequent use of proper nouns that were clear markers to Greek audiences familiar with myths, lineages, and other core information about the ancient world and underworld. To "hold the boards" in huge public arenas, these monologues had to be clearly centered in the actor's diaphragm, with muscular engagement of the vocal articulators and resonators. Key words that signified intention were declared with complete conviction. Thus, virtuosity of performance was borne through the theatrical display of language. Likewise, new playwrights need to point key words in their monologues, and provide a map for the performer to deliver language with conviction. The greatest achievement of new playwriting has been to reclaim the presence of language in the theater. While we tend to think of this as a radical breakthrough, we are, in fact, drawing upon the deeply encoded theatricality of antiquity which celebrated *logos* above all else.

Works consulted

Note: Play from author means that the playwright provided me with an unpublished, working copy of the play, usually before it was published. Subsequent to the first edition of this book, many of these plays are now in print. In these cases, the bibliography has been updated to include the published copy which is readily available.

Aristotle. 1954. *Poetics*, trans. Ingram Bywater. New York: Random House.

Artaud, Antonin. 1958. *The Theater and Its Double*, trans. Mary Caroline Richards. New York: Grove Press.

Bakhtin, M. M. 1968. *Rabelais and His World*, trans. Helen Islowsky. Cambridge, Mass.: MIT Press.

Bakhtin, M. M. 1981. *The Dialogic Imagination: Four Essays*, trans. C. Emerson and M. Holquist, ed. Michael Holquist. Austin, Tx.: University of Texas Press:

Bakhtin, M. M. 1986. *Speech Genres and Other Late Essays*, trans. Vern McGee, ed. Caryl Emerson and M. Holquist. Austin, Tx.: University of Texas Press.

Beber, Neena. 1990. "Dramatis instructus." *American Theatre*, January, 22–6.

Beber, Neena. Plays from author: *Hard Feelings* (1999), *Thirst* (1998), *Common Vision* (1998), *The Goddess* (1992), *Tomorrowland* (1997).

Benjamin, Walter. 1977. *Understanding Brecht*, trans. Anna Bostock. London: NLB.

Bentley, Eric. 1968. *The Theory of the Modern Stage*. Harmondsworth, UK: Penguin.

Bossier, Gregory. 2000. "Between East Coast and West End." *The Dramatist* (May/June), 24–31.

Brown, Scott. 2009. "The Story of Oh!" <http://nymag.com/arts/theater/reviews/62196>. November 16.

Castagno, Paul. C. 1993. "Informing the new dramaturgy: critical theory to creative process." *Theatre Topics*, 3:1 (March), 29–44.

Castagno, Paul. C. 1993. "Varieties of monologic strategy: the dramaturgy of Len Jenkin and Mac Wellman." *New Theater Quarterly*, 10:34 (May), 134–46.

Castagno, Paul. C. 1997. "The new dramaturg and the new playwright: an approach to the first draft," in *Dramaturgy in American Theater: A Sourcebook*. New York: Harcourt Brace.

Cohn, Dorrit. 1978. *Transparent Minds: Narrative Modes for Presenting Consciousness in Fiction*. Princeton, N.J.: Princeton University Press.

Colbert, Soyica D. 2010. "The Book of Grace. By Suzan Lori-Parks": *Theatre Journal*, 62:4 (December), 666.

Congdon, Constance. 1994. *Tales of the Lost Formicans and Other Plays*. New York: Theatre Communications Group.

Culler, Jonathan D. 1997. *Literary Theory: A Very Short Introduction*. Oxford: Oxford University Press.

Debré, Olivier. 1999. *Espace pensé, espace créé: la signe progressi*. Paris: Cherche midi.

Edson, Margaret. 1999. *Wit*. New York: Dramatists Play Service.

Ehn, Erik. 2000. *The Saint Plays*. Baltimore, Md.: Johns Hopkins University Press.

Fornes, Maria Irene. 1986. *Maria Irene Fornes: Plays*. New York: Performing Arts Journal Publications.

Fuchs, Elinor. 1985. "Presence and the revenge of writing." *Performing Arts Journal* 9:2/3, 163–72.

Gladwell, Malcolm. 2000. *The Tipping Point: How Little Things Can Make a Big Difference*. Boston, Mass.: Little, Brown.

Goffman, Erving. 1959. *The Presentation of Self in Everyday Life*. New York: Doubleday.

Goffman, Erving. 1974. *Frame Analysis: An Essay on the Organization of Experience*. New York: Harper & Row.

Gomez-Peña, Guillermo. 1996. *The New World Border*. San Francisco, Calif.: City Lights.

Gould, Christopher. 1989. *Anti-Naturalism*. New York: Broadway Play Publishing.

Gumperz, John J. 1982. *Discourse Strategies*. Cambridge, UK: Cambridge University Press.

Gussow, Mel. 1998. "Playwrights who put words at center stage." *New York Times*, February 11 (4:44).

Gussow, Mel. 1990. "Language as a Toy in One-Man Comedy." *New York Times*, January 12 (4: 5-6).

Hare, David. 1989. *The Secret Rapture*. London: Faber & Faber.

Hirschkop, Ken and David Shepherd. 1989. *Bakhtin and Cultural Theory*. Manchester: Manchester University Press.

Hirson, David. 2010, *La Bête*, New York limited run production. October 6.

Holquist, Michael. 1990. *Dialogism: Bakhtin and His World*. London: Routledge.

Horwitz, Andy. 2010. *Five Questions for Adam Greenfield* (http://culturebot. net/tag/adam-greenfield/).

Iizuka, Naomi. 2003. *36 Views*. Woodstock, N.Y.: Overlook Press.

Jenkin, Len. 1982. Dark Ride. New York: Dramatists Play Service.

Jenkin, Len. 1988. *Kid Twist*, in *7 Different Plays*, ed. Mac Wellman. New York: Broadway Play Publishing.

Jenkin, Len. 1993a. *Careless Love*. Los Angeles, Calif.: Sun and Moon Press.

Jenkin, Len. 1993b. *Dark Ride and Other Plays* (includes *Limbo Tales, American Notes, My Uncle Sam, Poor Folk's Pleasure*). Los Angeles, Calif.: Sun and Moon Press.

Jenkin, Len. 1996. Interview with author, San Francisco, Calif., March 18.

Jenkin, Len. 1999. Unpublished plays from author: *Candide* (adapted from Voltaire) (1989), *Tallahassee* (written with Mac Wellman, 1991).

Jenkin, Len. 2008a. *Kraken*. New York: Broadway Play Publishing.

Jenkin, Len. 2008b. *Margo Veil*. New York: Broadway Play Publishing.

Jennings, Michael W. 1987. *Dialectical Images: Walter Benjamin's Theory of Literary Criticism*. Ithaca, N.Y.: Cornell University Press.

Jones, Chris. 2010. *Chicago Tribune* online.

Jones, Jeffrey. Play from author: *Der Inka von Peru* (1992).

Jones, Jeffrey. 1985. *Seventy Scenes of Halloween*, in Mac Wellman, *Theatre of Wonders: Six Contemporary Plays*. Los Angeles, Calif.: Sun and Moon Press.

Kramer, Sherry. 1987. *The Wall of Water*. New York: Broadway Play Publishing.

Lane, Erin and Nina Shengold. 1997. *Take Ten*. New York: Vintage

Lee, Young Jean. 2009. *Songs of the Dragon Flying to Heaven and Other Plays*. New York: TCG.

Lee, Young Jean. 2010. *The Shipment* and *Lear*. New York: TCG.

Lindsay-Abaire, David. 2006. *Rabbit Hole*. New York. TCG.

Lodge, David. 1990. *After Bakhtin: Essays on Fiction and Criticism*. New York: Routledge.

Maguire, Matthew. 1995. *Phédra*. Los Angeles: Sun and Moon Press.

Maguire, Matthew. Play from author: *Throwin' Bones* (1998).

Mahone, Sydné. 1994. *Moon Marked and Touched by Sun: Plays by African American Women*. New York: Theatre Communications Group.

Mamet, David. 1985. *Speed the Plow*. New York: Grove Press.

Mamet, David. 1990. Interview in *Theater Week*. March 6.

Mann, Thomas. 1960. "Versuch über das Theater." *Gesammelte Werke* 10, 29. Frankfurt: S. Fisher.

Marranca, Bonnie. 1996a. *Ecologies of Theater*. Baltimore, Md.: Johns Hopkins University Press.

Marranca, Bonnie. 1996b. *Plays for the End of the Century*. Baltimore, Md.: Johns Hopkins University Press.

Matejka, Ladislav and Krystyna Pomoroska. 1978. *Readings in Russian Poetics*. Ann Arbor, Mich.: University of Michigan Press.

McDonagh, Martin. *A Behanding in Spokane*. As seen on May 4, 2010, Helen Hayes Theatre, New York.

Medvedev, P. N. and M. Bakhtin. 1978. *The Formal Method in Literary Scholarship*. Baltimore, Md.: Johns Hopkins University Press.

Messerli, Douglas. 1998. *From the Other Side of the Century II: A New American Drama (1960–1995)*. Los Angeles, Calif.: Sun and Moon Press.

Mukarovsky, Jan. 1977. *The Word and Verbal Art*, trans. John Burbank and Peter Steiner. New Haven, Conn.: Yale

Nelson, Richard. 2000. *American Theatre*. New York: TCG. (March, 25-26).

Overmyer, Eric. 1986. *On the Verge, or the Geography of Learning*. New York: Broadway Play Publishing.

Overmyer, Eric. 1987. *Native Speech*. New York: Broadway Play Publishing.

Overmyer, Eric. Play from author: *Alki* (Peer Gynt adaptation) (1997).

Overmyer, Eric. 1993. *Eric Overmyer. Collected Plays* (includes *Dark Rapture, In a Pig's Valise, In Perpetuity throughout the Universe, On the Verge, The Heliotrope Bouquet, Native Speech*). New Hampshire: Smith and Krause.

Overmyer, Eric. Personal interviews with author, March 1996 and spring 1997. Tuscaloosa, Ala.

Parks, Suzan-Lori. 1995a. *Imperceptible Mutabilities in the Third Kingdom*. Los Angeles, Calif.: Sun and Moon Press.

Parks, Suzan-Lori. 1995b. *Venus*. New York: Dramatists Play Service.

Parks, Suzan-Lori. 2001. *The Red Letter Plays*. New York: TCG.

Parks, Suzan-Lori. 2002. *Topdog/Underdog*. New York: TCG.

Parks, Suzan-Lori. 2006. *365 Days/365 Plays*. New York: TCG.

Patterson, David. 1988. *Literature and Spirit: Essays on Bakhtin and his Contemporaries*. Lexington, Ky.: University of Kentucky Press.

Petrey, Sandy. 1990. *Speech Acts and Literary Theory*. New York: Routledge.

Quinn, Michael. 1988. "Svejk's stage figure." *Comparative Drama*, 31:3 (September), 330–41.

Ramchandani, Ariel. 2009. <www.moreintelligentlife.co.uk/blog/qa-young-jean-lee-playwright-provocateur>, June 9.

Richards, Keith. 2010. *Life*. London: Little, Brown.

Robinson, Marc. 1989. "Don't fence them in." *American Theatre*, November, 28–34.

Robinson, Marc. 2009. *The American Play*. New Haven, Conn.: Yale University Press.

Ruhl, Sarah. 2006. *The Clean House and Other Plays*. New York: TCG.

Ruhl, Sarah. 2008. *Dead Man's Cell Phone*. New York: Samuel French.

Ruhl, Sarah. 2010. *In the Next Room, or the Vibrator Play*. New York: Samuel French.

Schoen, Walter. 1990. Personal interview with author, Washington, D.C.

Smiley, Sam. 1971. *Playwriting: The Structure of Action*. Englewood Cliffs, N.J.: Prentice-Hall.

Steiner, Peter. 1984. *Russian Formalism: A Metapoetics*. Ithaca, N.Y.: Cornell University Press.

Striar, Maria and Detrick, Erin. 2007. *Funny, Strange, Provocative: Seven Plays from Clubbed Thumb*. New York: Playscripts, Inc.

Svich, Caridad. 2005. *Divine Fire: Eight Contemporary Plays inspired by the Greeks*. New York: Backstage Books.

Tessari, Roberto. 1989. *Commedia dell'arte: la maschera e l'ombra*. Milan: Mursia.

Todorov, Tsvetan. 1984. *Mikhail Bakhtin: The Dialogical Principle*, trans. Wlad Godzich. Minneapolis, Minn.: University of Minnesota Press.

Turner, Victor. 1982. *From Ritual to Theatre: The Human Seriousness of Play*. New York: Performing Arts Journal Publications.

Weeks, Jerome. 1995. "Erik Ehn: Bowling for transcendence." *American Theatre*, January, 35–36.

Wellek, René. 1980. "Bakhtin's view of Dostoevsky: 'Polyphony' and 'Carnivalesque.'" *Dostoevsky Studies*, 1, 31–9.

Wellman, Mac. 1984. "Theatre of Good Intentions." Symposium on New Writing for the Theatre. Minneapolis, February.

Wellman, Mac. 1985. *Theatre of Wonders: Six Contemporary Plays*. (incl. Jenkin's *Gogol*). Los Angeles, Calif.: Sun and Moon Press.

Wellman, Mac. 1991. *Murder of Crows*. TCG *Plays in Process*. 13:3.

Wellman, Mac. 1992. "Figures of speech." *Performing Arts Journal*, 14:1 (Spring), 43–51.

Wellman, Mac. 1995. *The Bad Infinity* (containing *Harm's Way*, *The Bad Infinity*, *7 Blowjobs*, *Whirligig*, *Terminal Hip*, *Crowbar*, *Professional Frenchman*, *Energumen*). Baltimore, Md.: Johns Hopkins University Press.

Wellman, Mac. 2001. *Cellophane* (also includes other plays by the author). Baltimore, Md.: Johns Hopkins University Press.

Wellman, Mac. 2008. *The Difficulty of Crossing a Field*. Minneapolis, Minn.: University of Minnesota Press.

Wellman, Mac. Unpublished plays from New Dramatists and author: *Bodacious Flapdoodle* (1984), *Cleveland* (1986), *Dracula* (1990), *Hyacinth Macaw* (1994), *Second Hand Smoke* (1996),

Wellman, Mac and Young Jean Lee. 2006. *New Downtown Now: An Anthology of New Theater from Downtown New York*. Minneapolis, Minn.: University of Minneapolis Press.

Index